"While reading this book, I was so enthralled by what I was learning about Christ and his Word that I forgot I'm the one who makes the show they're referencing. Conversations like the ones in this fascinating book, even in the moments when I disagreed, are what I've always hoped the show would engender. We must go deeper in our relationship with and understanding of Christ, and this book is an essential tool in that pursuit."

—**Dallas Jenkins,** creator of the TV show *The Chosen*

"The groundbreaking, provocative series *The Chosen* deserves groundbreaking, provocative analysis. The contributors to this volume have done just that. They have demonstrated how philosophy and theology can successfully enhance, enrich, and challenge us in our engaging this extraordinary series on Jesus of Nazareth. Essential reading."

—**Charles Taliaferro,** St. Olaf College

"*The Chosen* probably presents Jesus's heart and life to more people in the world right now than any other medium. This book helps us understand and articulate in a more sophisticated way why that is the case. Granted, biblical scholars like myself will have quibbles here and there about some historical details (though overall *The Chosen* is careful); but had biblical scholars been in charge of the script, it would have been a different genre (documentary) with not a fraction of the impact! Like the ancient practice of *lectio divina* or medieval Corpus Christi plays, *The Chosen* engages our imaginations to enter the world of Jesus and invites us to consider for ourselves what it was like to be with our Lord in fully human form."

—**Craig S. Keener,** Asbury Theological Seminary

"This volume features scholarly yet accessible essays on *The Chosen*, perhaps the most remarkable cinematic depiction of the life of Christ in American history. The essays, addressing topics from Jesus's divinity to his interaction with women, demonstrate that the series stands alone not just because of its widespread popularity but also because of its theologically rich depiction of the life of Christ."

—**Thomas Hibbs,** Baylor University

Watching
THE CHOSEN

History, Faith, and Interpretation

Edited by

Robert K. Garcia
Paul Gondreau
Patrick Gray
Douglas S. Huffman

William B. Eerdmans Publishing Company
Grand Rapids, Michigan

Wm. B. Eerdmans Publishing Co.
2006 44th Street SE, Grand Rapids, MI 49508
www.eerdmans.com

© 2025 Robert K. Garcia, Paul Gondreau, Patrick Gray, and Douglas S. Huffman
All rights reserved
Published 2025
Printed in the United States of America

31 30 29 28 27 26 25   1 2 3 4 5 6 7

ISBN 978-0-8028-8546-3

Library of Congress Cataloging-in-Publication Data

Names: Garcia, Robert K., 1970– editor. | Gondreau, Paul, editor. | Gray, Patrick, 1970– editor. | Huffman, Douglas S., 1961– editor.
Title: Watching the Chosen : history, faith, and interpretation / edited by Robert K. Garcia, Paul Gondreau, Patrick Gray, and Douglas S. Huffman.
Description: Grand Rapids : William B. Eerdmans Publishing Co., 2025. | Includes bibliographical references and index. | Summary: "A collection of essays focusing on the meaning and message of the television series The Chosen, with special emphasis on issues of history, faith, and theology"—Provided by publisher.
Identifiers: LCCN 2024043614 | ISBN 9780802885463 (paperback) | ISBN 9781467470025 (epub)
Subjects: LCSH: Chosen (Television program : 2017–) | LCGFT: Christian television programs. | Essays.
Classification: LCC PN1992.77.C4965 W38 2025 | DDC 791.45/72—dc23/eng/20241015
LC record available at https://lccn.loc.gov/2024043614

Contents

Preface   ix

List of Abbreviations   xiii

PART ONE: IMAGINATION AND INTERPRETATION

1. Balancing Authenticity, Plausibility, and Relatability in *The Chosen*   3
   The Interaction of Three Key Principles
   DOUGLAS S. HUFFMAN

2. Imaginative Retellings, Serious Interpretation   14
   The Church Fathers and The Chosen *on John 1:43–51*
   DAVID KNEIP

3. Evil and Divine Hiddenness   25
   Feeding the Philosophical Imagination in The Chosen
   DOLORES G. MORRIS

4. The Dialectical Imagination, the Sacramental Imagination, and the Appeal of *The Chosen*   37
   Different Christian Approaches
   KENNETH GUMBERT

Contents

PART TWO: STORYTELLING AND NARRATIVE

5. The Knowledge Spiral in *The Chosen*   47
   How the Visual Medium Conveys the Relational Message
   M. ELIZABETH LEWIS HALL AND TODD W. HALL

6. The Sufficiency of Story   61
   Narrative, Theology, and The Chosen
   T. ADAM VAN WART

7. Strong Feelings and Potent Senses   69
   Three Johannine Moments in Conversation with The Chosen
   JEANNINE M. HANGER

8. Teaching with *The Chosen*   81
   Helping Students Connect with Scripture through Cinema
   JOHN HILTON III

PART THREE: CHRISTOLOGY AND HISTORY

9. Too Divine to Be Human?   93
   The Chosen's Portrayal of a Fully Human Jesus
   PAUL GONDREAU

10. The Voice of the Bridegroom   105
    The Johannine Biblical Theology of The Chosen
    DANIEL M. GARLAND JR.

11. *The Chosen* as a Contribution to the Debate over the Historical Jesus   115
    A Child of the Third Quest
    JAMES F. KEATING

12. Matthew, Mark, Luke, and John   126
    Portraying the Evangelists in The Chosen
    PATRICK GRAY

Contents

PART FOUR: EMOTIONAL RESONANCE, WOMEN, AND PERSONHOOD

13. "You Are Mine"   139
    Jesus and the Emotional Resonance of The Chosen
    JESSE D. STONE

14. Jesus as Personalist   150
    Recognizing the Other in The Chosen
    DEBORAH SAVAGE

15. Counting Sheep with Jesus   162
    The Significance of the Individual in The Chosen
    ROBERT K. GARCIA

16. "Behold the Handmaid(s) of the Lord"   176
    The Chosen's *Amplification of Women's Voices in Scripture*
    GAYE STRATHEARN

17. Meaning and Calling   188
    A Rhetorical Analysis of Jesus's Interactions with Women in The Chosen
    JOY E. A. QUALLS

Notes   201

List of Contributors   235

Index   237

Preface

The chapters in the present volume reflect upon various aspects of *The Chosen*, the first multiseason television show about Jesus Christ and his earliest followers. With over half a billion views on its free electronic media app, the show has amassed an impressively large worldwide following since its debut in 2019 and has now become available on cable networks, streaming services, and broadcast television platforms as well as in theatrical releases. Viewers are discovering that *The Chosen* is not quite like Hollywood productions for the big or small screen, yet neither is it the typical faith-based film experience. Much like *The King of Kings* (1927), *The Greatest Story Ever Told* (1965), *Jesus of Nazareth* (1977), and *The Passion of the Christ* (2004) before it, *The Chosen* appears poised to become the defining Jesus movie of the current generation. Its reach is all the more impressive given the fragmented media landscape—compared with previous decades—in which it has attracted a still-growing audience.

Most of the chapters appearing here were first delivered at a conference on *The Chosen*, held at Brigham Young University in Provo, Utah, in March 2024. Other essays were commissioned to focus on dimensions of the show that did not receive attention at the conference, though the editors make no claims to comprehensiveness; with several times the material of a standard film release, there is no shortage of material to be examined. The conference was the first-ever academic gathering devoted to *The Chosen*, and this volume is the first published collection of scholarly essays with the series as its focus. While one of the editors (Doug Huffman) serves as a script consultant for the television series, no other contributors have any formal or informal relationship with the show, nor has *The Chosen* provided any financial support or editorial guidance at any stage in the preparation of this volume.

This volume is an ecumenical project in two senses. First, the contributors come from a wide range of theological perspectives, representing many different Christian denominations and faith traditions. The roster includes Catholics, Baptists, Presbyterians, Pentecostals, and Latter-day Saints, along with members of other Protestant evangelical traditions such as the Churches of Christ and the Evangelical Free Church. Second, the volume is an interdisciplinary enterprise. Among the contributors are theologians, biblical scholars, philosophers, and psychologists, in addition to specialists in the fields of film studies, missiology, church history, and communications. The chapters reflect upon the portrayal of Jesus and his followers, the ideas and ideals presented in the series, the artistic license exercised in bringing the stories from the canonical gospels to the screen, and the relationship between medium and message in the vision of the show's creators. When the volume went to press, the first four seasons of *The Chosen* (of a projected seven seasons) were available, with the fourth season having just finished streaming. These chapters therefore provide an assessment of the series more or less at its halfway mark.

The chapters are divided into four sections. In part 1 ("Imagination and Interpretation"), Douglas S. Huffman clarifies three key principles that are frequently invoked in assessments of *The Chosen*—authenticity, plausibility, and relatability—and examines the ways in which the series attempts to keep them in a proper balance. David Kneip examines the story of Philip and Nathanael (John 1:43–51), demonstrating the ways in which the imaginative retellings of scriptural narratives that are a hallmark of *The Chosen* mirror the kinds of interpretation found in early Christian commentaries on the Gospels. Dolores G. Morris explains the show's capacity for fostering our philosophical imagination as it pertains to two philosophical challenges to belief in God, namely, the problem of evil and the problem of divine hiddenness. Connecting some different interpretive traditions, Kenneth Gumbert reflects on how the storytelling of Dallas Jenkins, a Protestant, appeals to the viewer's dialectical and sacramental imaginations as those terms are understood in Catholic systematic theology.

Preface

In part 2 ("Storytelling and Narrative"), M. Elizabeth Lewis Hall and Todd W. Hall approach the series from the discipline of psychology and examine its method of storytelling through the lenses of attachment theory and dual processing models of information. T. Adam Van Wart explicates the narrative theology of *The Chosen* and encourages viewers to "receive that story, in all its Christic beauty, as the story of our own lives." Jeannine Hanger focuses on two episodes from John's Gospel—the raising of Lazarus and the anointing of Jesus by Mary—to better understand how its rendering on the screen might move viewers toward the goal of ingesting "more of the word of God, which contains, for us, the words of life." In view of continuing the telling of Scripture's narrative, John Hilton III surveys the advantages of using *The Chosen* in the classroom and shares some suggested methodologies and resources for educators.

In part 3 ("Christology and History"), Paul Gondreau responds to criticisms that the series undercuts the doctrine of Christ's incarnate and sinless humanity by placing them in the context of long-standing christological debates. Daniel M. Garland Jr. explores the show's biblical theology through an examination of the two scenes in the Gospel of John that highlight Jesus as the bridegroom Messiah: the wedding at Cana and the Samaritan woman at the well. James F. Keating explores points of convergence between *The Chosen* as a work of history-based art and the ongoing quest for the historical Jesus. Patrick Gray takes the brief flash-forwards in which the evangelists are portrayed in the act of writing the Gospels and puts them into conversation with ancient traditions about Matthew, Luke, and John specifically as authors, and contemplates the historical and theological significance of these cinematically unique portrayals.

In part 4 ("Emotional Resonance, Women, and Personhood"), Jesse D. Stone considers the emotional resonance of *The Chosen* in dialogue with thinkers such as Augustine and Charles Taylor. Deborah Savage analyzes the interactions of Jesus with other characters with reference to the philosophy of personalism often associated with John Paul II. Robert K. Garcia focuses on how the life and teachings of Jesus, especially as imaginatively amplified in *The Chosen*, provide credible and compelling support for the idea that each person has irreplaceable and infinite value. Gaye Strathearn suggests that *The Chosen* utilizes creative dialogues to give known women in the story of Jesus a voice that the text of Scripture rarely does in order that especially modern women viewers will more easily connect with the divine narrative. From the perspective of interpersonal communications, Joy E. A. Qualls undertakes a rhetorical analysis of the interactions between Jesus and the many female characters in the series.

Throughout these chapters and across all parts of this volume, readers will encounter proposed answers to questions commonly encountered when viewing *The Chosen*. What is this television show really about? How does the portrayal of Jesus in this episode measure up to what the Bible actually says? What are the theological ideas and ideals supporting this imaginative representation? Why does this show resonate with me, and why do I find it so engaging and meaningful? These questions and many others are addressed by the contributors to this volume. We trust readers will find these interdisciplinary perspectives and interfaith reflections helpful as they continue to contemplate and connect with, wrestle with and enjoy *The Chosen*.

The Editors

Abbreviations

ANF	*The Ante-Nicene Fathers: Translations of the Writings of the Fathers Down to A.D. 325*. Edited by Alexander Roberts and James Donaldson. 10 vols. 1885–1887. Repr., Peabody, MA: Hendrickson, 1994
CBET	Contributions to Biblical Exegesis and Theology
CSB	Christian Standard Bible
ESV	English Standard Version
ESVCE	English Standard Version Catholic Edition
NABRE	New American Bible Revised Edition
NASB	New American Standard Bible
NIV	New International Version
NRSV	New Revised Standard Version
NRSVCE	New Revised Standard Version Catholic Edition
PG	Patrologia Graeca. Edited by J.-P. Migne. 162 vols. Paris, 1857–1886

Part One

IMAGINATION *and* INTERPRETATION

1

Balancing Authenticity, Plausibility, and Relatability in *The Chosen*

The Interaction of Three Key Principles

DOUGLAS S. HUFFMAN

With an impressively large worldwide following, the first-ever multiple season television show about Jesus called *The Chosen* has amassed over half a billion views on its free electronic media app and has become available on cable and broadcast networks as well as with theatrical releases. What has made this streaming TV show so popular? Rather than address the matters of social media, advertising, free availability, and other influences, this chapter discusses the balance of some of the show's broader internal attributes that I suggest have led to its wide-ranging appeal.

Introductory Disclaimers

At the outset, let me make two disclaimers regarding the television show and my involvement with it. First, a personal disclaimer: as one of three theological script consultants, I am not a disinterested party when discussing *The Chosen*. Each season before filming begins, the scripts are sent to three consultants for feedback and suggestions from their various Christian faith traditions:

Father David Guffey, a Roman Catholic priest; Rabbi Jason Sobel, a Messianic Jewish rabbi; and me, an evangelical New Testament scholar. After the episodes are filmed and edited, the creator and director of *The Chosen*, Dallas Jenkins, brings us script consultants together to discuss each episode. These Bible roundtable discussions are available on *The Chosen* app for all to enjoy. (Yes, that's right: a priest, a scholar, and a rabbi walk into a TV studio!)

My second disclaimer is somewhat pedestrian, but I find it helpful to point out that *The Chosen* is merely a television show. It is not part of the Bible and is not an attempt to add to Scripture any more than Leonardo da Vinci's painting of the Last Supper is intended to be Scripture. Like da Vinci's painting, *The Chosen* is a work of art intended to represent biblical truth. Audio recordings of the reading of Scripture have been produced, and some even have dramatic visual representations as well, but that is not the genre of *The Chosen*. The most fitting genre category for *The Chosen* is that of historical fiction: it is historical for what we have in Scripture and attempts to tie together those historical features with fictive connections for the longer story arc of the television show. While they can be helpful tools, such artistic representations of biblical truths should never be used to replace the Bible as God's word to us. Dallas Jenkins has commented on *The Chosen*'s artistic process: "We take Bible stories, we work our way backwards to add the context, to add backstory: some of it's historical, some of it's cultural, some of it's artistical imagination. All of it's intended to support the character and intentions of the Gospels."[1]

Indeed, the show is actually quite transparent about this feature with its own disclaimer screen at the beginning of the first episode (S1E1).

> *The Chosen* is based on the true stories of the gospels of Jesus Christ. Some locations and timelines have been combined or condensed. Backstories and some characters or dialogue have been added.
>
> However, all biblical and historical context and any artistic imagination are designed to support the truth and intention of the Scriptures. Viewers are encouraged to read the gospels.
>
> The original names, locations and phrases have been transliterated into English for anything spoken.

Elsewhere the writers declare, "*The Chosen* was created by lovers of and believers in the Bible as the inerrant Word of God. . . . Our intention is that

Balancing Authenticity, Plausibility, and Relatability in The Chosen

all biblical and historical content, as well as the artistic imagination, wholly support the truth and purpose of the Scriptures. Our deepest desire is that you would delve into the New Testament Gospels for yourself and discover Jesus."[2] Rather than critique the television show for what its creators are *not* intending to do (!), viewers would do well to heed these declarations, and any critiques should be offered in light of its stated intentions. This chapter is one such offering in that direction.

Three Principles to Keep in Balance

The show's own disclaimer screen at the beginning of the first episode is, in fact, a nice starting point. It demonstrates a mindfulness among the makers of *The Chosen* about keeping things in balance. The "broader internal attributes" I referenced earlier are what I see as three of the show's overarching principles—or perhaps even goals—that are to be kept in balance, and the title of my chapter declares these three principal goals: authenticity, plausibility, and relatability.

(1) By "authenticity," I mean the show's attempt to move the story of Jesus and his first followers from the pages of Scripture to the format of a television show and to do so in an accurate way. To what degree does the TV show faithfully render the written story into an audiovisual medium? The caution here is to be careful that the measure of "accuracy" is not merely one's own preferential imagination.[3]

(2) Whenever a story is moved from the written page to the screen (big or small), there are gaps to be filled. For example, a writer can comfortably avoid describing the color of clothing for a character in the story, but the audiovisual medium of a television show requires that the characters' clothes have a color of some kind, and good costumers try for the kinds of fabrics and colors that would be plausible for the time and place of the story being told. So, "plausibility" is the second principle for *The Chosen*, and we can ask how plausibly the show fills in the unknown but nonetheless necessary details of a story taking place in the first-century Middle East.

(3) A third principle at work in *The Chosen* to mention here is "relatability." Fans of the show often mention how they can relate to its characters. What are the features that give *The Chosen* this sense of relatability? For many, the

simple answer is that *The Chosen* showcases Jesus's humanity while remaining faithful in its depiction of his divine nature. The Jesus portrayed by actor Jonathan Roumie is not a standoffish character always alone or contemplative or preoccupied but is one who has friends and family and enemies, gets hungry and tired and weary, and experiences a wide range of realistic human emotions, including a hearty sense of humor. And this balance of Jesus's humanity with his divinity is more robust than merely "a relatable man with super powers," as Michael John Petty puts it.[4] But let us also note that, as a serial television show, *The Chosen* has time for character development not only for Jesus but also for imagining more fully the lives of his chosen disciples. While viewers might resist comparing themselves to Jesus himself, it is more natural to connect with Jesus's first followers, especially when they are portrayed as having the same sorts of life experiences, problems, and emotions as the rest of humanity—notwithstanding the centuries of difference in time and culture. This opens up the storytelling for exploring some issues and motivations unavailable to other Jesus film projects.

Balancing the Three Principles

But more than describe the three principles of authenticity, plausibility, and relatability, I want to discuss the interaction and balance of these principles in the production of *The Chosen*. It seems clear that these three principles work together to introduce people to the authentic Jesus and narrate a plausible storyline that encourages them to encounter Jesus for themselves in a more relatable way than they may have formerly imagined.

In the world of film, particularly when dealing with projects "based upon a true story," the balance of artistic license must be considered.[5] When can authenticity be sacrificed for the sake of relatability? How much imagined dialogue can be plausibly suggested in order to display more authenticity in the story? Social media has tracked several controversies about *The Chosen*, including questions about authenticity. Even well-intentioned viewers sometimes doubt the legitimacy of *The Chosen* because of its apparent departures from the authentic story of Jesus found in the Bible. Indeed, some of the sharper critiques have even leveled charges of blasphemy and heresy because of supposed attempts to add to the Bible.

Balancing Authenticity, Plausibility, and Relatability in The Chosen

In contemplating such questions as these for true-life film projects, there may be many realms to consider, but I have selected ten particular issues to focus on for *The Chosen*. Of course, director Dallas Jenkins recognizes that there are some places where they may have simply made mistakes in producing a particular episode, and as evidenced in the Bible roundtable discussions, he is more than willing to have those errors pointed out. And I suspect that other scholarly discussions of the show will oblige in addressing the show's occasional anachronisms and other missteps. But I want to discuss briefly here ten places where authenticity is intentionally encroached upon—even if plausibly so—precisely for the sake of relatability. The first few issues may well illicit some eye-rolling that I would even bother to mention them. To my mind, however, the willingness to sacrifice some authenticity in these areas for the sake of relatability sheds some light on the necessity of artistic license in creating plausibly authentic presentations for meaningful impact in works of art.

(1) Language

Of the various complaints I've heard about *The Chosen*, it is enlightening to observe that no one has complained about the fact that the TV show is in English. After all, if *The Chosen* was aiming to be absolutely authentic, the languages utilized in the show would be Aramaic, Greek, and perhaps a little Latin and ancient Egyptian. But no one has charged the show with inauthenticity—much less blasphemy or heresy—for filming the show in English. Why? Because viewers understand the desirability of having the show accessible in one of the world's current day international languages.[6] My point here is that most people recognize that both authenticity and plausibility in the realm of language can be sacrificed a little for the sake of relatability for modern viewers.[7] This might be instructive for us as we consider some other realms of artistic license.

(2) Miracles

Perhaps as blatant as the use of English in *The Chosen* is the simple fact that no real miracles are performed by actor Jonathan Roumie in his portrayal of Jesus. Rather than real miraculous deeds, *The Chosen* utilizes regular filmmaking special effects for portraying such things as the miraculous catch of fish, the changing of water to wine, the feeding of the five thousand, and Jesus walking on water. "Well, of course!" you declare. "That's what we expect of a TV show—regular filmmaking special effects. You can't tell the authentic story of Jesus without having some portrayal of the miraculous." And that is my point. The inauthentic special effects are necessary to portray in a more relatable manner the authentic story of Jesus.[8]

(3) Dates

First-century chronological studies face several dating difficulties. For many it is rather odd to suggest that Jesus was born sometime between 6 and 4 BC.[9] Even more significantly, scholars debate the precise dates for the public ministries of John the Baptist and of Jesus, that is to say, whether Jesus's crucifixion and resurrection are best dated to the year AD 30 or AD 33.[10] Because they occasionally utilize date captions in the show, the makers of *The Chosen* were compelled to make a choice on these dating matters. And the decision to go with the earlier dating of Jesus's ministry has ramifications for such things as who was in leadership of the Sanhedrin at the time. To me the earlier dating is quite plausible and lends to the authenticity of the show; but I am aware that some scholars have a preference for the later dating scheme and see *The Chosen*'s choice as less plausible. But personal preferences about plausibility cannot be the sole arbiter on matters of authenticity. Fortunately, for most viewers, this difference of three years has very little impact on their assessments of the show's authenticity or on the relatability they feel with a show that necessarily must navigate real historical dates.

(4) Storyline Selectivity

As a seven-season series, *The Chosen* has more airtime than other Jesus film projects; nevertheless, *The Chosen* cannot include every episode from all four of the canonical gospel records. Furthermore, the Four Gospels themselves do not record all the same stories, so the storyline selectivity of *The Chosen* has good precedent.[11] Viewers may not always appreciate the selection and ordering of the Jesus stories portrayed in the television show, but there is no threat to authenticity here in its relatable collection of episodes. And viewers are clearly encouraged to read the canonical gospels, and perhaps to do so with

Balancing Authenticity, Plausibility, and Relatability in The Chosen

a properly motivated imagination. After all, as the aphorism rightly proclaims, "The book is always better than the movie."

(5) Timeline Compression

Even if only subconsciously, anyone watching movies or television shows today is familiar with the use of timeline compression.[12] Storytelling is made more relatable to the audience by skipping over mundane happenings that are not relevant to the central storyline. Viewers are content to see Jesus begin the journey westward from Capernaum and then to jump a couple minutes later to his arrival in Cana; no one wants to watch him every minute of the hours-long walk that it would take in the real world.[13] Time compression is actually an issue for reading the Gospels properly. A quick reading of the tightly narrated events in Luke 24, for example, might lead some to presume that Jesus's ascension was on the evening of his resurrection. But Acts 1—written by the same author as Luke 24—makes clear that the ascension happened forty days after the resurrection. In a sense, time compression is merely another version of storyline selectivity with precedents in the Gospels themselves. In bringing greater relatability to the storytelling, such selectivity need not be a threat to authenticity.

(6) Character Development

I come now to areas where some informed viewers fear that artistic license decisions in *The Chosen* represent more serious threats to the authentic story found in the Gospels. Perhaps chief among the suspicions is the character development of some of Jesus's first followers. Content with the well-informed portrayal of Simon Peter, and perhaps tolerant of the limp of Little James and the martial arts of Simon the Zealot, more people have questions about the apparent autism of Matthew.[14] But the portrayal of Matthew as played by Paras Patel is a good exemplar for the approach of *The Chosen*'s writing team in exercising controls on their artistic license. In contemplating Matthew as described in Scripture, the writers asked what kind of a person would choose to reject his Jewish family and friends so as to work collecting taxes in his hometown for the occupying enemy Romans. In answer to that question, it seems quite conceivable that he was someone who did not care about family and social interaction and someone particularly gifted in an area of extreme focus like mathematics. Indeed, it is this kind of reflection that makes it at least plausible that Matthew might have been on the autism spectrum. With such character development as this, *The Chosen* seeks to emphasize relatability but to do so with plausibility and without sacrifice to authenticity.

(7) Names of Characters

Two other character-related issues are sometimes questioned with regard to artistic license in *The Chosen*. One has to do with the names given to some New Testament characters. A prime example here is the name of Eden given to the wife of Simon Peter. While his wife is not actually mentioned in the Gospels (cf. 1 Cor 9:5), the Synoptic Gospels are explicit that Simon Peter had a mother-in-law (Matt 8:14; Mark 1:30; Luke 4:38), and a spouse usually comes with one of those. As *The Chosen* explores what it might mean for a married person to be a follower of Jesus, the show could not realistically have Simon constantly referring to his spouse as "wifey," so giving her the Jewish name Eden (which means "delight") seems properly pragmatic as well as relatable. So too some of the close-up interactions imagined between Jesus and other anonymous figures in the New Testament seem likewise to warrant granting them names. Thus, characters like the woman at the well and the woman with a flow of blood are given the names found in church tradition, respectively, Photina and Veronica.

(8) Additional Characters

The other character-related issue is *The Chosen*'s focus on several additional persons not explicitly mentioned or otherwise implied in Scripture. Prime examples would be Shula and Barnaby, two neighbors who are healed by Jesus. Bible stories about Jesus frequently refer to the "crowds," and many readers may prefer the people in the crowds to remain nameless and out of focus. But the reality is that those people had names, and the miracles they experienced changed their lives in just as significant ways as those who are singled out or named in the Gospels. By suggesting personal names for some of the faceless people in the crowds, and by suggesting that Jesus had other individual interactions with first-century people not explicitly mentioned in the Bible, *The Chosen* invites its twenty-first-century viewers to consider the fact that Jesus can be interested in interacting with them, too, without being explicitly mentioned in Scripture. This use of artistic license brings a personal relatability to the audience, with no real threat to the authentic features of the television show.[15]

(9) Fictitious Events and Conversations

Related to the use of additional characters in the story is the issue of fictitious events and conversations that occur in *The Chosen*. The Gospel of John acknowledges lots of events that were not recorded (John 20:30–31; 21:25), so it is plausible to portray some such events. The medium of a television show calls for filling out details that a pure literary medium simply does not provide. But admittedly that does not explain all of the additions seen in *The Chosen*, so I suggest here three subcategories for explaining these embellishments.

First, some additions can be explained away as *natural representations of first-century life*. While not explicitly mentioned in Scripture, it takes very little artistic license to suggest that Nicodemus celebrated the Sabbath with his family (S1E2). Similarly, what we know of first-century child mortality rates would make it likely that the followers of Jesus knew someone who had experienced a miscarriage. With Simon Peter being the one apostle confirmed as married, it is somewhat sensible as well as relatable to have him and his wife portray this first-century reality (S3E5).

A second categorization of fictitious additions in *The Chosen* can be explained as *depictions of theological truths*. The fabricated conversation between Little James and Jesus about God's ability to work through hardships has been reported as one of *The Chosen*'s most significant portrayals of authentic biblical teaching (S3E2). On the other hand, arguably the most controversial scene in *The Chosen*'s first four seasons is the twenty seconds where Jesus is practicing the Sermon on the Mount (S2E5). Many viewers were scandalized by the idea that Jesus as the divine Son of God would work on constructing a sermon rather than merely knowing (omnisciently) what to say without any preparation at all. But the New Testament is clear that in his humanity Jesus "increased in wisdom" (Luke 2:52), which implies the usual learning processes of children. It seems that this would include things like walking, talking, eating, reading, writing, and so forth. Scripture even says that Jesus "learned obedience" (Heb 5:8) but is careful to note that he can "sympathize with our weaknesses" as "one who in every respect has been tempted as we are, yet without sin" (Heb 4:15).[16] Thus, it seems reasonable to presume that one who could learn to talk, to read, to write, and to obey without sinning could also learn how to construct sentences and put together a sermon without sinning.[17]

A third categorization of fictitious additions in *The Chosen* can be explained as *audience surrogacy*, which is actually a regular feature of film projects. A major example of this is the scene where Matthew is relearning how to fasten the traditional Jewish prayer tassels to his garment (S3E7). Even if he had completely renounced his faith altogether, it seems that a man raised as a practicing Jew would never forget this basic practice. But this scene is designed to teach the viewers about the tradition by way of reminding Matthew.

As with its use of extrabiblical characters in its portrayal of the story of Jesus and his followers, *The Chosen*'s use of extrabiblical dialogue and events is largely a restrained utilization of artistic license that is both plausible and relatable. These extra items are in keeping with expected representations of first-century life, acceptable depictions of theological truths, and normal instances of audience surrogacy.

(10) Anachronistic Practices

The makers of *The Chosen* are rather insistent about portraying Jesus as a first-century Jew, and in the assessment of some, the show is largely successful in this representation. Parents are referred to as "Eema" and "Abba," the Sabbath is referred to as "Shabbat," and characters greet one another with "Shalom, shalom." Nevertheless, for the more knowledgeable viewers, some of the Jewish customs portrayed in *The Chosen* fall short on the scales of authenticity. For example, in one episode (S3E6) Nathanael mentions that Simon Zee could make a weapon of his *kippah*—a wry compliment to the warrior disciple that he could turn a cloth head covering into a tool of warfare. This is unfitting to the first-century world, for while Jewish men have for centuries covered their heads in prayer and in Scripture study, the *kippah* (Hebrew) or *yarmulke* (Yiddish) is relatively new and did not become a common practice until the thirteenth century. Similarly, in several episodes (e.g., S3E8 and S4E7), there is an overabundance of wax candles in use, which seems dubious in first-century Israel where oil lamps were far more likely. But wax candles are a regular part of Jewish observances today, and what seems like a technically anachronistic portrayal is helping viewers appreciate afresh the authentic Jewishness of Jesus and his world. The everyday Jewish air about the show is palpable in its everyday expressions and depictions. And so it is that Jewish reviewers can conclude that *The Chosen* "presents the most intensely Jewish Jesus and the Gospels we've ever had."[18] As with the modernization of the language of the show, despite the occasional anachronism lowering the level of authenticity, the viewers are finding in it a proper relatability that might have otherwise been further out of reach.

Conclusion

All in all, it appears to me that *The Chosen* operates with sensitive awareness regarding both its message about Jesus and its modern-day audience. The use of artistic license in *The Chosen* is controlled by a tremendous concern for authenticity to its message, and with the demands and constraints of its audiovisual medium, *The Chosen* seeks the most plausible ways to make its first-century material relatable to twenty-first-century viewers.

Of course, there are places where *The Chosen* could have done better in balancing the principles of authenticity, plausibility, and relatability. Teasingly, I like to tell people that if there is something in a particular episode that they dislike, that is probably a spot in the script where the show did not take the advice of the consultants. Nevertheless, I appreciate very much the rigorous—even if imperfect—efforts *The Chosen* has made in submitting its artistic license to a proper balance of authenticity, plausibility, and relatability.

2

Imaginative Retellings, Serious Interpretation

The Church Fathers and *The Chosen* on John 1:43–51

DAVID KNEIP

From the first season of *The Chosen*, viewers have noted, sometimes critically, that the show's creative team adds material to the biblical narrative by fleshing out stories with dialogue and backstory.[1] What is less well known is that the practice of imaginative retelling is hardly original to *The Chosen*. In fact, since the birth of Christianity, Christians have been engaging in the practice as they have sought to understand and interpret scriptural narratives that sometimes do not tell as much as readers would desire. In the present chapter, I will examine one of those narratives—the story of Philip and Nathanael as found in John 1:43–51—and how it has been interpreted through imaginative retelling in season 2, episode 2 of *The Chosen* and in commentaries from the first few centuries of Christian history. Although a great deal of time and space separates the ancient writers from the modern television show, there are a number of intriguing parallels between them, including proposals of backstory for the narrative, conjectures about what was meant by various statements in the text, and choices about which lines in the story were invitations to interpretation. Yet there are differences between the two as well, including the specific details proposed to flesh out the narrative, as well as the meanings of various statements made by the characters in the story.

Imaginative Retellings, Serious Interpretation

First, however, I must comment upon the raw materials for this analysis. Ancient Christians engaged the Gospel of John in many different ways, including artwork, occasional sermons, quotations in larger works, and imaginative expansions on the text itself.[2] In this chapter, I have chosen to focus specifically on the sustained interpretations of John's Gospel found in written commentaries from antiquity. Their step-by-step interpretation of John's text mirrors the artistic approach of *The Chosen*. Unlike many popular Jesus films, the show is neither a focused depiction of a single event or group of events, nor an attempt at showing the entirety of Jesus's life and ministry in the order one finds in the Gospels. Rather, like most biblical commentaries, it proceeds in serial format, episode by episode, so that there is opportunity to engage more of the text and also foreshadow or recall future or past events. Some of the ancient commentaries discuss the entire gospel, while others are more selective in their treatment; in other words, as a group, they mirror the approach taken by *The Chosen*, which omits some episodes but includes most of them. I examine commentators from both the eastern and western churches, most of whom have been translated into English.[3] They include Ephrem the Syrian (fourth century), John Chrysostom (fourth century), Augustine of Hippo (fourth–fifth century), Theodore of Mopsuestia (fourth–fifth century), Cyril of Alexandria (fifth century), the Venerable Bede (eighth century), Step'anos Siwnets'i (eighth century), Moshe bar Kepha (ninth century), Isho'dad of Merw (ninth century), and Nonnus of Nisibis (ninth century).

PHILIP AND NATHANAEL IN *THE CHOSEN*

Season 2, episode 2 of *The Chosen* depicts the story of Philip and Nathanael, with two halves of very similar length, each encompassing one full day. Most of this material is an addition to Scripture, with the meeting of Philip and Nathanael not coming until near the end. The first half of the episode involves scenes from one day alternating between Nathanael's life (facing a traumatic work disaster) and that of the disciples (in conversation at their campsite). The second half of the episode is linear with the two narratives converging into one series of events, all apparently in another single day. As the episode comes to its climax, the director finally depicts Philip's and Nathanael's conversation, followed by their meeting with Jesus that evening.

David Kneip

From an artistic perspective, the episode contains a number of interesting elements. Three aspects merit special attention: (1) Nathanael's actions under the fig tree, (2) the question whether anything good can come out of Nazareth, (3) and Jesus's statement about seeing angels ascending and descending upon the Son of Man. These facets of the story are exemplary for comparing the artistic and theological interpretations found in *The Chosen* with the early Christian commentaries.

NATHANAEL UNDER THE FIG TREE

What happens to Nathanael under the fig tree? *The Chosen* answers the question early in the show's episode, but in the gospel text, the tree only appears later in Jesus's mention of it. This scene is a particularly poignant part of the episode even though it is an addition to the biblical text—Nathanael's presence under a fig tree is mentioned in John 1:48 only as something that happened prior to his interaction with Jesus, with no further details given. The fig tree location is introduced after Nathanael has been in the bar following a worksite disaster, and it is used in two scenes. In the first, Nathanael sets his drawings and renderings afire, saying to God, "This was done for you," a statement he repeats later with more feeling. He then cries out to God, starting with the standard Jewish blessing used many times in the show ("Blessed are you, Lord our God, King of the universe"), continuing with the Shema ("Hear, O Israel. . . ."), then the first verses of Ps 102, and finally Nathanael's heartfelt cry of "Do you see me?" In the second scene, the documents have been reduced to ash, and Nathanael puts them on his head in a traditional gesture of grief and mourning before walking away. He is alone throughout these scenes; no other humans appear at any point. Additionally, the tree itself is alone. It stands in the middle of a high-elevation grassland. In *The Chosen*, the tree is depicted as rather like Nathanael himself: remote, isolated, and alone.

This depiction is important because the ancient Christian commentators spent significant time wondering about what precisely Nathanael was doing or had done under the fig tree. Jesus mentions the fig tree in John 1:48, but he gives no explanation of it or of what Nathanael was doing under it.[4] Two questions occupied early commentators. First, what does this interaction tell us about Jesus? And second, what leads Nathanael to respond to Jesus with such an exalted confession of faith: "Rabbi, you are the Son of God; you are the King of Israel!" (v. 49)?[5] The commentators seem to have assumed that Nathanael's response was entirely appropriate rather than an overreaction, generally concluding that something about Jesus's knowledge of the fig tree led Nathanael to this bold conclusion.[6]

It should be noted that not all the commentators discussed here addressed the topic of the fig tree. Further, commentators such as Augustine made no remarks on the fig tree in a literal sense but proceeded directly to address its spiritual significance.[7] Those writers who did consider the fig tree in a literal way fall into three groups. First, three authors in the eastern Christian tradition (Theodore of Mopsuestia, Cyril of Alexandria, and Moshe bar Kepha) assumed that the fig tree was simply where Nathanael was located before Philip called him. They seem to have imagined the scene as though Nathanael was under the tree *immediately* before Philip called him, taking Jesus's words in John 1:48 at face value: "Before Philip called you . . . you were under the fig tree." For example, Theodore of Mopsuestia wrote that, by his statement, Jesus "clearly pointed out the place and the tree under which he [Nathanael] was before he had been called by Philip," with the intention being that "he might show the excellence of his power in this way."[8] After making a similar comment, Cyril of Alexandria noted that there was a purpose for this information: "It is quite helpful that he mentions both the fig tree and the occasion because they provide the proof that he saw him [Nathanael]."[9] The strength of this interpretation is that it builds on Jesus's words, and it certainly magnifies Jesus. On the other hand, it does not explain the depth of Nathanael's response.

A second group of commentators, also represented by eastern Christian writers (Moshe bar Kepha, John Chrysostom, and Nonnus of Nisibis), imagined that the fig tree was where Philip and Nathanael had their conversation about Jesus being the Messiah.[10] Chrysostom, the great fourth-century preacher from Syria, remarks that "no one else was present there, but only Philip and Nathanael, and they were carrying on their entire conversation in private." John's Gospel provides the detail that Jesus called to Nathanael as Nathanael was approaching (John 1:47). Chrysostom adds that this occurred "before Philip drew near, so that the evidence was above suspicion," presumably meaning that Philip could not have whispered anything about Nathanael to Jesus.[11] Nonnus connects this statement with Jesus's majesty, saying that Jesus thereby revealed to him "his all-seeing and all-comprehending power" by showing him "the place where Philip had met him" and naming the fig tree explicitly.[12] As before, this interpretation has in its favor that Jesus talks about the fig tree and Philip's call in the same verse, thus making sense in terms of the narrative itself, as well as making strong theological claims about Jesus's divine foreknowledge. However, it does not explain why Nathanael would respond the way he did.

One writer, however, built upon this theme of divine foreknowledge with an interpretation that aligns closely with what we see in *The Chosen*. It appears in only one extant author, Ishoʻdad of Merw, who wrote many biblical commentaries while serving as a bishop in what is now northern Iraq. In his commentary on John, he indicated that a tradition had been handed down to him about Nathanael, though it is unclear whether *all* of what he wrote was part of the tradition, or whether some of it was from his own imagination.[13] Regarding Nathanael, Ishoʻdad reported that "this man, in his youth, had committed a murder by himself and had buried [the body] under a fig tree, without anyone seeing him."[14] Unlike the previous two interpretive trajectories, this guess is one that has no basis in the words of the gospel narrative *except for* Nathanael's reaction. Whoever originally espoused this possibility was clearly thinking about what would motivate Nathanael to call Jesus "the Son of God" and "the King of Israel" based on Jesus's one statement to him. In the gospel, Jesus himself acts surprised: "Do you believe because I told you that I saw you under the fig tree?" (John 1:50). Obviously, the idea that Nathanael was someone who had committed a terrible sin is quite different from the notion depicted in *The Chosen*, that is, that Nathanael was in deep grief. What these two interpretations share is the possibility that something terrible had happened, that Nathanael was completely alone, and that Jesus's knowledge of him in that moment is what caught his attention and motivated his confession of faith.[15]

Taken together, the various early Christian commentaries on this matter grow out of a problem that *The Chosen* attempts to address, namely, that the biblical texts are *merely* text. In other words, the gospel narratives provide some dialogue but no information about such things as facial expressions or tone of voice. In this case, what is missing is backstory, specifically, what Jesus was referring to regarding the fig tree. Nathanael seems to have known what Jesus meant, given his response, but the reader is not told why Nathanael was under the fig tree to start with, or the way in which it was important for the story. But in both the early Christian commentaries and in *The Chosen*, the reason matters. For the ancient Christian commentators, Jesus's awareness of Nathanael shows Jesus's divine foreknowledge and power, his ability to read hearts and minds, and (in the case of Isho'dad) his discretion, since Jesus did not broadcast Nathanael's sin publicly but only discreetly referred to it by mentioning the place where it happened. In *The Chosen*, the way the artistic team fills in the gap helps viewers grasp the depth of Nathanael's awe and how *personal* it was that Jesus saw him there. In the imaginative dialogue that the show adds, Jesus says, "When you were in your lowest moment, and you were alone, I did not turn my face from you," which is a direct reference to Ps 102:2, one of the texts Nathanael quoted earlier in the episode. Only then does Jesus say, "I saw you . . . under the fig tree."

"Can Anything Good Come out of Nazareth?"

One of the most famous lines from this narrative comes from Nathanael: "Can anything good come out of Nazareth?" (John 1:46). In *The Chosen*, Nathanael delivers this line in what appears to be his house, when Philip has come to tell him about the Messiah. Nathanael is certainly dejected, very tired, and possibly hungover. (In S4E2 Philip says that Nathanael had "passed out.") These circumstances make him only *more* likely to speak his mind. When Philip says that "the One" is "Jesus of Nazareth, son of Joseph," Nathanael responds with an incredulous "Nazareth?!" and starts to laugh. He then adds, "Can anything good come out of Nazareth?" and disparages it as a backwater. When Philip challenges Nathanael's characterization with a gentle smile, Nathanael then says, "Hey—I'm just telling it like it is! Why can't I do that?"[16] After making more negative comments about Nazareth, he concludes, "Honestly, Philip, saying 'the One' is a Nazarene is practically heresy!" Eventually, Nathanael heeds the repeated invitation to "come and see," but what seems to motivate him is his friendship with Philip, as well as Philip's appeal to Jesus's piety, rather than anything about Nazareth. The scene communicates that, at least in Nathanael's mind, Nazareth is entirely laughable.

This characterization of Nazareth will be familiar to those who have seen earlier episodes of *The Chosen*. To be sure, characters refer now and again to "Jesus of Nazareth" in a merely descriptive way. Some mentions of Nazareth itself are not pejorative. In season 1, episode 3, Jesus tells the children Abigail and Joshua that he is from Nazareth, and in season 1, episode 5, Dinah says that Mary came all the way from Nazareth for the wedding. But far more frequent are the negative comments and perceptions, as in season 1, episode 2, when Barnaby jokes, "Apparently something good *can* come from Nazareth!" or in season 1, episode 5, when Dinah and Rafi are embarrassed at a wealthy individual's comment that Dinah grew up in Nazareth. There are many more such comments, and by season 2, episode 2, the scriptwriters have clearly set the mood: generally speaking, people think of Nazareth as insignificant at best and contemptible at worst.[17]

For the ancient commentators, multiple issues arise from Nathanael's words. First, some note that, in both Greek and Latin, Nathanael's line about Nazareth can be read as either a question or a statement. Because there were no question marks in either language originally, readers must depend on syntax and word order, and in both cases the meaning is ambiguous. Cyril of Alexandria, the fifth-century bishop from Egypt, took it for granted that Nathanael *affirmed* rather than questioned Philip's naming of Jesus of Nazareth as the Messiah, as if he had said, "Something good can come out of Nazareth!" For Cyril, "Nathanael readily agrees that what people expected to be revealed from Nazareth would be great and most fair."[18] The Venerable Bede read it similarly, taking Nathanael's words as a statement and then noting that it is "as if he were clearly saying, 'It can happen that from a city with such a great name something of supreme grace may arise for us.'"[19] Augustine wrote that he knew it as *both* a statement and a question, and the great African bishop argued that it made sense either way, in that Nathanael was either affirming Philip's comment with his statement or responding to that comment with doubt or questioning. He did note, however, that it is usually read as a question.[20] That is true among contemporary English translations, and it was also true among most ancient commentators.

Many of the commentators nonetheless understood Nathanael's Nazareth remark differently than does *The Chosen*, seeing it as evidence of Nathanael's close study of the Scriptures rather than a comment upon the village itself. Chrysostom thought that the dialogue between Philip and Nathanael showed that *both* men were well versed in the Scriptures. For Chrysostom, when Philip said, "We have found him of whom Moses in the Law and also the prophets wrote" (John 1:45), it was an indication that Philip knew the law well, and

Nathanael's question showed that he had even "examined into the prophecies more carefully than Philip" and knew that the Messiah was to be born in Bethlehem.[21] For Chrysostom, Nathanael's question was not borne of derision about Nazareth or a lack of faith in Philip's words but rather came from deep knowledge of the Scriptures. Ephrem the Syrian made the same point, saying that Nathanael's question meant that he knew the text, and Moshe bar Kepha argued that Nathanael was more learned in the law and the prophets, so that he had the prophet's statement about Bethlehem in mind.[22]

Two other ancient commentators addressed John 1:46 differently, postulating a background that would explain Nathanael's question. Concerning whether anything "good" could come out of Nazareth, Theodore of Mopsuestia wrote, "Among the Jews the name of that village was much despised because its inhabitants were truly pagans," possibly referring to Isa 9:1–2 or Matt 4:15, where Galilee is called "Galilee of the Gentiles."[23] Cyril of Alexandria took a different tack, saying that "an untrue conjecture prevailed among the Jews" to the effect that the Messiah would come from Nazareth, "even though Holy Scripture says that he is a Bethlehemite." As a result, Cyril wrote, when Philip referred to Jesus as being from Nazareth, Nathanael's affirmation of Philip's statement meant that "what people expected to be revealed from Nazareth" would be good.[24] (Modern scholars have not found any attestations to the tradition Cyril cites here.)

Finally, some commentators focused on Jesus's response to Nathanael's question. This choice is interesting, given that Jesus was not present when Nathanael made his statement; presumably, they thought Jesus's divine knowledge would have permitted him to be aware of Nathanael's words. Most ancient writers who explicitly considered this question viewed Jesus's response to Nathanael as positive.[25] Ephrem, for example, wrote that Jesus gives him "a good testimony on his behalf" since Nathanael is acting without guile, "not like the scribes who were acting deceitfully."[26] Furthermore, a number of the eastern writers noted that Nathanael did not respond to Jesus's praise in any particular way, as though he was not resting on his laurels but rather continuing to investigate who Jesus might be.[27] Others suggested that Jesus's purpose in speaking was to continue to lead Nathanael to faith. As Cyril of Alexandria wrote, Jesus "affirms Nathanael, not to control his dispositions by flattery but to prove by the things he knew that as God he knows hearts."[28] Chrysostom pointed out that Jesus never actually corrected the question of his origin but instead proceeded immediately to winning Nathanael over by demonstrating his divine knowledge.[29] In other words, whether the commentators discussed the grammar of Nathanael's statement, explained what might have been behind it, or focused on Jesus's response to it, the gaps in the text allowed them to use their imagination to explain its significance.

Angels Ascending and Descending

The final element of the narrative under consideration here is one that *The Chosen* does *not* choose to explain or embellish, namely, Jesus's comment that Nathanael will see angels ascending and descending upon him. After Nathanael confesses Jesus as the Son of God and King of Israel, the scriptwriters basically follow the gospel text: Jesus says, "Because I said to you, 'I saw you under the fig tree,' you believe? You are going to see many greater things than that. Like Jacob, you are going to see heaven open, and the angels of God ascending and descending upon the Son of Man" (John 1:50–51). The only addition to the gospel text is the phrase "like Jacob." There is no other expansion or comment on this line, and Nathanael does not react to Jesus's statement in any particular way.

In some of the early Christian commentators, however, this statement is one that receives a great deal of attention.[30] For some, Jesus is here demonstrating his own lordship or divine origin. To cite one example, Nonnus of Nisibis argued that Jesus here acted as a teacher for Nathanael in wanting him to "understand even more perfect things" about him: to call him "not only 'king of Israel' but of all the earth, and of heaven, and of the angels."[31] Some early commentators also wondered about the timing of the ascent and descent; in other words, they sometimes asked not *why* it would happen, but rather *when*.[32] Still others held that, as with the fig tree discussed above, the ascending and descending was figural or metaphorical, declining to search for literal referents to what seemed to be a prediction.[33]

In other words, while *The Chosen*'s scriptwriters elected not to engage this particular line, the early Christian commentators demonstrated that it was ripe with interpretive potential. It may be challenging to imagine how the show might have depicted it otherwise, but these ancient commentators can stoke viewers' imaginations and in so doing help them to become closer readers of the gospel text. The show's creators might have shown Jesus teaching Nathanael more explicitly, as they did with Matthew as Jesus's conversation partner regarding the Sermon on the Mount in season 2, episode 8. They could have used flashback to show angels ministering to Jesus in the desert, as they did in season 3, episode 3, with a nonscriptural narrative of Jesus as a boy with his father Joseph. Or they might have used a flash-forward to the future, with the disciples acting as effective messengers for the Jesus movement, as they did in the opening of season 2, episode 1, when the disciples were gathered to mourn the death of James, the son of Zebedee (Acts 12:2).

Conclusion

In this chapter, I have attempted to demonstrate that the interpretive practices deployed by *The Chosen*'s creative team closely mirror the practices of the ancient Christian writers who composed commentaries on the Gospel of John. These two sets of interpreters have come to different conclusions about certain elements of the narrative, such as what Nathanael was doing under the fig tree when Jesus saw him, the nature and import of the query about something good coming out of Nazareth, and what Jesus (or John) meant by the statement that angels would ascend and descend. However, both groups have sought clarity about the details of the gospel narrative.[34] They have imagined ways to flesh out the text, whether offering a possible backstory as the explanation for *why* an element under consideration took place, or attempting to help their audiences understand *how* something in the story happened or what a particular statement meant. As John J. O'Keefe and R. R. Reno put it, in seeking to understand why the scriptural text is the way that it is, *The Chosen* and the early interpreters look *into* the text for answers rather than seeking actual historical events *behind* it.[35]

For readers of faith, the similarities between the interpretations found in *The Chosen* and in the early Christian commentators evince a belief that was present in the early church, is common among preachers and Bible students in the church, and is a basis for the show itself, namely, that Scripture and its details matter. As Bede wrote, "We must not suppose that it was by chance, and without a mystical reason, that the evangelist wished to point out the name of the city Philip was from, and the fact that it was the same of Andrew and Peter."[36] Early Christian commentators believed that everything in the Bible was there on purpose, even if its import was not visible at first glance. As James L. Papandrea has expressed it, early Christians' conviction that the "ultimate author" of Scripture was God led them to believe that "every word in the text is there for a reason" and to search "for spiritual meaning in even the smallest details of a biblical story."[37] *The Chosen* and the early commentaries stimulate their viewers' and readers' imaginations about the narratives of Scripture, inviting reflection on the spiritual meaning of their smallest details.

3

Evil and Divine Hiddenness

Feeding the Philosophical Imagination in *The Chosen*

DOLORES G. MORRIS

As a Christian philosopher who is an active member of a local church community, I often find myself in awkward conversations about Christian media. "No," I say, "I'm afraid I have not seen that movie, though I have heard of it." The unfortunate truth is that I have a well-grounded aversion to a certain kind of Christian media. It isn't merely that I don't enjoy watching these movies; my objections are theological and philosophical. It is a difficult thing to do justice to the complexity of the Christian faith in a movie or show that has box office appeal. As a result, intellectual charity tends to go out the window in favor of a simplistic tale of Christian triumph. I understand that many people find these movies inspiring. Even so, I tend to find them problematic.

The Chosen is an exception by every measure. There is a reason for its unprecedented success. It is visually and dramatically engaging. Even setting aside the theology, it is good television. More significant are the ways in which it is an intellectual or philosophical standout. Where some Christian media offers a simplistic and narrow rendition of God's work in our world, *The Chosen* is expansive. It increases the imaginative possibilities. It reminds us that our vantage is just one of many, that Christ's mission has always surpassed and superseded any human conception thereof. *The Chosen* feeds our imagination.

Better still, it feeds our *philosophical* imagination. In what follows, I examine the success of *The Chosen* at fostering our philosophical imagination as it pertains to two philosophical challenges to belief in God: the problem of evil, and the problem of hiddenness.

The Philosophical Imagination

The term *philosophical imagination* may strike some readers as an oxymoron. The discipline of philosophy is often (mis)represented as a domain in which decisive proofs reign supreme and deductive reason is our only guide. The truth is more complicated. Taken literally, the word philosophy (from the Greek *philos* and *sophia*) means "love of wisdom." Just as *wisdom* is a broad category, spanning many areas of understanding, the discipline of philosophy is as well. In fact, many historic texts that we now classify as scientific or mathematical treatises were, at the time of their authorship, embarked upon as works of philosophy. Bertrand Russell captured this curious aspect of the history of philosophy well: "As soon as definite knowledge concerning any subject becomes possible, this subject ceases to be called philosophy, and becomes a separate science. The whole study of the heavens, which now belongs to astronomy, was once included in philosophy; Newton's great work was called 'the mathematical principles of natural philosophy.'"[1] Philosophy is, and has always been, the pursuit of understanding across domains. The love of wisdom gives rise to philosophical reasoning; the results are far-reaching, expansive, exploratory, and—at times—even messy and speculative. Philosophical proofs exist, of course, but they are just one type of philosophical reasoning among many.

Some kinds of philosophical reasoning rely on our ability to *imagine*. To be clear, when I write of the philosophical imagination, I do not mean to suggest that we have a special power that we ought to call by this name. It might be better simply to note that our ordinary imagination can reap significant philosophical dividends. There is even a case to be made for the use of a different word altogether. The philosopher Brie Gertler distinguishes *imagining* from *conceiving*.[2] Where the former involves a kind of mental imaging, the latter relies primarily on the content of concepts. Gertler captures a common form of philosophical reasoning under the heading of *conceivability tests*, whereby we "try to imagine or conceive a particular scenario, to determine whether it is possible."[3] To cite her examples, by imagining, we find that no single object could be simultaneously blue all over and orange all over; by conceiving, we determine that no bachelor could be married. My use of the term *philosophical imagination* is intended to include both conceiving and imagining. In short, I mean roughly this: the process of considering possibilities—how things seem to be, how they might otherwise be (or have been), and how they perhaps could never have been—all in the pursuit of wisdom.

The philosophical imagination is crucial. When we cannot know for certain how things *are*, we may nevertheless benefit from considering how they *might be*. For example, in the first season of *The Chosen*, we meet Mary Magdalene. Having been delivered from demonic possession, in season 1, episode 2, she invites members of her community—social outcasts—to a Sabbath dinner. There is, of course, no biblical evidence that this event occurred. Nevertheless, the scene is profoundly impactful. (It moved me to tears.) "Yes," I thought. "Something like this surely happened!" What I find most interesting here is that this depiction of a mere possibility raises the very question it sets out to answer: For those who encountered miracles, what came next? *Possibly*, Mary Magdalene went on to transform her community through radically gracious Sabbath celebrations. If not that, then something like it! In this way, an imagined account of what may have transpired points us back to a factual element of reality: that those who were healed were real people, living in community; that the effects of their healing surely spread beyond what Scripture has recorded. Viewers of *The Chosen* will note that the example of Mary Magdalene is just one of many. These carefully crafted imaginative additions are part of what makes this show so provocative and powerful.

Perhaps unsurprisingly, an impoverished imagination can be a source of philosophical and theological weakness. One's imagination is impoverished when it fails to consider the full range of relevant possibilities. When this happens, we run the risk of significant error. We can see this risk in the exchange between Jesus and Simon the Zealot by the Jordan River (S2E5). Simon has devoted his life to rigorous training of the sort he expects would be of use in service to the promised Messiah. He is ready to fight for the Messiah. He is ready to die for the Messiah. Now, convinced that Jesus *is* this Messiah, Simon is ready to fight, even unto death, for Jesus. Imagine, then, what he must have felt when Jesus tossed his prized weapon into the river! When Simon asks

Jesus, "You have no use for that?" we know what lies behind his question. The Messiah he expected would have valued his weaponry.

In this moment, we see Simon confronted with a choice: he could revise his conception of the Messiah, or revise his assessment of Jesus as Messiah. We all know what he chose, of course, but it is worth pausing to consider what he might have done—especially since this process would not have been unique to Simon. Instead, this fictional scene beautifully depicts precisely the kind of inner struggle that many of Jesus's followers must have faced. They expected a Messiah who would save them from the Romans. They expected an earthly triumph. When confronted by the baffling reality of Jesus, those who were unable or unwilling to *reimagine* the Messiah so as to broaden the scope of what a Messiah might be may have missed the Messiah completely.

In these examples, we see some of the ways that *The Chosen* feeds our imagination. We see, as well, that an impoverished imagination runs the risk of leading us into error. It is good that we reflect on the ways that Jesus may have changed the lives of those he encountered. It is good that we remember that his ministry was surprising, even to those who shaped their lives in expectation of the promised Messiah. Still, none of what I have so far addressed is especially philosophical in nature. In the next section, I will introduce two arguments in the philosophy of religion that require the engagement of our philosophical imagination: the problem of evil and the problem of hiddenness.

SUFFERING AND HIDDENNESS

The risks of an impoverished philosophical imagination are especially significant on matters pertaining to God. For my first example, consider one of the most widely discussed arguments in the philosophy of religion: the problem of evil. Broadly construed, the problem of evil holds that the existence of God is incompatible with the kinds of suffering we find in the world. Statements of the argument vary in significant ways, but all hold this one thread in common, namely, the claim that the world is not as it would have been had God existed and that a divinely created world would be better than the world in which we live. In this way, suffering is presented as evidence against the existence of God.

In response, Christian philosophers have worked to widen the space of possibilities, crafting accounts that seek to reconcile the suffering we find in our world with God's loving providence. Notably, most do not purport to tell the *true* account of why God has permitted suffering. Instead, as the philosopher Alvin Plantinga writes, "the aim is not to say what God's reason is, but at most what God's reason might possibly be."[4] To be clear, I do not mean to say that the problem of evil was eradicated by Christian philosophical responses. Rather, it has been transformed. Early statements of the argument set out to show the logical incompatibility of God and evil, claiming that it would be an outright contradiction for a good God to permit the evil we find in our world.[5] This argument has mostly been abandoned.[6] In its place, we find *probabilistic* arguments claiming that the suffering we see makes the existence of a loving God unlikely.[7] The reason for this shift is straightforward: many of the proposed accounts do, in fact, show that a loving God might *possibly* permit evil. By imagining or conceiving of reasons why a good God might permit suffering, philosophers demonstrated the real possibility thereof. Possibilities are powerful!

Now consider a second philosophical argument, one that is currently receiving a lot of attention among philosophers of religion. According to the argument from hiddenness, a loving God would never allow his creation to sincerely doubt the fact that he exists. At the very least, those who are not resistant to the idea of God would face no such doubts. After all, a loving God would desire a relationship with all of his creatures, and no creature can be in a relationship with a God in whose existence he does not believe. Using this notion of a *nonresistant nonbeliever*, what we might call a *sincere skeptic*, the argument runs as follows:

1. If a loving God exists, then there are no nonresistant nonbelievers.
2. There are nonresistant nonbelievers.
3. No loving God exists.[8]

There are other statements of the argument, some far longer than this one.[9] There are also many Christian responses to the argument.[10] My goal here is not to defend a robust response to the argument. Instead, I want to emphasize just one feature of this argument: it relies upon our ability to imagine or conceive of what a loving God would do.

As Michael Rea writes, "The problem of divine hiddenness, like the problem of evil, is fundamentally a problem of violated expectations."[11] In both cases, there is some tension between our understanding of God as loving and sovereign, on the one hand, and our experiences in this world, on the other. Our beliefs *about* God shape our expectations *of* God. When those expectations are not met—a heartbreaking death where we expected healing; feelings of loneliness and doubt when we expected comfort in prayer—we find ourselves wondering where we went wrong. In some cases, the exercise may be purely intellectual. For example, a philosopher who doubts the existence of God on the basis of suffering need not be motivated by disappointments in a former life of faith. For others, however, it is deeply personal.

Violated Expectations

When our expectations are unmet, we are forced to revisit those expectations. We do this all the time on insignificant matters. To use a silly example, one of my earliest memories involves a family wedding. (My mom is the oldest of nine children; there were a lot of weddings!) I remember sitting in the car and listening to the directions my parents were given, which were to take us from the church to the reception hall. I was very excited to hear that we were going to encounter a large fork in the road. Living on Long Island, I was familiar with two similar landmarks—a giant duck, and a giant witch. A large fork was a new one, and it sounded fun! Imagine my disappointment when we arrived at the reception, never having passed any fork at all. I was pretty sure my parents had gone the wrong way, and I let them know. They managed not to laugh too hard while they explained the source of my confusion, and I was convinced. Disappointed, but convinced.

In cases like this, we follow a rough process: What did I expect? What did I find? Where did I go wrong? In doing so, we are led to further questions. From What did I expect? we must then ask, And on what basis? Finally, Was that a good basis, were those good reasons, for that expectation? For ordinary matters, this is all routine procedure. I believed we would encounter a large statue of a fork. On what basis? My limited understanding of the word "fork." This impoverished vocabulary was not, it turns out, a reliable basis for my expectation. The matter was quickly and decisively resolved. In contrast, when our expectations about God are unmet, the process of untangling the source of our error can be more complicated.

This point is especially acute with respect to hiddenness. The argument from hiddenness tells us that a loving God would not hide from his creation.[12]

The philosophical conception of God seems, therefore, to foster the expectation that God would be obvious, that he would be readily *available*. In stark contrast, Jewish and Christian Scriptures very often depict God as hidden—as actively *hiding*, even (e.g., Isa 45:15).[13] When we base our expectation of God on Scripture, at least some degree of hiddenness is to be expected. The philosophical conception of God and the biblical one come apart in this respect. What are we to conclude? Is our God not a loving God? Is he not good? If he is, why does he allow us to experience divine hiddenness? To state the philosophical challenge more directly: it isn't merely that *reality* contradicts the expectations of God set by the argument from hiddenness; Scripture itself violates those expectations. If the argument succeeds, then the God of Abraham must not be a good and loving God. If the argument succeeds, he is no God at all.

There is a clear analogy here: the Jewish expectation of a Messiah. Across the board, Jesus violated expectations. The incarnation, death, and resurrection of the second person of the Trinity is an astonishing display of violated expectations, one after the other. Those who took him to be the Messiah were shocked at his death. They were shocked again at his resurrection! We can presume that his ascension, too, was unexpected. If there is a single theme that runs through the life of Christ, it could be captured by the phrase, "I did not see that coming!" For this reason, all those who believe that Jesus is God ought to be wary of adopting precise expectations of how God will act in the world.

Suffering and Hiddenness in *The Chosen*

Here, at last, is my primary point about *The Chosen*: over and over again, this show invites us to see the ways that Jesus surprised his followers. These surprises were not always good. Instead, they often disappointed those involved. In what follows, I want to look at a series of illustrations in *The Chosen* where we encounter precisely the kinds of unmet expectations that motivate the problems of evil and hiddenness. As we read in Scripture and see throughout this series, Jesus, like his Father, permits suffering and doubt.

I will begin with divine hiddenness. There are at least three ways in which the Christian God is, or seems to be, hidden: (1) his *ways* are beyond us; (2) a sense of his *presence* often eludes us; (3) his *existence* is not always obvious to us. Strictly speaking, the philosophical argument from hiddenness proceeds only upon the basis of this final kind of hiddenness. Nevertheless, all three are relevant. After all, if God's ways were transparent to us, if an experience of his presence were readily available to us, these would surely serve as further evidence of his existence.

We can see examples of each of the three in *The Chosen*. We have already discussed one clear example of a case in which God's ways might be hidden from us—that of Simon the Zealot. Of course, Simon was not the only one of the disciples to have expected a different Messiah. (The other Simon—Simon Peter—spends much of the first season practically looking for a fight!) We see this on display throughout *The Chosen*, in ways that are beautiful, powerful, and sometimes heartbreaking. When Nicodemus struggles to make sense of Jesus, torn between his expectations and this baffling reality, we understand his struggle. Here is a man who wants to honor God—if only he could figure out what doing so would require! We see more minor instances of a similar struggle throughout every season. *If Jesus is the Messiah, why is he contaminating himself with that unclean leper? Why isn't he fighting? Why won't he join me in confronting Herod? Why would he let my brother die? What kind of Messiah is this?*

We see a similar struggle in Jesus's private conversation with John the Baptist (S2E5). John's faith in Jesus is complete. He is wholly devoted to preparing the way for the kingdom of God and fully convinced that Jesus is the one who will bring that kingdom. Even so, he struggles with the pace at which Jesus works. In this poignant scene, we see him grapple with his own expectations—that Jesus would act, and act quickly, and act as John sees fit. John has the wisdom to hold his expectations loosely, trusting Jesus over his own plan. Even for John, this does not make it an easy endeavor. As a final example, consider Eden throughout the third season. How difficult it must have been to see her husband sent away so soon after his brief return. How heartbreaking to then endure a miscarriage, the loss of a hoped-for child, without her husband by her side. In each of these examples, we see faithful followers of God who are, nevertheless, puzzled by his ways.

The elusiveness of God's presence, or at least of what we expect his presence to feel like, is also clearly depicted in *The Chosen*. We see a glimpse of this when Eden confesses to Simon Peter that she sometimes forgets Jesus's face (S3E1). More significantly, when Jesus tells Nathanael that he saw him under the fig tree (S2E2), we hear Nathanael respond as he does in John 1:49: "Rabbi, You are the Son of God! You are the king of Israel!"[14] Here, the creators of *The Chosen* have again taken a line of Scripture and imagined its context. Are

Evil and Divine Hiddenness

we to believe that this is precisely what happened? Of course not! Instead, we are shown *one of many* things that might have happened. Above all, we are reminded of a clear biblical truth: however the details unfolded, when Jesus told Nathanael that he saw him under the fig tree, Nathanael felt seen in a way that eradicated all doubt. It is a small inference, indeed, to suppose that, before this, Nathanael had felt unseen.

Finally, though to a lesser extent, we even see examples of people sincerely doubting the existence of God. In the very first season, Simon Peter's struggles to maintain his hope in the promised Messiah reveal deeper doubts about the God of Israel. Many of the Romans, we can presume, act as they do because they believe that the God of Israel is no God at all.

In addition to hiddenness, we also encounter suffering in *The Chosen*—suffering that Jesus could prevent, but that he does not prevent. One clear case is the imagined conversation with Little James in the second episode of season 3. More striking to me is his farewell to John the Baptist. In that scene (S2E5), we watch Jesus wordlessly grieve his cousin. We know what John does not know, what his disciples do not know—that John's death is imminent. We see that Jesus knows this, that he could have prevented it. We watch as he does not prevent it.

The Power of These Examples

How do these examples help us in our efforts to make sense of suffering and hiddenness? They remind us of the limitations of our own understanding. In each of these examples, viewers of *The Chosen* stand in a peculiar vantage. We know how these stories end, but we do not know how *the* story ends—at least, not in any detail. To see what I mean, consider Simon Peter, Simon the Zealot, and John the Baptist. Each of these men wanted something good from God. They wanted the literal rescue of the Jewish people from Roman oppression. Not only was this a good thing; it was a thing promised by God. Further, it was something the Messiah was supposed to accomplish! We understand their frustration. We empathize with their disappointment. At the same time, we are not puzzled in the ways that they are puzzled. Instead, our empathy is tempered by the knowledge that theirs was, through no fault of their own, an impoverished vision of Christ's mission. From where we stand, we can see (more or less) what Jesus was up to. He wanted to overthrow more than Rome; he wanted to overthrow death. He wanted to liberate the Jewish people, but he also wanted to liberate all people, from all manner of oppression.

Furthermore, these examples and the series as a whole remind us of a difficult reality: that individual human responses to what we might call *evidence* vary greatly. The very same displays of miraculous healing convince some that Jesus is the Messiah, and others that he is a threat to the people of God. This is important, for it demonstrates the complexity of our expectation that God be more obvious. Obvious how? It is possible that this task is more complicated than we would like for it to be.

Consider once more the arguments from evil and hiddenness. In particular, note the manner of the reasoning involved. We began by considering the world as it is, or as it seems to be. There is suffering and doubt, and a great deal of it. Next, we asked how things *might* have been. Could there have been less suffering? Fewer skeptics? If so, how? At what cost? And what about God? Would a good God allow any suffering and doubt? If so, how much? And for what reason(s)? Finally, are there things that even God could not have brought about without some measure of suffering or doubt? (Things like free will?) That is, are there ways the world *could never have been*? In working through these questions and others like them, we examined the boundaries of possibility. When we fail to consider these questions in full, when we assume that we already know the full range of possibilities, we run the risk of being wrong about very important things.

There must, of course, be some boundaries to what we could expect of God. An evil God would be no God at all. Countless pages of philosophical writings have been devoted to logical deductions from the mere concept of God, where God is construed as something like "a being with every perfection." These arguments make little to no use of the imagination; they are expansions on the definition of a concept. These more recent arguments are not like that. Instead, they go beyond basic attributes of God—omnipotence, omniscience, omnibenevolence—and draw concrete conclusions about what God would do. In doing so, these arguments assume a certain hierarchy of values.

The problem of evil begins with the notion that a good God would want to prevent suffering. This is a reasonable assumption! Even so, it is an assumption that must be reconsidered in light of the sweeping variety of things that a good and loving God might value. If, for instance, free will, moral responsibility, and genuine worship cannot be had without some suffering, then a good and loving God might permit suffering on that basis. That is, he might not value the alleviation of suffering *above all else*. Likewise, the argument from hiddenness begins with the expectation that a loving God would do everything in his power to ensure that his creatures know, with confidence, that he exists. Again, it is easy to see where this expectation comes from. Why wouldn't a loving God want his children to know him? Careful reflection reveals that this is not the question we need to ask. Of course he would *want* that. The real question is, Might there be other goods that God also values? Could it be that some of those goods contribute to his willingness to allow some people to doubt his existence? From *goodness alone*, we cannot infer that the world will be as we think it ought to be.

This is just one of the many spiritual truths that *The Chosen* helps us to see. A good God will want good things. A loving God will care for his creation. This much *must* be true. Even so, the distance afforded by our historical perspective helps us to see the limitations we face in going much beyond these generalities. The Jewish people had special insight into who God is and what he had promised. Jesus's disciples had the astonishing privilege of walking alongside the Messiah, assisting him in his mission and learning, quite literally, at his feet. If *even they* got things wrong, how much more should we expect to have our own expectations violated? When we long for good things, when we ask for them in faith with confidence in God's loving providence, we will sometimes be disappointed. *The Chosen* helps us to see why that may be. God's ways are beyond ours; his plans are bigger than ours. The misunderstandings we see on display in Peter, Simon, John, and others should be a kind of guardrail to our own expectations. We can trust in God's goodness! We should be wary of placing too much trust in our own understanding of what that goodness will look like in our lives.

Epistemic Humility and the Limits of the Imagination

The philosophical term for the kind of caution I have encouraged here is "epistemic humility."[15] Those who are familiar with the word "epistemology" will see the meaning straightaway. Where epistemology is the study of knowledge, epistemic humility is humility about what we can know. I am a proponent of epistemic humility.[16] This is not to say that I advocate for complete skepticism. As the philosopher Nathan King writes, "Humble people don't underestimate their weaknesses—they avoid arrogance. But humble people also avoid *over-estimating* their weaknesses."[17]

Returning to *The Chosen*, Jesus's disciples were often surprised by his decisions. Even so, there are limits to the ways that he defied expectations. A Messiah who heals on the Sabbath and hugs a leper pushes the boundaries of what a Messiah might be. Had he, instead, stolen from the poor and used his miraculous power to harm the innocent, he would have shown himself to be no Messiah at all. We should take care not to assume that we know precisely when and how God will act. We can, nevertheless, remain confident in his goodness, his power, and his sovereignty.

I want to end by acknowledging some of the controversy engendered by *The Chosen*. In a blog post entitled, "'The Chosen' and the Sufficiency of Scripture," Travis Kerns succinctly captures a concern held by some viewers, writing, "*The Chosen* can be charged with breaking the Second Commandment, removing Scripture as the all-sufficient guide for Christian faith and practice, and ignoring multiple texts concerning the addition and deletion of texts of Scripture."[18] As I have made clear, I do not agree with this accusation. I do, however, think it raises a distinction that we must work to keep in mind: *The Chosen* is not, and does not purport to be, Scripture. If we take it as such, we will, in fact, violate the teachings of Scripture.

There are, in the end, two ways that the imagination can influence our philosophical and theological framework. If we are too rigid in our conceptions of God's activity in our world, we are likely to get things wrong. God is infinite; we are finite. He is transcendent. His ways are beyond our own. The imagination can be a helpful tool in reminding us of these truths, and *The Chosen* is an especially fruitful vehicle for these illustrations. God, through Jesus, has been defying our expectations from the beginning. We should expect some surprises still to come. Still, in working to broaden our imaginative landscape, we must not forget what the imagination is. *The Chosen* helps us to see some of the kinds of things that may have transpired in Jesus's life. It does not, therefore, give us *knowledge* about what transpired. The imagination yields possibilities. Possibilities are fruitful, they are philosophically powerful, but they are not *known actualities*. We must always keep this distinction in mind.

4

The Dialectical Imagination, the Sacramental Imagination, and the Appeal of *The Chosen*

Different Christian Approaches

KENNETH GUMBERT

It has often been argued that the most important contribution Christianity has made to Western civilization is the promotion of the individual as the foundation of all its cultural achievements.[1] This assessment is true in many ways; however, it more importantly reflects a particular worldview, assumptions that might not be universally shared. Others might argue that the most significant contribution Christianity made to the West is the formation of enduring institutions that created structures that eventually transformed society.[2] Both assessments are correct. But more significantly, they reflect two different worldviews that shape how individuals interpret practically everything around them, especially contemporary Christian practice.

Systematic theologian David Tracy explores the underlying worldviews of a variety of Christian denominations in *The Analogical Imagination: Christian Theology and the Culture of Pluralism*, an incisive analysis of the many strands of Christian practice in the United States within a pluralistic context.[3] His method involves an examination of classic texts produced by these various denominations. This "fundamentally hermeneutical" approach considers the seminal writings of Protestant and Roman Catholic theologians who represent the central tenets of their respective traditions.⁴ Tracy argues that classical Protestant Reformation texts often summed up in the principles of the five solae (*sola scriptura, sola fide, sola gratia, soli Deo gloria, solus Christus*) reject the authority and traditions of the Roman Catholic Church and promote an emphasis on personal salvation. In these texts, the reformers challenge the institutional church and amplify the role of personal faith and the individual's ability to study sacred Scripture as the only means toward salvation.

The Protestant Reform movement of the sixteenth century signaled a rejection of Scholasticism and paved the way for the Enlightenment of the seventeenth and eighteenth centuries. A hallmark of the Enlightenment and the early modern period was a focus on the individual and the natural rights of man. This movement emphasized rational thought and introduced the scientific method and materialist philosophies, as well as capitalism and Marxism. It favored a transcendent vision of God, where the natural world and the sacred realm are understood to be in opposition to each other. Tracy refers to this Reformation-derived worldview as the dialectical imagination. Obviously drawing from Hegel's dialectical method, Tracy associates the Protestant Reformers with a full-blown opposition to the various power structures of the sixteenth century that would lay the groundwork for a secular materialism that becomes characteristic of the modern era.

Tracy regards the Roman Catholic worldview as completely different from its Protestant counterpart. Classical texts in the Catholic tradition rely upon a more ancient, possibly even a more pagan worldview that emphasizes the primacy of communal institutions, ancient traditions, and rituals. He also identifies the necessity for mediators to guide the faithful toward salvation as the central idea germane to the Roman Catholic worldview. Tracy refers to this as the analogical imagination because, he argues, the classic texts of the Catholic Church posit a world that is mysteriously like the sacred realms where the divine immanently dwells with creation.

Another Catholic priest from Chicago, sociologist Andrew Greeley, writes about Tracy's theories in his 2000 book *The Catholic Imagination*.⁵ Greeley attends the distinctive elements of Roman Catholic liturgical practice combined with traditions associated with various ethnic Catholic cultures. He affirms Tracy's intention of interpreting Protestant and Catholic practice through a pluralistic lens that seeks to understand and respect the differences found among both branches of the Christian family. Greeley focuses on the specifically Catholic analogical imagination, which he renames the sacramental imagination because of the centrality of the sacraments in the Roman Catholic view of salvation. Catholics assume that to encounter the divine, one must go through the mediation of the sacraments. Unlike the Protestant worldview, salvation is not an individual or a direct experience.

Tracy goes into detail exploring the differences between the dialectical worldview and the analogical (or sacramental) worldview. For our purposes, we can focus on a few of these distinctions. According to Tracy, the dialectical imagination, as eventually influenced by Enlightenment ideas, championed the individual and his subjectivity as its primary value. As applied to Christian religious practice, he states the dialectical imagination posits a world where individuals can absolutely encounter the divine through direct faith in Jesus Christ. This act of faith is initiated by the person seeking God as a conscious act of the will. It is essential that the person chooses to accept Christ into one's heart. In this way, persons are "born again" and become children of God. This new relationship with the divine implies a radical distinction between one's old self and the newly saved self. Often the proof of this new personal relationship with Christ is a direct access to God's divine favors. This is manifested as real through personal success, which means material success as a sign of one's personal relationship with Christ. An interesting illustration of this stress on individuality can be readily detected in the realm of entertainment in, for example, the popular western films and television programs of the early to mid-twentieth century, such as Howard Hawks's 1948 masterpiece *Red River*. Those films and television programs appealed to the spirit of individualism popular at that time in American culture. The western cliché of the lone hero can be viewed as an expression—if not a product—of the dialectical imagination.

What does any of this have to do with the tremendous success of *The Chosen*? I suggest that what we have in *The Chosen* is something that appeals not only to dialectical imagination but also to sacramental imagination, and this gives the series a very broad appeal. Christians of all denominations love the series, and its audience continues to grow. Certain creative choices made in the first three seasons reveal the mindset of its creator, Dallas Jenkins.

Dallas Jenkins identifies as an evangelical Protestant Christian. He is very influenced by the success of his father Jerry B. Jenkins as the coauthor of the popular postapocalyptic *Left Behind* series (1995–2007). Central to the evangelical experience in America is personal acceptance of Christ, literal engagement with the Scriptures, and the living out of one's faith commitment through righteous behavior according to biblical standards. The mindset of the particular strand of evangelical Christianity that shaped Jenkins, sometimes referred to as dispensationalism, is most definitely associated with the dialectical imagination. Even though Jenkins consults theologians from Catholic, Jewish, and Protestant backgrounds, it is possible to see the influences of the dialectical mindset through storytelling choices throughout the first three seasons. However, it is also possible to detect elements of the sacramental imagination. The inclusive nature of the entire production may help account for the series's tremendous success among a wide audience.

The two most important story arcs that reveal Jenkins's imaginative leanings can be seen in the treatment of Mary Magdalene and Mary, the mother of Jesus. It is important to notice that Jenkins introduces Mary Magdalene and the miracle of her healing and ultimate professed belief in Jesus as the Messiah so early in the series. Jenkins takes liberties with the Scriptures and develops an extrabiblical narrative around the character as a prostitute who is possessed by a powerful demon. Her story becomes central to that of the call of the disciples as her affliction cannot be remedied by the Pharisees and the methods of the old dispensation. She can be healed only by Jesus, the Messiah hidden in plain sight among the Jews of Capernaum. Jesus, in his compassion and within his mission to reveal himself to certain individuals to fulfill God's will, heals Mary. This is noted as his first miracle in the series. And it makes absolute sense from a dialectical imaginative stance as the personal stories of Mary and all the disciples take center stage. (Indeed, Jesus does not appear until the very end of the first episode.) Personal salvation, including a moment in time where the individual encounters the Christ, believes, and accepts his presence in their life, is a central component of the dialectical mindset. The significance of this personal encounter is rooted in the centrality of the individual and one's subjective experience, especially of the divine. Mary's encounter is also significant because of the way her character displays the contrast between her old self—dissolute, immoral, demon-possessed—and her new, born-again self. The contrast between the old and the new, the earthly and the heavenly, the human and the divine are hallmarks of the dialectical imagination, an imaginative stance that underscores the transcendent nature of the Christ event.

Aspects of the dialectical imagination can also be seen when Mary is triggered and backslides into her old ways (S2E5–6). She disappears from the troupe of disciples and returns to the denizens and haunts of her former way of life. The distinction between righteousness, clean living and a sinful lifestyle is magnified here. The sacred cannot be commingled with the sinful. These worlds are incompatible, distinct realms. They are diametrically and dialectically opposed! The only approach to sin and the fallen nature of this world is to reject it, overcome it, and rise above it. And through the grace of God that comes through faith, individuals can transcend evil inclinations and become free of the shackles that hinder all human activity.

Consider the imagery of the cross in most evangelical churches. Here it is typical to find a cross but not a crucifix; the latter displays the body of Jesus as he nears his death, while the former does not. The imagery implies that the cross cannot contain the Christ. He died on the cross, yes, but he also overcame it. Jesus rose above the world and its sinful hold on creation. His followers must do the same!

The Chosen has a broad appeal because it embraces both the dialectical and the sacramental interpretation of the world. Evidence of Jenkins's adoption of the sacramental imagination may be seen in his inclusion of the Christmas narrative. At first glance, it seems the story of Jesus's birth is glossed over in the series. Even though the entire inspiration for the series grew out of a Christmas presentation for a Midwestern church community, the Christmas story was added onto the regular eighth episode of the second season, thus becoming part of the official canon of the series. Earlier in the series, Mary is presented as a member of a working-class Jewish household. In these early domestic scenes, Jesus spends most of his time with his father, who is training him in the woodworking trade. It is very instructive that the birth of Jesus narrative is glossed over here only to be added later for a Christmas special episode. Included in this special episode is Mary's prayer (Luke 1:46–55), known as the Magnificat in the sacramental tradition. The prayer is very important to sacramental Christians because Mary as *Theotokos* (literally, "God-bearer") is honored as the Mother of God. In this context, she is believed to be central to salvation history and the Gospels. She is also considered as the model for all Christians who, like Mary, are expected to give birth to the Word of God in their daily lives. The fact that Jenkins includes Mary's story and the nativity account in the series speaks to his desire and ability to reach out to all Christians from these two very different branches of the one faith.

The nativity narrative has often been problematical for Reformation theologians, who emphasize the death rather than the birth of Jesus. Calvinists especially have a history of criticizing Christmas celebrations as being nonbiblical and even of pagan origins. In Massachusetts, the Pilgrims outlawed the celebration of Christmas in their colony.[6] Similarly, there is not an established tradition of celebrating a specific liturgy on Christmas Day in the Church of Jesus Christ of Latter-day Saints. Understanding the different value placed on the nativity narrative in a dialectical framework versus a sacramental approach makes sense when considering the underlying meaning behind the Christmas story.

In the Christmas story, Christians celebrate the unity of heaven and earth. God sends his Son, through the birth of a child into a world of his creation. God is a little like the world, and the world is a little like God. The two realms are in harmony. This is the message of Christmas. It is an analogical message. This is probably why Catholics celebrate Christmas in such an elaborate manner. In fact, judging simply by the way Catholics celebrate Christmas versus the way they celebrate Easter, one might conclude that Christmas is the more important feast. Of course, theologically this is not true. But what is important is sometimes revealed not by what is said but by what is done. This makes sense for Catholicism because of its sacramental emphasis. The Catholic sacraments are things of this earth—bread, wine, water, oil, and human touch that are used and transformed to reveal Christ in particular ways for the believer. It is through the sacraments that Catholics believe they encounter Christ. It is a mediated experience through the church, the priest, the sacraments, its rituals, and its traditions.

The foundation for this incarnational worldview is found in the Christmas narrative. Christmas announces the immanent presence of God in our world. In fact, it asserts the necessary dimension of creation in man's search for the divine. The Christmas narrative announces that God can be encountered only through engagement with the world, mediated particularly through the sacraments and incidentally through encounters with nature. Therefore, it is possible to view the celebration of Christmas as the foundation for the entire sacramental theological system. Hence, its importance in Roman Catholic theology and practice.

The Appeal of The Chosen

In conclusion, the influence of both the dialectical imagination and the sacramental imagination can be detected in the creative choices made in *The Chosen*. This makes sense as the excitement of the gospel and the early spread of Christ's message is meant to appeal to the individual. The gospel message is itself a call to consider something new and different being introduced to humanity and salvation history. Yet it is also the story of the birth of a new institution, namely, the church. The dynamics of Christian storytelling, beginning with the Acts of the Apostles, shift after the resurrection with the institution of the church in Jerusalem and the spread of Christianity to the pagans of the Roman Empire. Because of these historical developments, it is possible to sense traces of both dialectical and analogical elements in the Christian tradition. *The Chosen* has successfully incorporated both strands of the gospel story. More than savvy marketing or inspired casting decision, this is the key to its broad audience appeal and unexpected success.

Part Two

STORYTELLING *and* NARRATIVE

5

The Knowledge Spiral in *The Chosen*

How the Visual Medium Conveys the Relational Message

M. ELIZABETH LEWIS HALL AND TODD W. HALL

Liz first viewed *The Chosen* in her role as a leader in the young adults ministry at her church. She was struck by how often the young men and women in the group commented on how seeing Jesus and the other apostles as real people impacted the ways in which they were able to see the presented gospel truths as relevant to them. As she reflected on this, she recognized that the depictions of Jesus, in particular, were also challenging her. She had never imagined a Jesus who could laugh, make jokes, or enjoy whittling wood in his spare time. She realized that her implicit image was of a serious man, very focused, a little distant from real life happening around him, and silent except when he opened his mouth to deliver profound, mysterious sayings. The Jesus of her imagination was someone she admired and followed, but he was not particularly approachable.

The Westminster Catechism, a foundational document in Reformed theology, begins by articulating the ultimate purpose of human existence: "Man's chief end is to glorify God, and to enjoy him forever."[1] This succinct statement encapsulates the centrality of relational intimacy with God to the Christian faith. Throughout the ages and across diverse Christian groups, this kind of intimacy with God has been pursued, using the language of "union" in the Catholic tradition, and "intimacy" in the Protestant tradition. For example,

Thomas Aquinas, writing in the thirteenth century, said, "Now the end of the spiritual life is that man be united to God, and this union is effected by charity, while all things pertaining to the spiritual life are ordained to this union."[2] However, for many believers, achieving and maintaining this relational intimacy with God can remain an elusive goal, despite earnest efforts and sincere desires.

In this chapter, we explore how the television series *The Chosen* may serve as a means of facilitating relational intimacy with God in Christ. Created by Dallas Jenkins, *The Chosen* offers a unique and compelling portrayal of the life and ministry of Jesus, inviting viewers to encounter the Gospels in a deeply personal way. Its vivid characterizations, emotional depth, and imaginative storytelling bridge cultural and linguistic divides in ways that promote a sense of relational connection.

To understand how *The Chosen* might fulfill this role, we examine the series through the lenses of attachment theory and dual processing models of information. Attachment theory, which describes the dynamics of close interpersonal relationships and the impact of early experiences on later relational patterns, provides a framework for understanding how individuals relate to God and how their perceptions of God can be shaped by their attachment histories. Dual processing models, on the other hand, distinguish between two interrelated systems of information processing—one implicit and intuitive, the other explicit and analytical—and highlight the importance of engaging both systems in the process of spiritual transformation.

We propose that *The Chosen*, through its evocative storytelling and relatable portrayal of Jesus and his followers, may serve as a powerful tool for helping viewers overcome barriers to intimacy with God. By inviting viewers to enter into the gospel narrative in a way that engages both their implicit and explicit ways of knowing and challenges dysfunctional attachment filters, the series has the potential to undermine unhealthy perceptions, foster a deeper sense of God's presence and love, and encourage a more authentic and transformative relationship with God.

By considering *The Chosen* in light of these psychological frameworks, we aim to shed light on how the series may assist viewers in their pursuit of the ultimate purpose of human existence—glorifying and enjoying God forever. We will first explore two barriers to intimacy with God: the historical split between theology and spirituality in the Protestant tradition, and the prob-

The Knowledge Spiral in The Chosen

lem of God's incorporeality. We will then examine how attachment theory can help us understand the way viewers' relational histories and attachment styles influence their perception of God, and how *The Chosen*'s portrayal of Jesus can challenge and expand these perceptions. Next, we will delve into dual processing theory, explaining how the series's evocative storytelling engages both implicit and explicit ways of knowing, thereby facilitating a deeper internalization of spiritual truths. Ultimately, we hope to encourage further reflection on the transformative power of visual media in cultivating a more intimate, authentic, and transformative relationship with God.

Barriers to Intimacy with God

One of the reasons relational intimacy with God is challenging for many people in multiple traditions within Protestantism has to do with the historical split between theology and spirituality. This split has placed a wedge between explicit and implicit ways of knowing, prioritizing the former. Protestants (and perhaps others) are heirs to a form of Christianity in which the early church's understanding of theology as encompassing both implicit relational knowledge and explicit propositional knowledge was challenged by medieval Scholasticism and exacerbated by the Enlightenment's emphasis on rationalism and the split between faith and reason.[3] The result has sometimes been an overemphasis on explicit propositional knowledge at the expense of implicit relational ways of knowing God. This imbalance can contribute to a rationalistic approach to spiritual formation that neglects the importance of experiential, embodied knowledge in fostering intimacy with God. In this context, resources like *The Chosen* serve as a much-needed corrective, inviting viewers to engage with the gospel narrative and the person of Jesus in a way that integrates both implicit and explicit ways of knowing.

A second challenge to experiencing relational intimacy with God is his incorporeality. As embodied creatures, our relationships with others are profoundly shaped by our bodily existence. Our bodies serve as a primary vehicle for relating to others, facilitating connection, communication, and understanding.[4] The growing prevalence of social media, while seemingly offering an alternative to embodied relating, ironically highlights the importance of physical presence in relationships. Research has shown that, while social media can facilitate certain kinds of social connection, it can also lead to feelings of loneliness and disconnection when used as a substitute for face-to-face interaction.[5] Moreover, studies have found that the lack of nonverbal cues in online communication can contribute to misunderstandings and decreased empathy.[6] These findings underscore the centrality of the body in human relationships and the limitations of attempting to maintain intimacy through disembodied means.

Yet, as Scripture teaches, "God is spirit" (John 4:24), and as such, he does not possess a physical body.[7] This presents a challenge for humans seeking to cultivate intimacy with God. How can we experience the presence, closeness, knowing, and being known that characterize our most intimate human relationships with a God who is incorporeal?[8]

The Christian response to this dilemma is found in the person of Jesus Christ. As the incarnate Word, Jesus took on human flesh and lived an embodied existence (John 1:14). In his life, death, and resurrection, Jesus provided a tangible manifestation of God's love and character. Through his physical presence, Jesus modeled perfect humanity and offered salvation to a fallen world. As Heb 1:3 declares, "He is the radiance of the glory of God and the exact imprint of his nature."

While the incarnation provided a means for humans to encounter God in bodily form, Jesus's ascension poses a fresh challenge. With Jesus no longer physically present on earth, believers once again face the question of how to cultivate intimacy with an incorporeal God. The New Testament's answer to this quandary is twofold. First, we experience God in a mediated way through the church, which is described as the body of Christ (1 Cor 12:27; Eph 4:12). As members of Christ's body, Christians are called to manifest God's presence and love to one another and the world. Second, the indwelling of the Holy Spirit facilitates intimacy with God, as "the Spirit himself bears witness with our spirit that we are children of God," moving in us and allowing us to experience God in an intimate way as our Abba Father (Rom 8:15–16).

While affirming the vital roles of the church and the Holy Spirit in facilitating believers' growth and intimacy with God, we propose that visual storytelling, as exemplified in *The Chosen*, can serve a complementary function in helping to embody God in Christ in a way that facilitates intimacy. Just as our bodies enable us to connect with others through nonverbal communication, shared experiences, and emotional attunement,[9] visual media can engage our senses, emotions, and imagination in a way that makes the biblical narrative and its characters more tangible and relatable. By bringing the Gospels to life through compelling characterizations, authentic emotion, and rich historical context, *The Chosen* invites viewers to encounter Jesus and his followers in a more embodied way and to potentially overcome some of the barriers posed by God's incorporeality.

To further explore how *The Chosen* might facilitate intimacy with God, we turn now to the insights of attachment theory and dual processing models of information. These frameworks shed light on how the series's portrayal of Jesus and his relationships can shape viewers' internal representations of God and their ways of relating to God.

Attachment to God

One of the challenges associated with God's incorporeality is that God might present a kind of blank canvas, on which it is easy to project attachment dynamics. Attachment theory, developed by psychologist John Bowlby, describes the dynamics of close interpersonal relationships and the impact of early experiences on later relational patterns.[10] According to attachment theory, the quality of an individual's early interactions with primary caregivers shapes their internal working models of self and others, influencing their expectations, emotions, and behavior in future relationships. These attachment patterns—which can be classified as secure, anxious, fearful, or avoidant—tend to persist throughout life.

Research on attachment to God suggests that many people experience God as an attachment figure, in that, like other attachment figures, they seek proximity, comfort, and security in their relationship with God.[11] An individual's attachment style can significantly impact their perception of and relationship with God. For example, people with secure attachment styles tend to view God as loving, responsive, and reliable, while those with insecure attachment styles may struggle with doubts about God's love or fear of abandonment, or have difficulty trusting in divine provision.[12]

Moreover, an individual's attachment to God is often influenced by their attachment experiences with early caregivers. In other words, people may unconsciously view God through the lens of their human attachment relationships, projecting their experiences of love, rejection, or inconsistency onto their experience of God.[13] This can create challenges when reading biblical accounts of Jesus, as the relational lens through which these narratives are viewed can limit one's ability to accurately perceive and connect with him. For example, when Jesus provides his disciples with a model of prayer in Matt 6, is he inviting them into a trusting relationship with God the Father, or is he dictating the right way to interact with a busy God who needs to be approached carefully? The interpretation might depend on the attachment filter the reader brings to bear.

Further complicating matters, the interactions described in the Gospels reflect a cultural context and modes of interaction that are culturally distant from modern readers. Farming and fishing are commonly used as examples, but not many people in contemporary culture earn their living in these ways. Gender, ethnicity, and other social distinctions influence interactions in ways unfamiliar to modern readers. Translations, particularly those that closely follow the original languages in a word-by-word manner, can sometimes read in formal or stilted ways. All of these factors can contribute to difficulties in relating to Jesus on a personal, emotional level and in experiencing the depth of his love and compassion.

This is where *The Chosen* can play a valuable role in challenging viewers' attachment lenses and presenting a fresh, relatable portrayal of Jesus. By bringing the gospel narratives to life through compelling characterizations, authentic dialogue, and rich historical context, the series invites viewers to encounter Jesus in a way that feels more accessible and emotionally resonant.

Moreover, *The Chosen* has the potential to facilitate what attachment theorists call "earned security" or "earned attachment."[14] This concept refers to the process by which individuals with insecure attachment styles can, through corrective emotional experiences and supportive relationships, develop a more secure attachment style over time. In the context of spiritual growth, this suggests that viewers who may have had emotionally painful or inconsistent experiences with early caregivers, which led to insecure attachment patterns, can benefit from being emotionally drawn into depictions of Jesus. This may then allow them to open up more fully to experiencing God, directly and mediated through the church, in ways that facilitate earned secure attachment.

By depicting Jesus as a consistently loving, attuned, and compassionate presence, *The Chosen* offers viewers a model of secure attachment that can challenge their existing relational templates. Throughout the series, Jesus is portrayed as a fully embodied, emotionally expressive person who laughs, cries, and experiences the full range of human emotions. He is shown as someone who values relationships, spending time with his disciples, engaging in heartfelt conversations as well as light-hearted banter, and demonstrating empathy and compassion for those he encounters. This depiction of Jesus as a relatable, emotionally attuned figure can help viewers to form a more secure attachment to him and to experience his love and presence in a way that feels tangible and transformative. Through ongoing exposure to Jesus's unconditional love and acceptance, as well as his ability to meet characters in their deepest struggles and vulnerabilities, viewers may begin to internalize a new, more secure attachment to God.

Viewers may also benefit from finding characters in *The Chosen* with whom they identify, and from seeing how meeting Jesus changes them. Mary Magdalene is a character who displays characteristics of an anxious attachment style. Anxiously attached individuals have learned that caregivers are unreliable; they often have histories of abandonment. Mary's past traumas and experiences of rejection have left her feeling unworthy, ashamed, and desperate for love and acceptance. When she first encounters Jesus in the series premiere (S1E1), she is drawn to his compassion and understanding but struggles to believe that she is truly deserving of his love—a theme that continues for several seasons. Her continued insecurity leads her to overwork, perhaps in an attempt to earn Jesus's approval (S2E8). Later she confesses that she does all she can but worries she will "never be enough" (S3E6), and another character notes Mary's ongoing struggles with shame. Her shame leads to a relapse, but she ultimately returns to Jesus (S2E6). In a poignant scene, Jesus gently confronts Mary's deep-seated shame and fear of abandonment, assuring her of his unconditional love and acceptance.

Research on the development of secure attachment in early childhood emphasizes the importance of attunement, in which the caregiver genuinely sees the child.[15] In adulthood, this internalized ability facilitates intimacy through the capacity to genuinely attend to the other person. These episodes intuitively capture this dimension of attachment. In the series premier, Jesus sees Mary and calls her by her real name—something that no one has done for many years: "I have called you by name, you are mine" (Isa 43:1). In the reconciliation scene after her relapse, the culmination of the scene is when Jesus repeatedly encourages her to look up at his face (S2E6). Once again, as Mary meets his eyes, she is seen for who she is and is accepted. Jesus's consistent, unconditional love and acceptance help her to gradually internalize a more secure attachment, allowing her to find peace, purpose, and a deep sense of belonging in her relationship with him.

In contrast, Matthew, the tax collector, exhibits traits of an avoidant attachment style.[16] This attachment style is characteristic of people with experiences of rejection. *The Chosen* hints that Matthew was isolated from his peers from an early age and that he had learned to protect himself by maintaining emotional distance and viewing relationships as transactional rather than intimate. Perhaps he is willing to endure the social rejection due to his profession as a tax collector because he is already resigned to his isolated state. As he says to Gaius, "When you realize that nobody else in the world cares what happens to you, you think only about yourself" (S1E7). His tendency to downplay his emotions and experience the world primarily through a rational lens is an avoidant trait that leads him to discount his own emotional experiences. After seeing Peter and Andrew's miraculous catch of fish, he says, "I don't believe what I saw. I need to know: was I deceived?" to which Andrew answers, "What good is our answer if you don't even listen to yourself?" (S1E6).

When Jesus first calls Matthew (S1E7), Matthew thinks Jesus has made a mistake. But Jesus informs him that there is a celebration they are preparing for. "I'm not welcome at dinner parties," he tells Jesus, to which Jesus responds that there will not be a problem: "You are the host." In a moment, Jesus takes Matthew from social outcast to social insider. However, his problems do not instantly disappear. Among the disciples, he is portrayed as an outsider and an observer. His interactions with the other disciples are not always smooth, as some, most significantly Simon Peter, continue to struggle with hostility toward him because of his involvement with the Roman imperial authorities (e.g., S2E3). Slowly, however, we see signs that Matthew is learning to reconnect. He makes friends among the disciples, including Mary Magdalene and Philip. He becomes more emotionally aware. In the most prominent example in the series, Jesus's teachings about reconciliation in the Sermon on the Mount strike home. It is clear that Jesus's teachings have touched him emotionally as well as intellectually—a sign of internal integration. Immediately afterward, he returns to his family home to seek reconciliation (S3E1, S3E2), enacting the changes in his attachment system.

Simon Peter, one of Jesus's closest disciples, demonstrates a mix of attachment styles throughout the series. His primary attachment style seems to be secure, as evidenced by his close relationships with his wife Eden and his brother Andrew. However, as with many people with secure attachments, in moments of stress or uncertainty, Peter can also display anxious tendencies that are projected onto God. Ambivalence is characteristic of his relationship with God the Father and with Jesus. His struggles to trust God are seen in an early scene when he cries out to God, "You know, if I didn't know any better, I'd say you enjoy yanking [the people of Israel] around like goats and can't decide whether we're chosen or not!" (S1E4). Even after witnessing Jesus's miracles and hearing his teachings, his wife's miscarriage sends Simon Peter into a tailspin. He tells John, "I trusted Jesus.... I'm furious. I'm so angry.... He can do anything. How could he let this happen to Eden?" (S3E7).

The most dramatic enactment of his struggles, and the turning point, occurs when Jesus approaches the disciples as he is walking on the water. Simon Peter challenges Jesus, "If it is you, command me to come to you on the water. If you are who you say you are, bid me to step out of this boat." His ambivalence here gets him into trouble. While he does step out in faith to walk on the water, Simon Peter's lapse in faith makes him sink. Ultimately, he learns the profound lesson that Jesus is worthy of his faith as Jesus lifts him up and embraces him (S3E8). The scene ends with Peter recognizing that the solution to his insecure ambivalence lies not in himself but in Jesus. He cries out to Jesus, "Please. Don't let me go!"—to which Jesus responds, "I'm here. I'm always here." The root cause of insecure attachments is rejection or unstable caregiving. The path to earned attachment is consistent, attuned care, which Jesus tangibly demonstrates. Jesus's patient, consistent presence in Peter's life helps him to develop a more secure attachment, empowering him to confess that Jesus is the Christ and to become a key leader in the early church (S4E2).

For viewers who may struggle with their own attachment wounds or insecurities, seeing this transformative process unfold on screen can be deeply resonant and encouraging. By witnessing the way in which Jesus meets each character in their unique struggles and lovingly guides them toward greater security and wholeness, viewers may find hope and inspiration for their own spiritual journeys. *The Chosen*'s portrayal of these attachment dynamics can serve as a powerful reminder that, no matter one's relational history or current struggles, Jesus's love has the power to heal, transform, and provide a secure foundation for a deepening relationship with God.

Furthermore, by providing a window into the lives and struggles of Jesus's disciples and other biblical characters, *The Chosen* normalizes the experience of spiritual doubt, questions, and relational challenges. Viewers can see themselves in the struggles of Peter, Matthew, and Mary Magdalene, recognizing that even those closest to Jesus grappled with fears, insecurities, and relational wounds. This can foster a sense of identification and empathy, helping viewers to feel less alone in their own spiritual journeys and more open to receiving God's love and grace.

In summary, attachment theory provides a valuable framework for understanding how individuals' relational histories and internal working models can shape their perception of and relationship with God. *The Chosen*, through its emotionally resonant storytelling and authentic portrayal of Jesus, offers a powerful means of challenging viewers' attachment lenses and facilitating a more secure, intimate connection with God. By presenting Jesus as a relatable, compassionate figure who meets people in the depths of their human experience, the series invites viewers to encounter him anew, opening their hearts to the transformative power of his love.

Dual Processing Theory

We now turn our attention to another psychological framework that sheds light on the series's potential for spiritual impact: dual processing theory. This theory provides valuable insights into how the show's evocative storytelling and character portrayals engage viewers' cognitive and emotional processes and ultimately foster a more holistic and transformative encounter with the gospel message. By considering *The Chosen* through the lens of dual processing theory, we can gain a fuller understanding of how the series works to bridge the gap between intellectual knowledge and experiential faith, between theology and spirituality, and to invite viewers to internalize and apply biblical truths in a way that touches both heart and mind.

Dual processing models of cognition distinguish between two interrelated systems through which individuals take in information, process it, and arrive at conclusions. The first system, often referred to as the implicit or intuitive system, operates automatically, rapidly, and with little conscious effort.[17] This system relies heavily on emotional cues, heuristics, and past experiences to guide decision-making and behavior. The attachment filters mentioned in the previous section are an example of the kinds of learned information processing that occur in this system. In contrast, the second system, known as the explicit or analytical system, is slower, more deliberate, and requires conscious effort. This system engages in logical reasoning, critical thinking, and problem solving, drawing upon factual knowledge and rational analysis.

While both systems play essential roles in human knowing, the implicit system is generally more influential in shaping our perceptions, attitudes, and behaviors, particularly in the realm of interpersonal relationships and spiritual experiences. However, the explicit system is crucial for critically evaluating our intuitive responses, integrating new information, and making well-reasoned decisions. Effective functioning and growth require a healthy interaction between these two systems, allowing individuals to balance their emotional and intuitive experiences with rational reflection and understanding. When both systems impact each other in a dynamic way, it creates a knowledge spiral, leading to a more holistic way of knowing.[18]

In the context of spiritual growth and development, dual processing theory highlights the importance of engaging both the implicit and explicit systems in the process of internalizing and applying spiritual truths. While explicit knowledge of theological concepts and biblical narratives is essential, it is often the implicit, emotionally laden experiences that most powerfully shape an individual's felt sense of God's presence and love. This is where the evocative storytelling of *The Chosen* can play a vital role in facilitating spiritual growth by engaging viewers' implicit processing systems and fostering a deeper, more intuitive connection with Jesus and his message.

Throughout the series, *The Chosen* brings the gospel narratives to life in a way that speaks directly to viewers' implicit processing systems. For example, in the episode "I Am He" (S1E8), Jesus's encounter with the Samaritan woman at the well is depicted with a depth of emotional nuance and psychological realism that draws viewers into the heart of the story. As Jesus gently reveals the woman's past and offers her living water, viewers are invited to experience the power of his compassion and the transformative nature of his love on an intuitive, emotional level.

The show also models someone who is attempting to integrate their implicit and explicit knowledge. Throughout the first season, the character of Nicodemus is shown grappling with the tension between his explicit knowledge of religious law and his growing intuitive sense of Jesus's divine nature and authority. This tension culminates in his discussion with Jesus under the cover of darkness (S1E7). Early in the scene, Nicodemus clearly expresses his dilemma when he says, "There are many things we are drawn to without our thinking or our ability to explain why." Jesus confronts him with the need to experience the Spirit instead of simply struggling to understand: "How do you know it's the wind?" "Because I can feel it, and I hear its sound." Jesus continues, "Do you know where it comes from? Do you know where it's going? . . . The Spirit may work in a way that is a mystery to you." Jesus gently prods his intellectual defenses through his questions before challenging him to become a follower. Nicodemus's journey illustrates the process of integrating explicit and implicit ways of knowing, which eventually results in his acknowledgment that Jesus is the Messiah.

The knowledge spiral refers to the process of linking our intuitive, emotionally laden experiences with our rational, propositional understandings.[19] In the context of faith, it allows for a more holistic and transformative engagement with spiritual truths. There are two aspects to the knowledge spiral. First, we can link the implicit system with the explicit system, or interpret our experience.[20] The implicit system is nonverbal, and consequently the process of making the implicit explicit is facilitated by the use of imagery, metaphor, and story. *The Chosen* provides these in abundance—as did Jesus, who often communicated important truths through stories and metaphors. Note, for example, the use of the analogy of the wind to explain the actions of the Spirit in the account of Nicodemus above (see John 3:1–21). This imagery is further embedded in the story of Nicodemus's unfolding faith journey. Through the use of imagery and storytelling, *The Chosen* creates opportunities for individuals to experience the gospel message in a way that feels personally relevant and emotionally impactful. This emotional engagement can then serve as a catalyst for deeper reflection, discussion, and integration with explicit knowledge of biblical truths through the process of interpreting our experience.

In the second aspect of the knowledge spiral, we can feel an idea, or feel God's truth. The series's focus on the relational dynamics between Jesus and his followers provides a powerful model for the kind of experiential learning that facilitates spiritual growth. As viewers witness the transformative impact of Jesus's love and presence in the lives of characters such as Mary Magdalene, Simon Peter, Matthew, and Nicodemus, they are invited to feel the idea of

Jesus's love in their own spiritual journeys. By fostering a sense of identification and emotional connection with the characters, *The Chosen* encourages viewers to apply the lessons and insights gleaned from these stories to their own lives, bridging the gap between implicit and explicit ways of knowing.

In summary, dual processing theory provides a valuable framework for understanding how *The Chosen*'s evocative storytelling can facilitate spiritual growth and transformation. By engaging viewers' implicit processing systems through emotionally resonant narratives and authentic character portrayals, the series creates opportunities for individuals to experience the gospel message in a way that feels personally relevant and deeply impactful. As viewers are drawn into the relational dynamics between Jesus and his followers, they are invited to consider how these same experiential truths might shape their own spiritual journeys, fostering a deeper integration of implicit and explicit ways of knowing. Ultimately, by engaging both heart and mind, *The Chosen* offers a powerful tool for spiritual formation, enabling viewers to internalize and apply biblical truths in a way that transforms both their understanding and their lived experience of faith.

Conclusion

In this chapter, we have explored the potential of the television series *The Chosen* to facilitate a deeper, more intimate relationship with God. By considering the show through the lenses of attachment theory and dual processing models of knowing, we have argued that its compelling storytelling, authentic character portrayals, and emotionally resonant themes can help viewers overcome barriers to spiritual intimacy and foster a more secure and transformative connection with Jesus.

Through its narrative approach and the presentation of Jesus and his followers in realistic, relatable ways, *The Chosen* has the power to bypass the intellectualizing tendencies of an overly rationalistic approach to faith, speaking directly to the heart and engaging viewers' implicit relational knowledge. By portraying Jesus as a fully embodied, emotionally attuned, and consistently loving presence, the series offers a compelling model of secure attachment, inviting viewers to experience the transformative power of divine love in a way that challenges experiences of insecure attachment projected onto God.

Moreover, by engaging both implicit and explicit ways of knowing, *The Chosen* encourages a more holistic and integrative approach to spiritual formation, one that values the interplay between experiential knowledge and propositional truth. As viewers are drawn into the gospel narrative and the lives of its characters, they are invited to reflect on their own spiritual journeys, integrating the insights gained from the series with their explicit knowledge of Scripture and theology. They are challenged to see the Christian life as primarily a relational journey with a loving God.

The insights of dual processing theory suggest that church practices that seek to connect implicit and explicit forms of knowing through the knowledge spiral are essential for spiritual growth and transformation. The use of discussion groups and small group curriculum aimed at incorporating explicit knowledge with experiences evoked by *The Chosen* can serve this function. The importance of spending time explicitly reflecting on the knowledge gained through implicit channels is supported by educational research demonstrating that debriefing (involving the explicit system) is essential for people to make sense of their experience (involving the implicit system) and to integrate new knowledge into their existing understanding.[21] By engaging both implicit and explicit ways of knowing, churches can create opportunities for believers to experience a deeper, more authentic connection with God that goes beyond mere intellectual assent.

In a world that often feels fragmented and disconnected, where faith is frequently reduced to a set of propositions or intellectual assent, *The Chosen* offers a powerful reminder of the relational heart of the Christian message. By engaging our hearts and minds, our implicit and explicit ways of knowing, the series invites us to encounter Jesus anew, not merely as an object of study but as a living, loving presence who desires to transform us from the inside out.

6

The Sufficiency of Story

Narrative, Theology, and *The Chosen*

T. ADAM VAN WART

It was only with great reluctance that I eventually agreed to watch an episode of *The Chosen*. I had been urged more than once to give it a try, but, like a dog who has learned to suspect there is a pill in the peanut butter, I was certain it would be just another tedious instance of manipulative evangelical artifice masquerading as entertainment or art. Dallas Jenkins himself could not have said it any better: "Christian films suck."[1] Despite my protests, however, my mother eventually wore me down.

By the end of the first episode, I was hooked.

In this chapter, I aim to offer a theological account of how *The Chosen* has won me, and so many others, over. More specifically, I want to give a theological account of what *The Chosen* quite evidently seems to grasp that so many other purveyors of Christian media miss: the sufficiency of story. What sets *The Chosen* apart and makes it so viscerally compelling is its confidence not just in the *didactic content* of the biblical witness but the art of its *narrative form*. In clearly opting to focus on plot rather than proselytizing or propaganda, that is, *The Chosen* displays an implicit awareness of (1) divine wisdom with respect to scriptural inspiration and composition in that, by some estimates, over two-thirds of the Bible consists of narrative, and of (2) vital truths essential to any properly theological anthropology, especially with respect to human identity, desire, and truth. This awareness, rooted as it is in keen insights regarding divine revelation and human nature, is a major factor in *The Chosen*'s success. I will conclude with a brief sketch of how Christians might variously apply the same awareness in living out their own roles within the ongoing story of God's creative and redemptive work in Christ.

The Art of Trusting the Narrative Form

When asked in interviews about his motivations in launching *The Chosen*, Dallas Jenkins frequently comments on his extreme dissatisfaction with the lack of authenticity and inattention to the craft of storytelling that he finds so frequently in media targeted to popular Christian audiences. Unsurprisingly, Jenkins attributes the success of *The Chosen* in no small part to his resolute commitment to avoid these deficiencies in his own storytelling and filmmaking. As he says in a recent interview in *Outreach Magazine*, "I decided to do my best to focus on making great art. . . . It's the story that most resonates."[2]

In taking the approach to telling the stories of Christ's life and ministry the way that he has, Jenkins displays a tacit recognition of what so many post-Enlightenment engagements with Scripture clearly overlook: the indispensable centrality of the Bible's narrative form(s).[3] That Jenkins and the producers of *The Chosen* appreciate the significance of the Bible's narrative form(s) may be seen in the way they avoid three key mistakes, all too common when it comes to modern re-presentations of the biblical stories of Christ's incarnation, ministry, passion, and resurrection.

The first modern pitfall *The Chosen* avoids is that of seeking the significance of the gospel narratives in something other than the stories themselves. In describing the rise of modern biblical hermeneutics in the eighteenth and nineteenth centuries, for example, Hans W. Frei notes how, in debates about whether to interpret a given narrative of Scripture as history, allegory, or myth, it was not long before "the *meaning* of the stories was finally [thought to be] something different from the stories or depictions themselves, despite the fact that this is contrary to the character of a realistic story."[4] In his landmark work, *The Eclipse of Biblical Narrative*, Frei traces the ways in which the meaning or significance of the Bible's various narratives began to be sought by modern readers by reference to things either *behind* or *beyond* the stories themselves.[5]

The Sufficiency of Story

Within this framework, for some the meaning of the Bible's stories was to be found in their antecedent histories, the facticity (or lack thereof) of the events depicted. For other modern readers, the significance of biblical tales was to be discerned in whatever religious significance or social value they happened to have within a given community. Still others located the heart of the scriptural narratives in the implied doctrinal truth-claims they contained, objective propositions hidden in the text only needing to be mined, refined, and plied. Whether the text's supposed historical, social/religious, or propositional/didactic significance was in view, however, with each of these approaches to biblical narratives, the stories themselves were treated as something either reducible or ancillary to what was presumed to be of far greater significance. (Whereas the first two misguided hermeneutical strategies were and still are common in Protestant and, though late to the party, Catholic liberalism, the third is characteristic of theological conservatism.) With respect to meaning, the narratives themselves were no longer deemed sufficient as such, and the relationship of meaning to story became that of kernel to husk, to borrow an analogy popularized in 1899 by Adolf von Harnack.[6]

The Chosen avoids this pitfall. In distinguishing *The Chosen* from the mistakes outlined by Frei, however, I am not suggesting that Jenkins and the others involved in producing the show are indifferent to the historical, social, or propositional/didactic significance of the gospel stories. Nor do I mean to imply that, in their pursuit of the art of good storytelling, Jenkins and others do not sincerely revere the letter of the biblical texts themselves or have shown any evidence of casual disregard for the Bible or its literal sense. On the contrary. As Jenkins himself has said, "Do we believe it's okay to tell Bible stories and fill in all those gaps with historical data and artistic imagination? Some people don't. We do (obviously). I'm a Bible-believing evangelical. I have zero desire to mess with Scripture or make some sort of new theological point. This is about telling these stories in a way that makes the moments in Scripture even more impactful."[7] To be sure, there is a strong evangelistic component at work behind the show, as well as a desire to inspire current practitioners of Christianity to greater discipleship. There is more at work here, in other words, than a conscious desire to honor the art of storytelling. But, crucially, there is not less than that either.

The second and third common mistakes that *The Chosen* happily avoids are, in a sense, two sides of the same all-but-valueless coin. For if *The Chosen* refuses to treat the gospel stories reductively, it treats the biblical witness neither totemically (or, if you like, fetishistically), on the one hand, nor as a museum piece to be displayed but never touched, on the other.[8] Briefly, the totemic/fetishistic use operates as if the Bible's exact words—either in a particularly cherished translation, like, say, the King James Version, or as faithfully re-presenting a long lost original manuscript—were imbued with something like magical properties. The view of biblical inspiration at work here treats the text of Scripture as if each letter or word or phrase or proposition contained a power analogous to that of the sorts of spells one finds in fairy tales, though an outright comparison to magic would be anathema to individuals who subscribe to this view of inspiration. The museum model, by contrast, avoids magical thinking but, like an archaeologist who has unearthed priceless stone tools dating from the Mesolithic period, treats the text as an artifact to be meticulously preserved and put on display safely beyond the reach of ordinary people who might attempt to handle or make use of those same tools for themselves. In any case, as with the first mistake, what these mistakes share in common is, again, a fundamental misunderstanding of the sufficiency and central function of the Bible's narrative form. Rather than operating as if the storied form of Scripture was dispensable to its meaning, however, these treatments tragically, if unwittingly, block any imaginative engagement with the plot and thereby drain the very life out of these stories' intrinsically artistic nature. It would not be going too far to say that they treat the Bible docetically. By ossifying the Bible and its stories in this way, these approaches fail to appreciate what was once so exquisitely put by comedy legend Norm Macdonald: "It takes a powerful imagination to see a thing for what it really is."[9]

As a result of mistakes such as these, there have been countless presentations of the life of Jesus or other Bible stories in Christian or Christian-adjacent media over the years that, radically unlike Scripture itself, appear completely indifferent to the art form of storytelling: sterile, lifeless, wooden portrayals that, to all appearances, have been consciously produced in such a way that not the slightest deviation or interpretive embellishment of the biblical accounts was thought permissible for apparent fear of sacrilege or textual desecration. The faces of the actors are expressionless—terrifyingly so in the case of Robert Powell's unblinking Jesus in *Jesus of Nazareth* (1977)—the dialogue is delivered in unrelatable King James English, and the costumes and set pieces are either wholly utilitarian or designed in seeming ignorance of their bearing any inherent aesthetic value. Whatever the particular shortcomings of artistry they embody, these approaches all fail to appreciate that the biblical stories are presented as such precisely because they are intended to invite us to enter them as characters ourselves, to find our place within the Scripture's grand narration of the Lord's creative and redemptive love. The role of narrative as a form of art is to envelope the audience imaginatively in the world being depicted, to invite and enfold its readers in the action as participants in the plot. The stories of Scripture are meant to be lived in. *The Chosen*, in contradistinction to so much Christian media that has fallen victim to modern hermeneutical assumptions, manifestly displays a recognition that the stories of Scripture are meant to be lived in and works in concert with the Bible's own narrative artists in drawing others into the drama of divine love. Its unparalleled popularity is attributable, in large part, to its success in winsomely coaxing so many of us into that drama by honoring its artistic character and telling those stories well.

While not obvious, I would submit that each of these three mistakes, all of which *The Chosen* successfully avoids, is ultimately theological in nature. To wit, each of these errant approaches presupposes a view of divine inspiration that, intentionally or not, ultimately undercuts the intentionality of human and divine authorship alike and, with it, the significance of the Bible as God's written word. The narrative art form of Scripture can be treated as superfluous or incidental to the revelation to which it witnesses only at the expense of that selfsame witness. It is not accidental, in other words, that God's word has been delivered to us in the form that it has. Dallas Jenkins and the producers of *The Chosen* clearly grasp this profound theological truth of biblical inspiration and, consequently, recognize the sufficiency and indispensability of the Bible's narrative form(s).

The Narrative Form of Trusting the Art

In addition to understanding this deep theological truth regarding Scripture, *The Chosen* likewise (at least implicitly) exhibits a solid theological grasp of what it means to be human. In his groundbreaking book, *After Virtue*, for example, the Catholic philosopher Alasdair MacIntyre argues that, at root, "man is in his actions and practice, as well as in his fictions, essentially a story-telling animal."[10] He makes this point in arguing a position similar to Frei's, not with respect to modern philosophy's impact on biblical hermeneutics, but to its role in shaping common modern conceptions of what constitutes personal identity and moral action. MacIntyre shows, however, that "all attempts to elucidate the notion of personal identity independently and in isolation from the notions of narrative, intelligibility, and accountability are bound to fail."[11] Whatever else it means to be human, in other words, the fact that our lives and identities are gifted to us by the narrative(s) in which we find ourselves is a truth that is difficult to deny. As MacIntyre convincingly shows, to offer any compelling—to say nothing of coherent—account of who we are or what we are doing necessitates the telling of a story of some kind or another in which we play a role as central characters. Narrative thus suffices not only for God's revelatory purposes in Scripture, it suffices, as well, for gifting or revealing us to ourselves.

By contrast, many modern notions of what it means to be human exhibit markedly different anthropologies. The audiences targeted by much Christian and Christian-adjacent media are ostensibly presumed to be little more than consumers, or a random assembly of contingent facts, or a malleable amalgamation of vacillating self-preferences, or some other variety of implicitly modern, narrative-negating anthropology. Saying so, of course, is not meant to disparage the character of, or attribute maleficent intentions to, those producing this material. Rather, it is simply to recognize what MacIntyre clearly shows, namely, that (1) philosophically modern anthropological theories have become culturally pervasive and that (2) what one understands human persons to be has a profound influence on how one engages and interfaces with them.[12]

If MacIntyre's narrative-centered anthropology is correct, then it should not be at all surprising that the principal witness to God's revelation to us in Christ—the Bible—should open with narrative, close in narrative, and have the story of Jesus as its most central narrative feature. Scripture reveals, in fact, that we are a people whose identities have been constituted by story, the very reason of our existence having been delivered to us via the cosmic narrative of divine creation, redemption, and re-creation.[13] Thus, while MacIntyre's argument regarding the narrative construction of human identity is primarily philosophical in character, his insight, influenced in large measure by Thomas Aquinas, points to the heart of any properly *theological* anthropology. We are introduced to ourselves in the carefully stylized story of creation in the opening chapter of Genesis. We begin to become acquainted with ourselves and God's inescapable love in the tension-filled drama of Israel. We discover

The Sufficiency of Story

ourselves truly in the climactic narration of Christ's incarnation, passion, resurrection, and ascension. And we fully become ourselves in the unfolding conclusion of the Lord's new covenant re-creation of all things. Theologically speaking, that is, the deep grammar of what it means to be human, the central truth and ultimate good of each and every one of our lives is given to us authoritatively in the story of Scripture.[14]

Again, I would submit that, whether they know it or not, Dallas Jenkins and the producers of *The Chosen*, in reflecting the ostensible artistic narrative preferences of the Lord himself, tap into this crucial theological truth regarding what it means to be human persons. Said differently, in so conscientiously honoring the narrative form of Scripture, *The Chosen* cooperates in the Bible's strategy of introducing us to the Lord and to ourselves through the story of God's love for us in Christ. Because it follows Scripture in so carefully presenting each of its central characters—most especially Jesus—*in their* stories *as its* story, with all the moral, social, and other complexities requisite for an authentic display of human being, *The Chosen* speaks to us in the depths of our human existence. If we are, to borrow a phrase from Luigi Pirandello, "characters in search of an author," *The Chosen* follows the Bible's artistic lead in familiarizing us with that Author and directing us toward the roles we have been created and re-created to play.

Conclusion

The Chosen enjoys its incredible appeal largely because it adheres so closely to the narrative character of the biblical witness itself. Intentionally or not, its writers and producers thus display an implicit trust in the Holy Spirit's own preferred method of introducing us both to the Lord and to ourselves. Unlike post-Enlightenment hermeneutics and so much other Christian or Christian-adjacent media, the series acknowledges that the meaning of the biblical narratives is inseparable from the narratives themselves, and it artistically invites us to recognize its stories as our own. In short, *The Chosen* perceives and embraces the sufficiency of story.

Of course, to speak of the sufficiency of story is to invite the logical question, Sufficient *for what* exactly? Once that question is asked, it becomes quickly apparent that narratives will not suffice for everything. This is, no doubt, why God's revelation in Scripture includes numerous additional literary genres beyond narrative. It is also why the church has been recurrently led by the Holy Spirit to formulate its (often narratively derived) normative rules for correctly engaging with Scripture through creeds and councils. In his critique of the methods of certain "narrative theologians," then, Matthew Levering is not incorrect that in speaking of "the highest mysteries" like the Trinity, "theologians can describe more than an abstraction that functions as a regulative, grammatical norm."[15] But they certainly cannot do less than that either. The choice is never one between the grammar of Christian doctrine and its truth; these things come together or not at all. And, of course, neither the grammar of Christian faith nor its attendant truth-claims can have existence without the narrated drama of Scripture as it has been given to us.[16] So, no, the narrative of Scripture does not suffice for everything, but it certainly suffices for a great many (and perhaps the most important of) things and is, in any case, indispensable to any endeavor properly identified as Christian. By Scripture's own lights, after all, biblical narrative can suffice for introducing us to the one in whom we may have life through faith: "These are written *so that you may come to believe* that Jesus is the Messiah, the Son of God, *and that through believing you may have life in his name*" (e.g., John 20:31 NRSVCE, emphasis added).[17]

We who would seek to receive ourselves by way of the biblical narrative and to play the various roles therein to which we are daily being invited would do well to follow *The Chosen*'s example in following the example of Scripture. For while *The Chosen* certainly makes for excellent entertainment, the story it tells so well is both borrowed and true. We should, therefore, avoid the mistake of thinking that the significance or meaning of the story told by Scripture is to be found in anything else than itself, or that the beauty and artistry it exhibits is of no genuine consequence in its designs. Moreover, we should receive that story, in all its Christic beauty, as the story of our own lives, individually and as a whole. The biblical story, the one that *The Chosen* seeks faithfully to narrate, is in progress, streaming for free right now and ongoingly, season after season until the Lord returns finally to complete the new creation of the new covenant inaugurated by his resurrection. May the stories of our own lives, then, embrace the sufficiency of that story and, like *The Chosen*, draw others to assume their own roles within it.

7

Strong Feelings and Potent Senses

Three Johannine Moments in Conversation with *The Chosen*

JEANNINE M. HANGER

As a New Testament professor, I focus much of my reading, teaching, and writing on the Gospels, especially the Gospel of John. Therefore, I was curious to see how *The Chosen* would portray the events narrated in John 11 and 12, namely, when Jesus calls Lazarus from the tomb (S4E7), followed by Mary anointing Jesus's feet with perfume (S4E8). My interest in these specific scenes is motivated by the combination of emotional and sensory elements represented in these two events—in textual form, these are among the most explicitly emotion- and sensory-rich depictions of Jesus's life and ministry.

As I anticipated viewing how *The Chosen* interpreted and portrayed details often debated among scholars, I wondered whether the show would match my own convictions about these interpretive nuances. As it turns out, these details did not always match; nevertheless, I was not disappointed. This chapter will explain why. Ultimately, my goal is to draw attention to how Jesus interacts with his followers as he embodies his claim, "I am the resurrection and the life" (John 11:25).[1] By exploring the emotional tenor and sensory qualities of three specific moments within these two scenes, we will observe what *The Chosen* portrays so vividly: Jesus embodies this claim not only according to what onlookers see but also because of what they hear, smell, and touch.

Jeannine M. Hanger

The Role of Imagination and Our Sensory Approach

We all use our imagination when we read texts. Some suggest that engaging *The Chosen* may condition viewers to let the show do all the imaginative work for us.[2] The concern is that we not allow our conception of the true Jesus to be replaced by Jonathan Roumie's Jesus. I do not disagree with this caution. As Doug Huffman comments in his chapter in the present volume, we should bear in mind that this series understands itself to be a work of historical fiction, remaining aware that these episodes are not meant to replace the biblical accounts. *The Chosen* is nevertheless a compelling medium for inspiring profound reflection on these stories that Christians regard as Scripture.

The genius of this series is how it fuels the imagination to ponder the finer contextual details of familiar biblical accounts. The show does this by creatively filling in plausible backstories and characterization to achieve greater effect and *affect*. While many of these elements are fictional, it is precisely these imaginative moments that highlight the gospel stories in ways that help us when our own imagination is underdeveloped either by our rote familiarity with these texts or by our complete *un*familiarity with them. These details remind us *that* there is a backstory, even if we cannot say exactly what it is.

Three moments in these two scenes (in S4E7 and S4E8) merit close attention in terms of their emotional tenor and sensory qualities. First, we will explore how *The Chosen* interprets and depicts Jesus's strong display of emotion and tears (John 11:33, 35, 38), a perennial puzzle for scholars given that Jesus knows all along that he is going to bring Lazarus to life. Second, we will explore the raising of Lazarus, both its auditory and olfactory qualities (John 11:39–44). Finally, we will address Mary's anointing of Jesus's feet—her tears, the fragrant perfume, and the humble, tactile quality of her gesture (12:1–8).

Visiting Lazarus, Expressing Grief

Danger and foreboding are in the air as Jesus leads his friends to Bethany to visit Lazarus. John's Gospel presents this as the final public sign of Jesus's ministry. It is the event leading to Jesus's arrest.[3] *The Chosen* captures this dynamic along with Jesus's emotion as he engages with his friends.

Jesus in John 11:33, 35, 38

As Jesus arrives, Martha and then Mary come to greet him, each with the grief-laden complaint, "Lord, if you had been here, my brother would not have died" (11:21, 32). Jesus declares to Martha that Lazarus will rise again, stating, "I am the resurrection and the life" (11:25). Martha responds with belief (11:27), but her understanding seems limited to the assumption that Jesus is speaking about the final resurrection of all the faithful. Then when Jesus encounters Mary, he is overcome by emotion, which John narrates with three emotional expressions. Seeing Mary and the other mourners weeping prompts Jesus to become deeply disturbed (Greek: *enebrimēsato*) (11:33). John uses this same word a second time in v. 38 when Jesus arrives at the tomb. This word is uncommon and notoriously difficult to translate. It indicates a troubled grief intermixed with anger.[4] The text presents this expression of grief as distinct from his tears, since after its first reference, Jesus asks where they laid Lazarus (11:34), and it is only after the onlookers invite Jesus to "come and see" that John narrates, "Jesus wept" (11:35).

Jesus's Angered Grief

Jesus's strong emotion is puzzling given his declaration to Martha that Lazarus will rise again. Some interpreters have postulated that Jesus's first expression of angered grief in John 11:33 is directed toward Mary and the mourning bystanders for their tears; he is disturbed at their lack of faith.[5] *The Chosen* perhaps conveys a hint of this interpretation, although it is easy to miss since it is presented in an order different from that in the biblical text. In the show, it happens before Mary arrives. When Matthew and Peter ask whether they are supposed to understand his words to Martha, Jesus utters a troubled sigh. Is he annoyed? Disappointed? Jesus then responds, "I suppose not yet."

I have long disagreed with the interpretation suggesting Jesus is grieved over Mary's and the bystanders' unbelief, although in theory it makes sense: this sign occurs at the end of Jesus's public ministry, *after* people witness Jesus enact multiple signs. Shouldn't they anticipate what he would do?[6] Jesus's exasperated sigh in *The Chosen* suggests he hoped they would. Notice how it is not directed at Mary and the anonymous bystanders but at the disciples. If anyone could anticipate Jesus's actions it would be them, especially since Jesus leads them to Bethany to "awaken Lazarus" (John 11:11).

Regardless of whether or how others' unbelief figures into Jesus's angered grief, *The Chosen* consistently portrays the varying levels of developing belief in these miraculous moments, capturing also the wonder of the bystanders—including his disciples—every time Jesus performs a sign. It never gets old. They rarely presume how Jesus will respond as they exchange knowing yet always hopeful glances (cue the background music), which foreshadows the delight that dawns when he *does* heal, restore, and raise to life.

Jesus's Tears

Presuming Jesus's tears are in part the culmination of his angered grief (John 11:33), we focus next on answering the question, Why did Jesus begin to weep (11:35)? Many interpreters believe—rightly, in my view—that Jesus is sharing in the grief of his friends, his tears indicating his complete investment in the moment.[7] Even more, Jesus is struck by the finality and the absolute interruption that death represents. Sickness, death, and sin are the result of the fall, of Satan ferociously at work against God. As Jesus encounters death firsthand, he is not only saddened, but he is grieved with anger over the havoc that death has wrought upon the earth. Even though Lazarus will be raised, humanity still must contend with death for years to come. And so, John narrates, Jesus weeps. This is the world in which we live, and it is a reality Jesus feels.[8]

The Chosen captures this dynamic, but it seems as though there is another layer of meaning feeding Jesus's tears, and it lands with stunning effect.[9] The text states that Jesus is troubled and weeps after he sees "Mary and the Jews" weeping (11:33). *The Chosen* draws this moment out, as Jesus first looks at Mary, then his mother, then Martha, until finally he pivots around to slowly survey his disciples. Everyone stares back at him blankly with wonder. It is the culmination of these shared looks that seems to lead Jesus to crumple into tears, which gives viewers pause to ask, What was Jesus thinking about that led him to weep?

My own interpretation of *The Chosen*'s rendering of this moment? Jesus's tears appear to be in part related to his anticipated death. Perhaps he dreads the coming suffering, but he seems especially disturbed over how it will devastate his loved ones. This scene, flanked by the disciples' conversations and backstories peppered throughout the episode, conveys the danger Jesus faces by traveling to Bethany. Viewers of the show (and rereaders of the Gospels) perceive that *Jesus* is aware of the suffering ahead. But Peter's blank stare, Andrew's agitation, and others' looks of wonder indicate that they are not.

As Jesus dissolves into tears, it is poignant to see his mother run to comfort him and put her arms around his head as only a mother can do. Jesus grasps onto her through his sobs. Perhaps the familiarity of the singular, short verse, "Jesus wept"—the shortest in the English Bible—has conditioned us to imagine him emoting alone. John's Gospel does not mention her in this scene.

His mother's presence accomplishes two things. First, it accentuates Jesus's humanity and his vulnerability in his moment of need. Second, his mother may be the only one who is somewhat attuned to the suffering ahead. Her presence and her embrace, therefore, comfort Jesus all the more. As Jesus's tears subside, he cups his mother's face with shaking hands and near panic on his face. It is only when he looks over to a sobbing Mary that he seems to snap back to the present moment and collect himself. Then Jesus, his mother, Martha, and Mary struggle to their feet, interlink arms, and begin walking to Lazarus's tomb. If you have grasped that Jesus is grieved over what is ahead, you realize that he is beginning a march toward two tombs: Lazarus's and his own.

Understanding Jesus's tears to be about his impending death is a valid (if less common) interpretation of the text.[10] I have always waved away this explanation, considering it uncharacteristic of Jesus to cry for his own suffering in a moment focused on the Bethany family. However, many interpreters believe John is drawing parallels between the raising of Lazarus and of Jesus.[11] Moreover, Thomas reflects the danger they face in traveling to Bethany, saying (11:16), "Let us also go, that we may die with him." John Chrysostom suggests that Jesus's emotion here resembles the grief of the synoptic Jesus at Gethsemane. Since there is no Gethsemane scene in John, Chrysostom and others propose that this intense grief is John's way of depicting Jesus's anticipation of the cross.[12]

The Chosen's dramatization of this scene is compelling. It makes sense that Jesus's looming death could play into the overall significance of the moment. It seems possible that Jesus's emotion is related to several things at once. Is this not the way of human grief and tears? How many of us have ever been emotionally moved about the matter immediately in front of us, only to have it remind us of a related heartache, which triggers yet another point of anguish, until the floodgates are fully opened for a good, hard cry about it all? Jesus sees the tears of Mary and the mourners and is moved to tears over their grief for Lazarus, which triggers grief over the human condition of sickness and death. This, in turn, leads to the solution for all this suffering: Jesus's own impending death. As Jesus anticipates the suffering ahead, he feels how devastating it will be for his loved ones, and he is devastated by their lack of understanding. Jesus is on the brink of a critical shift: once he calls Lazarus from the tomb, the wheels will be in motion for his own demise. Jesus's tears indicate how deeply he knows this.

Ultimately Jesus's grief puts his full humanity on display and makes him utterly relatable. Perhaps he grieves his coming death as he considers its effects on his loved ones, while he also grieves more broadly over the sickness, death, and sin of the human condition. While his death will ultimately bring about an end to this curse, he must walk through suffering to get there. In a similar fashion, we must also weather the storms of an inaugurated but not yet consummated kingdom. As we see in John 11, *The Chosen* also presents Jesus as one who grieves and weeps, just like us. In the second moment within this scene, weeping will soon give way to rejoicing.

The Silence and Stench of Death

When Jesus arrives at the tomb, John tells us he is deeply moved once again (11:38), and he directs bystanders to take away the stone. Memorably, Martha protests (11:39): "Lord, by this time there will be an odor, for he has been dead four days." Jesus reminds her that if she believes, she will see the glory of God. And so, John reports, they take away the stone. Jesus then lifts up his eyes and prays to the Father (11:41–42). After this prayer, "with a loud voice," Jesus cries, "Lazarus, come out" (11:43). And "the dead man," John narrates, emerges from the tomb!

This is a climactic moment, both in John's Gospel and in *The Chosen*. Our focus here will be the sensory qualities of this scene. We typically engage texts silently, with our eyes. Sometimes we listen to these words as they are read aloud. *The Chosen* gives us the opportunity to see and hear texts acted out, expanding our understanding of (and appreciation for) the effects of words. As for additional sensory details, imagination must fill in the rest. Here I want to augment our understanding further by briefly inspecting the sounds and smells of this particular scene.

The Sound of Death

First, what does death sound like? If we are talking about the *response* to death, we might think of weeping, or we might imagine musical lamentations that aid the funerary process. Mourners in the ancient world might imagine the sound of a stone being rolled over the entrance of a tomb. But consider the sound of death itself: what is profound is its absolute stillness and silence. There is no more movement. There is no more life. Lazarus's tomb, before everyone descends upon it, houses the utter stillness of death.

The Smell of Death

Second, what does death smell like? Many of us today do not actually know. We live in a world of refrigeration and professional funeral homes. Many of us inhabit urban spaces, where it is unusual to encounter even animal remains (save for occasional roadkill we drive past on the highway). But ponder the smell of death in the ancient world, where families acted as their own funeral directors, literally handling their deceased loved ones. Jewish families were accustomed to applying funerary spices and aromatics to dead bodies.[13] This would cover over the smell of death at first, but not for long. The tomb in which Lazarus was placed would be located outside of town to avoid crossing purity boundaries. Practically, the dead were left to decompose in silence.

Not all interpreters believe we should make too much of Martha's comment about the stink when Jesus tells onlookers to roll away the stone (11:39). Some suggest there would not be any smell, and the text never goes on to indicate whether there *was* an odor.[14] All we have is Martha's protest anticipating it. However, after four days in a tomb, it is difficult to imagine there *not* being a stench escaping from the tomb when the stone is rolled away. *The Chosen* does not omit this detail. Bystanders—including Jesus—visibly react, using their arms to shield their noses. Jesus's own disciples are the closest to the odor as they roll away the stone. Notice how it is only *after* the stone is removed that Jesus prays to the Father, elongating the moment that extends the reach of the stench as it escapes from the tomb. Everyone knows Lazarus is dead—the onlookers see and hear it, and they also smell it.

And now, we come to the moment when Jesus calls—bellows—to Lazarus in the tomb, "Lazarus, come out!"[15] Readers of John 11 might not include in their imaginative rendering of these words how long it would have taken for Lazarus to hear Jesus's voice, to arise, and to hobble amid his grave clothes to the entrance of the tomb. Witnesses both see and hear signs of life. What neither the text nor *The Chosen* can communicate is how the stench of death hangs in the air even while signs of life are seen and heard.

What a spectacular moment! *The Chosen* captures it so dramatically. There is celebration and a wonderful reunion of Lazarus with his sisters. But there is also an understandable level of fear: one woman screams and runs away, terrified. As in John 11, *The Chosen* depicts those who respond to Jesus with belief, and those who, in their unbelief, spread the word and seal Jesus's fate.

Martha's mention of the odor of death is a critical contribution to our reflection on the theological weight of the moment. Lazarus was dead—everyone could hear, see, and smell it. Then Jesus, the resurrection and the life, calls Lazarus from the tomb. The prophetic words of John 5:25 are fulfilled in this moment, carrying an audible quality: "[The hour] is now here, when the dead will *hear the voice* of the Son of God, and those who *hear* will live" (emphasis added). Lazarus likewise *hears* Jesus's voice rouse him from death as he emerges from the stench of death to life.

In the final scene, a new smell will be associated with the themes of death and life.

The Fragrance and Emotions of Life and Death

In the aftermath of the raising of Lazarus, there is consternation and celebration. John tells us that this event prompts the religious leaders to meet (11:45–53), and this leads them to plot Jesus's arrest and ensuing death. We then read about a celebratory meal at which Lazarus's sister Mary anoints Jesus's feet (12:1–8).

Before *The Chosen* portrays this meal, viewers accompany Mary on a journey to search for the perfect gift for Jesus. At a perfumer's shop, Mary coaxes a reluctant supplier to show her the most valuable perfume in stock. To the perfumer's surprise, Mary plunks down almost a year's worth of wages and insists on purchasing the entire alabaster jar of pure nard. What we learn from this fictional exchange is the purpose for such a valuable ointment—it is used to anoint royalty. What a creative way to explain the significance of John's simple narration, "Mary therefore took a pound of expensive ointment made from pure nard, and anointed the feet of Jesus and wiped his feet with her hair" (12:3a). Modern readers might not pick up on what an anointing with such costly nard would signify: Mary's gesture suggests a royal anointing, one fit for a king.

The Anointing in John 12:1–8

John's narration of the anointing scene differs somewhat from Matthew's and Mark's.[16] John is unique for his distinct mention of the fragrance that fills the house (12:3b), which is significant for several reasons. First, this detail may be intended to evoke God's glory "filling the house" of the temple (1 Kgs 8:10–11) and tabernacle (Exod 40:34–40).[17] Second, Dominika Kurek-Chomycz observes that this mention of the fragrance (Greek: *osmē*) is "superfluous," since the reference to nard (Greek: *myron*) would in itself already indicate fragrance.[18] Finally, it is not accidental that this is the second and only other reference to smell in John, placed so close to the mention of the odor of 11:39.[19]

As Judas protests the extravagance of Mary's gesture, Jesus defends her, interpreting it as a kind of preburial anointing (12:7): "Leave her alone, so that she may keep it for the day of my burial."[20] With Jesus's comment, we get a fuller understanding of how smell is intertwined with themes of death and life. When the stone was rolled away from Lazarus's tomb and the stench of death wafted out, Lazarus awakened from death, emerging from the tomb to life. Then, in the celebration of Jesus raising Lazarus to life, we observe Mary anointing Jesus with an exquisite fragrance that Jesus in turn associates with his own death. Finally, it is Jesus's death that will ultimately lead to life for the world. As Dorothy Lee suggests, the perfume presents a "sublime expression of sensuous beauty counteracting the previous stench of death."[21] John's two references to smell thus hover around themes of death and life in a somewhat counterintuitive manner.[22]

The final noteworthy element of John's portrayal of Mary anointing Jesus is how she utilizes the sense of touch to pour the ointment on Jesus's feet and to wipe them with her hair. This tactile gesture of handling feet is recognized for its humility, signifying the quality of Mary's devotion and love for Jesus. In that context, letting down her hair would have raised a few eyebrows, along with the startling choice to use her hair to wipe his feet. This uniquely conveys her love and affection for Jesus, perhaps even foreshadowing the humble, tactile, and intimate qualities marking Jesus's own washing of his disciples' feet (John 13).

In summary, Mary's anointing of Jesus's feet would have carried several layers of significance. From an anointing connected to his death and burial, to its royal connotations, to its humble expression of love and devotion for Jesus: this was a significant gesture.

The Anointing in The Chosen

Mary's anointing of Jesus in *The Chosen* closely matches the primary layers of significance that John's account articulates. First, it is evident that Mary considers this a royal anointing. She spends an enormous amount of money on the perfume, commenting that this is a gift for the "most important king the world has ever known." These royal hues come across in the actual anointing, where Mary addresses Jesus directly with a prayer typically offered to God, "Blessed are you, King of the Universe." Second, Jesus interprets Mary's gesture as preparing him for burial (cf. John 12:7). Finally, as Mary pours out the perfume on Jesus's feet and lets down her hair to wipe them, she expresses her affection, love, gratitude, and devotion in a manner consistent with the biblical account.

There are some minor differences with the text of John's Gospel in this portrayal, such as how *The Chosen* includes details from Matthew's and Mark's parallel accounts. Matthew and Mark mention that it is an alabaster jar (Matt 26:7; Mark 14:3), and both narrate that her gesture will be remembered throughout the world wherever the gospel is preached (Matt 26:13; Mark 14:9). I also wondered, at first, whether the show was attempting to integrate Luke's anointing too (Luke 7:36–50). This was a bit perplexing since Luke seems to depict a different scene altogether: the anointing in Luke takes place early in Jesus's ministry when he is invited to eat with a Pharisee. Luke features an unnamed woman who has lived a sinful life, and while the woman similarly anoints Jesus's feet, she does so initially (and uniquely) with her tears, and only after that with perfume. *The Chosen* portrays Mary also coming to Jesus in tears. Yet Mary's affection and gratitude to Jesus for Lazarus could conceivably prompt joyful tears in the midst of the anointing, even if John does not mention it.

The second detail that hints at the Lukan account is how *The Chosen* adds a Pharisee, Shmuel, to the dinner table. However, Jesus's conversation with Shmuel differs from Luke's account of his exchange with Simon the Pharisee. Shmuel's role is an inventive way to highlight the impropriety of Mary letting down her hair and handling Jesus's feet. As Shmuel judges her gesture immodest, he verbalizes what is implicit in John's account: Mary's action would be viewed by dinner guests as disruptive and improper. Like the scene at the perfumer's shop, *The Chosen* creatively highlights contextual details of the biblical texts typically discernible only after conducting more extensive study. These imaginative additions help viewers understand why Mary's gift is significant.

Finally, *The Chosen* does not miss the significance John ascribes to the fragrance of Mary's anointing. As the fragrance escapes from the jar, several dinner guests wrinkle or cover their noses. Judas in particular recognizes its expensive quality. It provokes his disdain for how wasteful he considered Mary's gift. The fragrance thus functions to highlight how interruptive and inappropriate Mary's anointing was viewed by some of those witnessing it.

Ultimately this episode presents Mary as tearfully joyful in her devotion and love for Jesus as she anoints his feet. Jesus welcomes her sacrificial expression of love as he defends her actions amid the protests of Shmuel and Judas. This underscores the strength of Mary's love for Jesus, as she risks her reputation to express her devotion. She thus provides a model of love and commitment to Jesus for viewers to emulate.

Conclusion

Recently, while my daughter was away from home at university, I entered her empty bedroom and encountered an overpowering, unidentifiable, horrible smell. My husband and I searched until we found the culprit: a tiny, dead lizard. Presumably dragged in by the cat, it had obviously been dead long enough to decompose. How could such a tiny little creature create such a big stink?

As readers of biblical texts, we might be tempted to overlook details like Jesus's tears, Martha's protest about an odor, or Mary grasping Jesus's feet. But when we really meditate on a text and imagine the implications of these sensory, emotion-laden moments, we realize that the smell of death and tears of loss are veritable elements of a story deserving our attention. *The Chosen* is an artistic medium that encourages our imagination toward greater understanding of the biblical accounts of Jesus's words and works. It presents embodied depictions of characters, helping us to connect with the emotive and sensory elements of texts that might otherwise remain words on a page.

My hope is that our exploration of these sensory, emotional moments will stimulate viewers of *The Chosen* to seek out the biblical texts with renewed curiosity and excitement. Reciprocally, it is a valuable exercise for Bible readers to stoke the imagination by engaging with artistic portrayals of these texts like *The Chosen*. By putting biblical texts in conversation with the series, we get a glimpse into not only *what* Jesus says and does but also *how* he says and does. In so doing, believers have the potential to ingest more of the word of God, which contains, for us, the words of life.

8

Teaching with *The Chosen*

Helping Students Connect with Scripture through Cinema

JOHN HILTON III

Cinematic portrayals of historical events can have a powerful impact on viewers, which is why they are often used in pedagogical contexts. For example, nonprofit organizations created curriculum guides for *Schindler's List* (1993), recognizing that Steven Spielberg's film could play a crucial role in reminding the public about the horrors of the Holocaust. In a similar way, educational organizations developed interactive lesson plans around Ava Duvernay's *Selma* (2014) to capitalize on its compelling depiction of the struggles and triumphs of the civil rights movement.[1]

Film portrayals of Jesus have likewise been widely used in classroom settings. There are advantages and disadvantages to using cinematic depictions when teaching historical or religious topics. For example, my earliest memory of watching a movie about Jesus was as a young adult in an auditorium with fellow students who were taking classes on becoming more effective gospel teachers. As I saw Jesus nailed to the cross, the Spirit washed over me and testified that what I was seeing was a portrayal of something that really happened. From my own experience, I believe that the Holy Spirit can use movies to teach us.

But in that same movie, those crucifying Jesus used a complicated pulley system to hoist him up on the cross. For years afterward, I imagined this as the method by which Jesus was brought up to his cross and put to death. But the complicated system of pulleys came more from the director's imagination than from archaeological evidence about crucifixion. The historical reality is that on some days, the Romans crucified hundreds of people; they almost certainly did not build scaffolds and pulleys for each of them. In fact, the most ancient images we have of crucifixion, such as the Puteoli graffito dating to the late second or early third century AD, depict the person being crucified as only a little bit shorter than the cross itself.[2] In other words, if the average person in Galilee was five and a half feet tall, crosses would be only about six or seven feet tall.[3]

This experience demonstrates some of the opportunities as well as the drawbacks to using film to teach about Jesus. On the one hand, creative storylines and character development can increase the relatability of biblical figures and the stories in which they appear. They can invite inspired questions as teachers and students think about the text in new ways. Introducing variety in the cinematic depictions of Jesus used in the classroom can also prevent students from fixating on any one portrayal of Jesus and instead direct them back to the text for closer reading and deeper reflection. On the other hand, cinematic depictions of Scripture can cause individuals to develop inaccurate ideas about Jesus. Some may also worry that film might inappropriately replace or distract from Scripture itself. In this chapter, we will explore these questions as they relate to *The Chosen*, ultimately showing that the benefits outweigh the risks.

Pedagogical Benefits of *The Chosen*

The Chosen is a television drama series that portrays the life of Jesus through a multiseason, episodic format. Created, directed, and cowritten by Dallas Jenkins, the show presents the story of Jesus in a unique way by deeply exploring the biblical narratives and imagined backstories of the individuals who came to be his disciples. Jenkins has made significant efforts toward historical plausibility, regularly consulting a panel of advisors that includes a Catholic priest, an evangelical Protestant biblical studies professor, and a Messianic Jewish rabbi. Motivated by a desire to remove "the veil and the walls that [we] sometimes put up between us and the authentic Jesus," Jenkins has chosen to artistically elaborate on what is recorded in Scripture.[4] After all, if one were to take the Gospels and plot the sequence of events on a timeline, fewer than one hundred days from Jesus's mortal life are recorded! Jenkins remarks, "Movie Bible projects are usually stiff, formal—they go from Bible verse to Bible verse, and everything is very, very black and white. I think we have to round the edges a little bit making this show feel a lot more human [by adding backstories, humor, and human interactions]."[5]

These creative additions to the narrative recorded in the Bible provide powerful tools for educators. I see at least three ways that *The Chosen* is helpful in educational settings: (1) for increasing the relatability of Scripture for students, (2) for stimulating incisive questions in the classroom, and (3) for providing variety and alternatives to media depictions of Jesus that already exist.

(1) In *The Chosen*, Jenkins has developed a diverse cast of characters who face a variety of challenges and thereby endows the stories in the Bible with a lifelike quality that makes them more relatable for viewers. The series develops in-depth characters for many of the women who followed Jesus, including Mary the mother of Jesus, Mary Magdalene, and Lazarus's sisters Mary and Martha. It also carves out space for women mentioned only briefly or by implication in the New Testament, such as Joanna and Peter's wife (named Eden in *The Chosen*). The faith portrayed by the women in this series can be a powerful way to reach female students who might be grappling with specific questions about what it looks like to be a woman and a follower of Jesus.

Characters are also portrayed as coming from a variety of backgrounds. For example, Little James, one of Jesus's disciples, is played by Jordan Walker Ross, an actor with severe scoliosis and minor cerebral palsy. After casting Ross, Jenkins rewrote the role to feature his disability rather than asking him to hide it.[6] These types of portrayals used in conjunction with Scripture can help students see the followers of Jesus as real people who made real choices to follow Jesus, and feel empowered to make similar choices in their own lives.

(2) The creative storylines of *The Chosen* can also evoke penetrating questions that might not otherwise arise from a cursory encounter with the text. Readers tend to form mental images of characters and settings included in written texts that may or may not correspond to descriptions provided by the author. While readers typically do this subconsciously, filmmakers cannot avoid asking questions and making decisions about a character's appearance,

the size and orientation of physical settings, the tone of voice used, and similar issues. Examining the decisions made by Jenkins in translating the written life of Jesus into the visual medium of film can help students cultivate close reading skills. Attention to such details may also enable students to engage with theological, spiritual, and ethical questions in a more meaningful way.

For example, *The Chosen* builds a storyline around Mary Magdalene (played by Elizabeth Tabish), showing her transformation from being possessed by devils to being a faithful disciple of Jesus (Luke 8:2). Mary is portrayed as having relatable moments of discouragement, and even relapse, which she overcomes by turning to Jesus for help. While it seems certain that Jesus's followers faced moments of discouragement, Mary's experience isn't drawn directly from the New Testament. However, this plausible portrayal could help students better appreciate the Bible as a resource for persevering in faith in the face of personal setbacks and stumbling blocks in that it indicates that not even those who walked with Jesus were free from challenges.

Another fascinating example is the backstory constructed for Matthew (played by Paras Patel). As an awkward tax collector on the autism spectrum, Matthew is portrayed as having made a comfortable life for himself by working for the Roman Empire. This is a plausible characterization given the historical evidence suggesting that, while it was often seen as a betrayal of the Jewish people who resented those who collaborated with their imperial oppressors, working as a tax collector had the potential to be personally profitable.[7] Matthew's backstory in *The Chosen* allows the viewer to imagine, first, the emotional toll of losing the approval of his own family and, later, what it might have been like for someone to walk away from comfort and wealth to follow Jesus. This portrayal could invite inspired questions about the kinds of sacrifices required to follow Jesus in our day, and why discipleship is nonetheless worth the cost.

(3) For better or worse, many students today are drawn primarily to visual media—a trend that has accelerated over recent decades with computer and laptop screens becoming nearly ubiquitous. This trend presents a range of educational challenges, as a number of critics have observed.[8] Nevertheless, visual media can hold students' attention when their focus might lag during discussions of the biblical text. The engaging nature of film can therefore be used to help draw students into the biblical world and increase their interest in learning more.

Teaching with The Chosen

Media representations of Jesus such as those in *The Chosen* can also be used to challenge ingrained assumptions about the biblical text. When it comes to the Bible, a common obstacle instructors must navigate is the students' familiarity (both real and imagined) with the subject matter. It can be a challenge to get students to read something that they assume they already know. The fresh visual perspective offered by *The Chosen* can remind viewers just how astonishing the claims made by and about Jesus were for the original audiences. Having students watch scenes from *The Chosen* thus helps make the strange familiar and the familiar strange and expands our ideas and insights into the Gospels.[9]

CHALLENGES IN TEACHING WITH *THE CHOSEN*

One concern many religious educators have with using cinematic depictions of nonfiction events is that students will develop historically or textually inaccurate ideas from the conjectured details of the film. How does a director balance being historically accurate with creating a compelling narrative? How does a director handle contested details or the many events that lack historical documentation?

These concerns are not unique to *The Chosen*. For example, although *Selma* was acclaimed by viewers and critics alike, director Ava Duvernay received criticism regarding some perceived historical inaccuracies in the film. In response, she reflected on her distinctive goals as a filmmaker: "This is a film. I'm not a historian. I'm not a documentarian. I am an artist who explored history. And what I found, the questions that I have, the ideas that I have about history, I have put into this project that I have made. I understand people wanting to see history through their own gaze, through their own lens, and this is the way that I see it. This is the way that I interpret it."[10] For believers, the issue of accuracy is particularly acute when dealing with matters of theological significance. There is a risk that individuals will believe that, because something is portrayed in *The Chosen* in a particular way, the depiction is necessarily supported by biblical evidence. It is important to guide students through recognizing which elements of a scene can be found in Scripture and which elements employ artistic license, as well as questions about whether and how such discrepancies matter.

Imaginative portrayals of Jesus on the screen raise unique questions for viewers approaching them from a faith perspective. Matthew J. Grey, reflecting on his experience as a believer, teacher, and scholar, explains, "For me, placing Jesus films, the New Testament text, and historical sources into thoughtful conversation has prompted valuable questions that I might not otherwise have asked about a wide range of issues, including Jesus's appearance, personality, teachings, and ongoing social relevance, as well as the nature of scriptural writings. Often these questions come as I find myself wondering why film directors made certain decisions, how I might have presented things differently as a believing historian, and what the implications of those decisions might be for the spiritual experience of the viewers."[11] Although he acknowledges the special challenges posed by Jesus films, Grey speaks for many religious educators when he concludes that they can promote powerful academic and spiritual experiences for both learners and teachers.

To use my earlier example, if I were to take the clip showing Jesus hoisted up to the cross by pulleys and place it alongside historical sources that indicate crosses were only slightly taller than the person being crucified, I could ask myself, "What is the effect of portraying Jesus so high off the ground? Why did the producers choose to film it that way?" Perhaps they wanted to dramatize his statement, "I, when I am lifted up from the earth, will draw all people to myself" (John 12:32 NRSV). Even if the visual depiction is not historically accurate, as I see Jesus high off the ground, I can contemplate Jesus drawing me toward himself—physically, but also spiritually—and ultimately toward heaven. I could also ask, "How might the crucifixion scene in this movie be different if its depiction aligned more closely with historical facts?" With a six-foot cross, Jesus would have been at eye level with the onlookers. That might change the way I see the conversation between Jesus and his mother, where he is looking at her and she is looking at him, almost face-to-face (see John 19:25–27). Thus, while historical and biblical accuracy are very important, thoughtful educators can help students distinguish between fact and fiction, make more nuanced observations about what they find on the page and on the screen, and tease out the implications of the interpretive choices made by authors and directors.

An additional concern religious educators might face in using *The Chosen* (or any other media representation of Jesus) in the classroom is that students will conclude that such representations are adequate substitutes for studying directly from the Scriptures. Dallas Jenkins addresses this concern at the very beginning of the first episode of the series. Before the action opens, a disclaimer states, "*The Chosen* is based on the true stories of the gospels of Jesus Christ. Some locations and timelines have been combined or condensed. Backstories and some characters or dialog have been added. However, all biblical and historical context and any artistic imagination are designed to support the truth and intention of the Scriptures. Viewers are encouraged to read the scripture and the gospels." Rather than replacing Scripture, clips from *The Chosen* can be used in conjunction with Scripture to pique curiosity and drive viewers back to the original source.

An Approach for Teaching with *The Chosen*

One strategy for teaching with *The Chosen* is to (1) isolate specific scenes that are drawn directly from biblical text, (2) invite students to read the passage(s) on which that scene is based, (3) have them watch the scene, either ahead of time or in the classroom together, and then (4) respond to questions (as a whole class, in small groups, or in writing). Questions for discussion might include the following:

- Which elements of this portrayal are directly drawn from the Scripture passage?
- What artistic license was taken in this portrayal?
- Is there anything from the biblical text that this film omits from its portrayal?
- What does this film add to its portrayal that is not explicitly in the text?
- What looks or sounds different from what you had imagined when reading the text? Is there a basis in the biblical text for preferring one rendering over another?
- Are there particular scenes, characters, or speeches that this film, in your view, gets wrong? In what respect or to what degree?
- Is there anything about the biblical text that this film helps you see that you did not see or appreciate previously?
- What is your reaction to the film's portrayal of Jesus?
- Are there motifs that are repeated that you had not noticed when reading the Gospel(s)?

- Does the film present a recognizably Jewish Jesus, as one finds in Matthew's Gospel? What details contribute to this characterization?
- Does the film do a good job of conveying, for example, the misunderstanding motif that recurs throughout Mark's Gospel? In what ways did the apostles and other figures fail to grasp Jesus's identity, and why or how do they misconstrue his person or his message?
- To what extent does the film reproduce the densely scriptural texture of the many speeches that appear in Luke's Gospel (e.g., the Annunciation, the Magnificat, the Benedictus)?
- How well does the film capture the dualistic imagery (e.g., light and darkness, true and false, life and death) that pervades John's Gospel?
- How does the film depict the interaction between Jesus and those plotting against him?
- What about the language? Does the translation used by the screenwriters lend a more realistic feel to the action and dialogue? Does it feel stilted? Is it easy to follow? Are there particular lines that seem to work very well or very poorly?
- If you were the director of this scene, what would you do differently?
- What questions or insights does this scene bring up for you?
- What does the video add to your feelings and understanding about this scene?
- Where do you see yourself in relation to this scene?

Many of these questions will be applicable to any scene one might choose. Instructors can frame questions tailored specifically to individual scenes or characters. Of course, different pedagogical settings will lend themselves to different sorts of questions, be they historical, literary, theological, or spiritual.

By my count, the first four seasons of *The Chosen* contain more than fifty discrete scenes that are based on specific passages from the New Testament, plus additional scenes drawn from the Hebrew Bible. To assist educators in identifying material from *The Chosen* that is directly drawn from Scripture, I have curated a collection of these video clips that are publicly available online and can be used in classroom settings.[12] This simplifies the process of quickly identifying where a specific passage is depicted in *The Chosen*. Moreover, due to time constraints imposed by the class schedule, the brevity of the clips makes them easier to incorporate into lessons.

Personally, I have found that using clips from *The Chosen* can illuminate principles that students might otherwise miss. For example, in a recent class, we studied John 5:2–13 and watched the scene in which Jesus heals the man at the pool of Bethesda (S2E4). Students were particularly interested in *The Chosen*'s depiction of a discussion between Matthew and John about whether carrying a mat on Shabbat was an actual violation of Jewish law. While this exchange is not present in John 5, the narrator of John's Gospel appears to assume that Jewish oral law that was later codified in rabbinic literature was present and applicable at the time of Christ. This background information provided my students with an opportunity to discuss the difference between the Oral and Written Torah.

After viewing the scene, one student shared a conversation with a friend who was struggling to eliminate pornography from his life. The student said, "Although some of the words from Jesus in the show weren't from the Scriptures, they really speak to my friend's situation." When I asked him to elaborate, the student responded,

> In *The Chosen*, Jesus told the sick man, "This pool has nothing for you, it means nothing, and you know it. But you're still here. Why?" I can see Jesus saying that to my friend: "This porn means nothing to you. But you're still looking at it. Why?" The sick man didn't know why he was still trusting in the pool, that couldn't help him. And so the Savior's words, "You don't need this pool—you only need me," are powerful. If we can realize that we find joy and hope not in worldly entertainments, but in Jesus Christ, then we can feel great peace.

As we discussed the clip as a class, I reminded students that although these lines are not directly taken from Scripture, they do align with Jesus's teachings—"You don't need this pool [or insert whatever temporal thing we want so badly]—you only need Jesus."

Conclusion

At the time of this writing, *The Chosen* video clips that I've curated have been viewed more than two million times (the video of Jesus healing the man at the pool of Bethesda has been viewed more than 250,000 times). I have heard from several teachers who have used these clips in a variety of different religion classes. Some report that students enjoy them simply for their entertainment value. Others, like a teacher at a Jesuit high school who contacted me, appreciate their potential to foster a deeper level of engagement. He wrote, "I think the value of the video clips is mostly in getting the students to consider these events as a real drama of history—as true human experiences which come out of Judaism and terminating in the establishment of a divine institution—rather than as a mere fantasy or abstraction that is more or less a code of ethics wrapped in some disconnected storybook tales." My suspicion is that, even though he is aiming to produce a work of art and not a lesson plan, Dallas Jenkins would be gratified to hear this.

I believe movies about Jesus are successful when they draw us closer to him and motivate us to study the Scriptures with greater intensity. By this definition *The Chosen* has been a success, no doubt because it was the part of Dallas Jenkins's express purpose in starting the project. Jenkins says, "We hear every day from literally thousands of people around the world who say, 'I'm reading my Bible more than I ever have before. I feel closer to Jesus than I ever have before from watching this show, and it's causing me to want to dig in more in my prayer life and in my Bible reading.' And I don't see how that can be a bad thing."[13]

Notwithstanding certain pitfalls, the use of cinematic portrayals of Jesus has enormous pedagogical and spiritual potential. By responsibly using scripturally based video clips, religious educators can help the Scriptures come alive and facilitate fruitful thought, discussion, and application.

Part Three

CHRISTOLOGY *and* HISTORY

9

Too Divine to Be Human?

The Chosen's Portrayal of a Fully Human Jesus

PAUL GONDREAU

The considerable acclaim *The Chosen* has enjoyed since its release has not shielded the series from sharp criticism—sometimes even virulent condemnation. A common object of censure includes the way the show supposedly portrays a "false Christ" in blasphemous, flippant, and heterodox ways and seemingly undercuts the doctrine of Christ's incarnate and sinless humanity.[1]

There are many issues endemic to efforts to condemn the series, not least of which that nearly all the gainsayers—at least that I've encountered—have watched nothing more than snippets of isolated scenes, or that they insist on playing armchair theologian without the necessary theological competency to do so in their passing judgment on the series. Worse still and undergirding nearly all condemnations of the show is the logical fallacy of the category error. *The Chosen* represents a form of Christian art—cinematic Christian art. But the gainsayers routinely judge the show not as a form of Christian art but as a kind of theological treatise or cinematic Bible study. In this way, they conflate Christian art (employing as it does artistic license) with Christian doctrine or with biblical exegesis. Hence, the category error.[2] So, just as it would be misplaced to accuse, say, Caravaggio's famous painting *The Call of St. Matthew* of giving short shrift to historical accuracy or of using the technique of tenebrism to portray Christ in an ill-suited and irreverent manner by leaving him who is the light of the world in the shadows with only his hand emerging (barely) from the darkness, so is it the same for dismissing *The Chosen* on the grounds, for instance, that it employs fictional narrative (deemed as irreverent) in the way it treats the gospel story.

Granted, the subject matter of Christian art—nearly always, as in the case of *The Chosen*, the gospel narratives and the person of Christ—*is* theological, and so any form of Christian art worthy of the name must respect the boundaries of defined doctrine. In my judgment and as I argue in this chapter, *The Chosen* easily meets this standard, in that the way it portrays the person of Jesus accords with the biblical witness and with defined christological doctrine. Even if *The Chosen* is not impervious to criticism—I have some criticisms of the show myself, mostly of a minor sort—I argue that condemnations of the show on theological or doctrinal grounds, especially as they relate to the humanity of Christ, are fundamentally misguided and without warrant.

To be sure, in what follows, I argue the case considerably more strongly. In my view, *The Chosen* not only accords with defined christological doctrine relative to the humanity and divinity of Christ, it excels at the way it presents both, but especially at the image of Jesus as fully human, due in no small degree to the exceptional performance of Jonathan Roumie. Christian tradition has ever struggled with accepting and affirming the full humanity of Christ, and to this end, *The Chosen*, as a form of cinematic Christian art, proves an invaluable service. Efforts to dismiss the show for portraying a "false Christ" ironically fall prey themselves to a "false Christ," since they betray the awkward relationship that countless Christians have always had with a fully human God-man, from the very apostolic age, in fact. And since a fully human Jesus sits at the heart of the Christian faith—and by extension at the heart of *The Chosen*—this proves problematic, to say the least, especially when it comes to allergic reactions to *The Chosen*. To put the matter plainly, I aim to provide not only theological justification for the way *The Chosen* depicts a fully human Jesus but a full-throttled theological defense of it.

This chapter proceeds in three steps. First, I offer a rapid overview of the foundation for the doctrine of the full humanity of Christ: the biblical witness and the ensuing witness of the ancient church, especially the teachings of the christological councils (notably, the First Council of Constantinople in 381 and the Council of Chalcedon in 451). This section, a christological primer of sorts, includes cursory consideration of the heresies that directly undercut belief in Christ's true and full humanity and that the above-mentioned councils (and the biblical witness in the case of the first heresy) responded to: Docetism, Apollinarianism, and Monophysitism. Second, I give focused attention to season 1, episode 3 of *The Chosen* in order to highlight the way the show, in the mode of cinematic art, harmonizes with this biblical and conciliar witness. Third, I show how criticisms of the show's portrayal of a fully human Jesus emerge as nothing other than recycled iterations of Docetism (or semi-Docetism) and Monophysitism (a kind of crypto-Monophysitism). The former manifests itself in relation to many aspects of the show, but especially a mirthful, playful, jocular Jesus and a Jesus and a John the Baptist who fail to see eye to eye on certain mission-related matters. The latter may be seen with regard to how critics take issue with the way that season 2 shows Jesus laboring at composing the Sermon on the Mount. At bottom, I contend, these critics prefer a glorified view of Christ's humanity, ever the scourge of adherence to the full concrete reality of the incarnation.

A Christology Primer: Christ's Full Humanity in the Biblical and Conciliar Witness

There is a manifold witness in the New Testament relative to Jesus's true and full humanity. In simple narrative terms, all four gospels make plain that Jesus ate, drank, slept, grew weary, and was moved by wonder, anger, and sorrow, as well as fear, desire, and joy, all of which, as Augustine of Hippo and Thomas Aquinas observe, attest to his true humanity, that is, to his having a true human body and human soul.[3]

"The Word Became Flesh"

Beyond these references, there are a few texts, especially from the Pauline and Johannine writings, that stand out in relief. A historical—and adjacent theological—reason accounts for this: both Paul and John were responding to that first of Christian heresies, Docetism. From the Greek *dokeō*, "to seem," Docetism posits a ghost or phantom incarnation (a fake incarnation, we might say today), that is, it asserts that Christ only *appeared* to have come in the flesh but did not in truth or reality.[4] Docetism (or semi-Docetism, in its softer variety) refers, then, to the heretical tendency to deny or downplay Christ's full humanity—a problem for Christianity at its very beginning and, as we shall see, a problem for Christianity still today.

In order to counteract the docetic currents that had already emerged in their day, both Paul and John have recourse to the suggestive term "flesh"—*sarx* in Greek, *caro* in Latin (whence incarnation)—in their referencing Jesus's humanity. Signifying the "stuff" of this world (more so than the more abstract "man"), "flesh" attests to the concrete reality of the humanity taken on by the Son of God. Hence, Paul professes that Christ "was manifested in the flesh" (1 Tim 3:16).[5] And in Rom 1:3, he states that he, Paul, proclaims "the gospel concerning [God's] Son, who was descended from David according to the flesh."

John, for his part, openly alerts his readers to the presence of the Docetists in his second epistle: "Many deceivers . . . will not acknowledge the coming of Jesus Christ in the flesh" (2 John 7). Wasting little time putting Docetism squarely in the crosshairs when composing the prologue to his gospel, he delivers the most robust antidocetic line in the entire New Testament when he announces, "And the Word became flesh and dwelt among us" (John 1:14.)

Other biblical passages could be cited for the manifest way they attest to Jesus's true and integral humanity, including Heb 2:14–17: "[Christ] himself likewise partook of the same nature [as the children of flesh and blood]. . . . Therefore he had to be made like his brethren in every respect." The biblical witness leaves little doubt that Jesus was truly and fully human, that is, that he is the God-*man* in every sense of the term, and that affirming this tenet must not be left merely in the abstract or confined to the ethereal.

"What Was Not Assumed Was Not Healed"

Concerns over upholding Jesus's true humanity at the time of the New Testament's writing did not end with the closure of the apostolic age but continued—indeed, they intensified—into the postbiblical period, even as the threat of Docetism, the tendency to deny or downplay Christ's full humanity, continued apace. By the third century, there arose a principle, profoundly seminal in the thought of many early Christian writers, that has become known as the soteriological principle. Predicated on the understanding that the very purpose of God's becoming man was for the sake of human salvation, the principle asserts in its classic formulation: "What was not assumed was not healed." For the whole of man to be saved, we might say, Christ had to take on everything essential pertaining to human nature. Possibly tracing all the way back to Irenaeus's theory of recapitulation late in the second century, the principle originates more than likely with the third-century writer Origen, who puts it thus: "Man would not have been saved entirely if Christ hadn't clothed himself in man entirely" (*Discussion with Heraclitus* 7).

"To Become Man"

The soteriological principle played a crucial role in the patristic response to Apollinarianism (named after Apollinaris of Laodicea), a docetic-like heresy that denied a human rational soul, or *nous*, in Christ. In 381, the First Council of Constantinople was convened to respond to this heresy. Apollinarianism was officially condemned, and the crucial term *enanthrōpeō*, "to become man," was employed, becoming enshrined in the credal profession that the council issued.[6] Outside the Bible, this would mark the early church's clearest attestation up to that date of Christ's full humanity. Still today Catholics recite this credal profession, the Nicene-Constantinopolitan Creed, at every Sunday liturgy, with the key line reading, "was incarnate of the Virgin Mary, and became man."

"Consubstantial with Us as Regards His Humanity"

Things would come to a head at the Council of Chalcedon in 451, where the early church's determination to proclaim the full truth of Christ's humanity (and divinity) would reach its high point. Chalcedon was convened in response to still another heresy attacking Jesus's full humanity (and his divinity), the heresy of Monophysitism. From the Greek meaning "one nature," this heresy posits in Christ not two natures, a human nature and a divine nature, but one blended or mixed nature (a blend of both human and divine elements). In this way, it compromises Jesus's full human nature. If, for a loose comparison, we consider the piece of cutlery known as the spork, we can see that the aptness of the comparison derives from the fact that a spork is neither fully a spoon nor fully a fork, but a blend of elements from both. So, too, Christ, according to Monophysitism, is neither fully human nor fully divine but a blend or mixture of elements taken from each; he is a third thing altogether, a kind of theandric mutant.

To counter this teaching, Chalcedon appropriated the celebrated term of the Council of Nicaea from 325, *homoousios* (consubstantial), used to affirm Christ's divinity at Nicaea, and applied it also to Christ's humanity: "Christ is consubstantial [*homoousios*] with the Father as regards his divinity [per the profession of Nicaea], and [as we council fathers at Chalcedon now assert] consubstantial [*homoousios*] with us as regards his humanity."[7] Christ shares in our human nature fully, not partially.

Not stopping there, Chalcedon employed another, even more crucial turn of phrase in its response to Monophysitism: "One and the same Christ, Son, Lord, only-begotten, acknowledged in two natures which undergo no confusion [*asygchytōs*], no change [*atreptōs*], no division [*adiairetōs*], no separation [*achōristōs*]." Christ's human nature was not compromised or diluted by its being joined to the divine nature, his humanity was not swallowed up or washed out by his divinity, since "the property of both natures is preserved, [while] com[ing] together into a single person and a single hypostasis."[8] The integrity and distinct identity of Christ's human nature were preserved.

A Fully Human Jesus: Camping outside Capernaum (Season 1, Episode 3)

With the doctrinal truth of Christ's true and integral humanity (human consubstantiality) fully established, we turn to *The Chosen*, especially the first season, in order to see how the show aligns with this tenet. Although the first two episodes of season 1 provide brief snapshots of what is to come in this regard, it is episode 3 of season 1 where the show lets fly with the cinematic image of the fully human Jesus that the series opts to set its course upon. It is a glorious course, in my opinion. Readers will recall this episode as the one that showcases Jesus's interaction with the children from Capernaum as he camps outside the town.

Striking Christological Gold

I draw attention not to his interaction with the children per se, beautiful and original though it be, but to the images of Jesus alone in his camp, where we see him laboring through sweat and vocal grunts in the effort at starting a fire, preparing his dinner, stretching his tight shoulder muscles, bandaging a cut on his wrist, and fashioning a lock and key before retiring for the night. If the first two episodes of season 1 make evident the powerful cinematic drama and beauty and the first-rate acting that would come to define the show, it is this episode, episode 3, that would define the show for its theological or christological content. As a viewer who has spent his entire professional theological career reflecting upon Christ's full humanity, this episode proved to be the theological hook that convinced me of the show's unique christological quality—and made me a devoted fan as a result.[9]

In my view, season 1, episode 3 exhibits the show's temerity and imaginative genius in portraying a side of Jesus's humanity (a Jesus who cooks, a Jesus who stretches his sore muscles, etc.) that has rarely, if ever, been depicted or imagined in the history of Christian art. In the process, it strikes nothing short of theological or christological gold. Bold and fresh, it is revelatory of the christological direction of the series. Simple and almost understated though it may be, showing the incarnate Son of God cutting garlic and stretching his sore muscles breaks new artistic ground. It is vintage *Chosen*, by which I mean the use of fictional narrative to offer a plausible cinematic presentation of what the gospel accounts leave the door open to but that, given the nature of the Gospels as providing bare-bones sketches, the biblical text fails to mention.

"Also Human"

We get much more of this fully human Jesus throughout the entirety of the series, of course. The warm, smiling, mirthful, and even playful—and eminently relatable—Jesus (done tastefully and judiciously, I find) appears throughout. In season 4 (the most recent as of this writing), there is a tender scene in episode 5 between Jesus and his mother Mary while both are at the home of Lazarus. Loving Jewish mother that she is, Mary offers to wash her son's hair in this imaginative scene, and at a certain point, Jesus finds himself explaining to her how his disciples still are not quite understanding his "mysterious new way" of discipleship.[10] Mary observes, "They're only human, what did you expect?" Pointing to himself with emphasis, Jesus replies, "Also human." Nothing underscores better the strides *The Chosen* makes in giving full, antidocetic weight to the concrete reality of Jesus's humanity than this short phrase uttered by Jesus to his mother.[11]

All the same, it is episode 3 of season 1, because it is the first, that sets the christological tone and shocks and awes with its fresh and bold portrayal of a fully human Jesus. This is something akin to Mel Gibson's *The Passion of the Christ*, which for its part depicts such memorable images as a Jesus offering a warm smile at the Last Supper or enjoying a playful moment with his mother in their home in Nazareth. These cinematic images were noteworthy at the time of the movie's release twenty years ago because they were bold and fresh. Enjoying the advantage of being a multiseason series, *The Chosen* succeeds in bringing this bold and striking portrait of a fully human Jesus to another level altogether.

"Jesus Offered Up Prayers and Supplications, with Loud Cries and Tears" (Heb 5:7)

The final feature of season 1, episode 3 that merits special acclaim is in the very opening scene, where we see Jesus alone at night at his campsite and praying to his Father with tears of anguish. Normally, one sees images of Jesus in prayerful anguish only in connection with the agony in the garden of Gethsemane on the night before his death—not at other times in Jesus's ministry, let alone even before his public ministry has begun, as this episode depicts. Yet the New Testament expressly affirms this very experience. In striking antidocetic language that connects closely with this iconic scene from *The Chosen*, Heb 5:7 states, "In the days of his flesh, Jesus offered up prayers and supplications, with loud cries and tears, to him who was able to save him from death, and he was heard for his godly fear." To view this passage from Hebrews rendered cinematically in such a powerful, imaginative way is to behold yet another example of the christological gold that the show offers its viewers.

Cinematic Anti-Docetism

Daring to show the incarnate Word of God embracing the ordinariness of human fatigue, of human muscle soreness, of simple cuts to the skin, of the need to start a fire in order to cook his own meal (Jesus *can* make his way in a kitchen, it turns out!)—in short, daring not to leave the incarnation in ethereal stained glass, as Dallas Jenkins prefers to say, but to put concrete flesh and bones on the doctrine of the incarnation, and thereby show cinematically the full concrete ramifications of God-made-man—*this* is no small part of the show's genius. That genius, if I can so put it, is what I would term cinematic anti-Docetism; it is to provide viewers with a cinematic glimpse into what the Council of Chalcedon means when it professes, "Christ is consubstantial with us as regards his humanity."

I use the word "daring" purposefully. To repeat, Christian tradition has ever struggled to embrace the full tangible reality of the incarnation, preferring instead to leave this doctrine in the abstract—or again in stained glass—if not to downplay it or deny it outright. Too often Christians still today fall prey, if not to docetic leanings straight up, then at least to soft docetic leanings (semi-Docetism), whereby the doctrine of God's becoming man remains affirmed in the abstract but goes little further. Docetism, it turns out, dies a hard death. As does its close cousin Monophysitism, as I will now detail in the final section of this chapter as we consider the way critics gainsay *The Chosen*'s depiction of Jesus.

"Blasphemy!": The Latent Semi-Docetism and Crypto-Monophysitism in Criticism of *The Chosen*

Is a Mirthful and Bantering Jesus Blasphemous? Lessons Learned from the Heresy of Docetism

Evidence for how Christians, however inadvertently, can slip into harboring a kind of semi-Docetism is seen in the way critics react allergically to the various ways the show depicts a concretely human, relatable Jesus.[12] Often without any argument, they charge *The Chosen* with blasphemy for showing a jocular, playful Jesus, such as when he makes animal flatulence sounds in order to help the children Abigail and Joshua feel at ease in his presence as they espy him from a distance at his campsite in season 1, episode 3. Unless one wishes to argue that playfulness and risibility belong to our sinful, fallen condition as such—they don't, since risibility is a property that follows immediately upon our rationality, and thus upon our God-given design—dismissing out of hand such features in the life of Jesus has no merit.[13] One can quibble about *how* a show might portray a mirthful, playful Jesus, but to oppose it in principle, as critics often do, is purely and simply to advance a latent semidocetic view of Christ.

Equally objectionable, so certain critics assert, is a Jesus and a John the Baptist who fail to see eye to eye on certain mission-related matters and who, after some bantering, have need for a meeting of the minds (see S2E5). Such an objection also lacks merit, particularly if we recall the misunderstanding that occurred, in Luke's account, between Jesus and his mother Mary (and his putative father Joseph) and the subsequent need for their own meeting of the minds: "'Son, why have you treated us so? Behold, your father and I have been looking for you anxiously.' And he said to them, 'How is it that you sought me? Did you not know that I must be in my Father's house?'" (Luke 2:48–49). Sinlessness does not necessarily preclude misunderstanding, miscommunication, or difference of opinion, nor does sinlessness equate with omniscience or with infallible judgment. (Catholic tradition holds, of course, that both Jesus and his mother were sinless.)

Simply put, those who gainsay *The Chosen* on such grounds show themselves more comfortable with a semidocetic Christ. They prefer a glorified view of Christ's humanity, a view of Jesus that washes out or dilutes his full and real humanity. They favor a Jesus who, yes, is human, but only so much.

Did Jesus Know All Things? Lessons Learned from the Heresy of Monophysitism

If Docetism (or semi-Docetism) still lurks among many of the faithful, so does a crypto-Monophysitism. In the case of *The Chosen*, the crypto-Monophysitism rears itself in the way critics object to how season 2 portrays Jesus laboring at composing, editing, and rehearsing the Sermon on the Mount in episodes 5, 7, and 8. They assert that, as the Word of God, Jesus knows all things and so never would have labored at composing a sermon, let alone taken redactional suggestions from others (as he does from Matthew in S2E8).

The christological error here is obvious, at least if we pay heed to the doctrine of the two natures in Christ. Jesus's two natures, per the Council of Chalcedon, remain distinct, even if united in the one person of the Son or Word. And because he had two natures, and since intellect (or mind) is a power pertaining to nature, Christ had two intellects, a divine intellect and a human intellect, and thus two types of knowledge, human and divine. (He also had two wills, as the Third Council of Constantinople in 680–681 professed.) These two intellects, and by extension two types of knowledge, did not fuse together, just as the two natures did not blend together.

Too Divine to Be Human?

To assert that Jesus knew all things because he was God—how often do we hear Christians say this?—is to collapse his human intellect (and thus his human knowledge) into his divine intellect (and so into his divine knowledge), as if his divine mind fused with his human mind and washed it out. To say Jesus knew all things because he was God is to superimpose the infinite knowledge of his divine mind onto his finite human mind. It is to affix omniscience to a knowing faculty (a human intellect) that, by virtue of its finite, limited nature, cannot know all things. Omniscience can in no way be a property of a human mind—any human mind—as there is no proportion between the two.

Beware the Trap of Epistemological Monophysitism: Christ's Human and Divine Intellects Did Not Blend

Put simply, when Christ was speaking and teaching as a man, he was using his human mind and human knowledge. His divine intellect and divine knowledge, per the two-natures doctrine, could not mingle with or butt into his human mode of knowing and speaking (recall Chalcedon's "no confusion" and "no change"). And his human knowledge would have been finite and limited, as with all human knowledge, even if, as Savior and Son of God, he had things revealed to him that were revealed to no other human being. Yes, Jesus knew things that no other human being knew, especially regarding truths about God and about human salvation, but this does not equate with omniscience. He did not know all things, at least in the way that only the infinite divine mind does. To suggest otherwise is to commit a form of psychological or epistemological Monophysitism. His infinite divine knowledge did not service or superimpose onto his finite human knowledge. Again, the two intellects were not blended.[14]

Now, the mode of human knowledge is discursive (step-by-step). Human intellects form mental and verbal constructions. They put concepts and sentences together, in a discursive manner. Is it *possible* that when he was preparing a sermon like the Sermon on the Mount Jesus labored at composing and rehearsing it? Yes. Chalcedon's condemnation of Monophysitism and its affirmation of the two-natures doctrine, I would assert, leave room for something like this. Is it *necessary* that it happened this way? No—nor does Dallas Jenkins claim that it did (he has voiced this disclaimer many times).

What *The Chosen* depicts by way of Jesus's sermon preparation is a form of (cinematic) Christian art—a different category from Christian doctrine! For the record, in my view, Jesus's sermon preparation did not happen in the way that *The Chosen* imagines. His sermons, including the Sermon on the Mount, certainly could have flowed from his mind effortlessly, similar to what writers experience when they speak of their being inspired by the muse. But hardly is *The Chosen* distorting Christ's humanity by choosing to portray it in the manner that it does.

At bottom, then, whether one gainsays *The Chosen* either in a crypto-Monophysite manner or on latent semidocetic grounds, the end result is the same: a sabotaging of Christ's full humanity.

Conclusion

The Chosen honors in cinematic art form both the biblical witness and the conciliar teaching on Christ's full humanity in a beautiful and brilliant way. *The Chosen* helps to drive home in a powerfully antidocetic manner the real humanity of Jesus, and thereby affirm in concrete cinematic art form what Christian doctrine has always professed: that the divine person of the Son truly became man ("consubstantial with us as regards our humanity") and that his human nature was in no way diluted or compromised, let alone canceled, by its substantial union with his divinity. As such, then, the authoritative weight of both the biblical witness and the conciliar witness, I would argue, stand fully behind *The Chosen*, while allowing for artistic license. The artistic license may not appeal to all tastes, but that does not mean that it crosses the line of theological heterodoxy. *The Chosen* is a gift that deserves to be a centerpiece in the long and venerable tradition of Christian art.

10

The Voice of the Bridegroom

The Johannine Biblical Theology of *The Chosen*

DANIEL M. GARLAND JR.

The great patristic exegete Origen of Alexandria famously stated that the Gospels are the firstfruits of Sacred Scripture and that among the Gospels, John's was the firstfruit of the firstfruits (*Commentary on John* 1.6 [*ANF* 9:300]). The Fourth Gospel presents readers with a deep theological depiction of the life of Christ that captivates the imagination. With *The Chosen*, the events of John's Gospel are incarnated, as it were, for the screen, which allows the viewer to visualize the text in new ways. A particular feature of *The Chosen* is that episodes often open with an Old Testament event that is relevant to the particular episode. In doing so, the writers of *The Chosen* are showing how the Old Testament finds its fulfillment in the New and are engaging in a form of cinematic biblical theology.

In this chapter, I will examine two scenes found only in the Gospel of John, the wedding at Cana (John 2:1–11) and the Samaritan woman at the well (John 4:1–42), in order to analyze their faithfulness to the biblical text and to highlight how the Old Testament background helps to flesh out the scenes depicted on the screen. My contention will be that, although there are some instances of dramatic license and slight divergence from the biblical accounts, on the whole *The Chosen*'s presentation of these scenes is faithful to the Johannine text and its theology.

Daniel M. Garland Jr.

The Wedding at Cana (Season 1, Episode 5)

This episode happens to be one where the opening teaser is not a scene from the Old Testament. Instead, this episode begins with a flashback to the finding of Jesus at the age of twelve after he teaches in the temple (Luke 2). The wedding at Cana scene in *The Chosen* will close with an intertextual allusion to this story (see below), but there is an Old Testament reference that may escape the notice of the casual viewer. While Ramah, Thomas's business partner supplying the wine, is counting the guests and realizing that there are eighty instead of forty, we hear the guests singing the *Od Yishama*:

> It shall be heard again in the cities of Judea
> And in the streets of Jerusalem:
> The voice of joy and the voice of gladness,
> The voice of the bridegroom and the voice of the bride.

These lyrics are taken from the seventh blessing from the Sheva Brakhot (the seven blessings) said at a traditional Jewish wedding. This blessing can be found in the Babylonian Talmud tractate Ketubbot:

> Blessed are you, O Lord our God, King of the Universe, who created joy and gladness, bride and groom, mirth, song, delight and rejoicing, love and harmony, peace and companionship. *O Lord our God, may there ever be heard in the cities of Judah and in the streets of Jerusalem voices of joy and gladness, voices of bride and groom*, the jubilant voices of those joined in marriage under the bridal canopy, the voices of young people feasting and singing. Blessed are You, O Lord, who causes the groom to rejoice with his bride. (Ketubbot 8a, trans. J. Neusner, emphasis added)

This in turn is based on the prophecy of Jeremiah (33:10–11):

> Thus says the Lord: In this place of which you say, "It is a waste without man or beast," *in the cities of Judah and the streets of Jerusalem* that are desolate, without man or inhabitant or beast, *there shall be heard again the voice of mirth and the voice of gladness, the voice of the bridegroom and the voice of the bride*, the voices of those who sing, as they bring thank offerings to the house of the Lord:

The Voice of the Bridegroom

> "Give thanks to the LORD of hosts,
> for the LORD is good,
> for his mercy endures for ever!"
> For I will restore the fortunes of the land as at first, says the LORD.[1]

Jeremiah here speaks of the messianic bridegroom who will bring joy and gladness to God's people. In *The Chosen*, the singing of these verses sets the stage for Jesus to reveal himself as this bridegroom.

The singing of this song resonates with John 3:29, where John the Baptist proclaims, "He who has the bride is the bridegroom; the friend of the bridegroom, who stands and hears him rejoices greatly at the bridegroom's voice; therefore this joy of mine is now full." Here John is designating himself as the "friend of the bridegroom," who is Jesus Christ. The Baptist has heard the voice of this messianic bridegroom, and in accordance with the prophecy of Jeremiah, his joy is now full.

An additional example of nuptial imagery in the account of the wedding at Cana in the Gospel of John is related to its setting "on the third day." This reference has led scholars to see a connection with the giving of the law at Mount Sinai in Exod 19, where the phrase "on the third day" occurs repeatedly (Exod 19:11, 15, 16).[2] God commands Moses in Exod 19:10–11, "Go to the people and consecrate them today and tomorrow, and let them wash their garments, and be ready by the third day; for on the third day the LORD will come down upon Mount Sinai in the sight of all the people." The Jews saw Sinai as a nuptial between Yahweh and Israel.[3] We read in Tractate Bakhodesh of the Mekilta of Rabbi Ishmael, a midrash on Exod 19:17: "Judah used to expound: 'The Lord came from Sinai' (Deut. 33.2). Do not read it thus, but read: 'The Lord came to Sinai' to give the Torah to Israel. I, however, do not interpret it thus, but: 'The Lord came from Sinai' to receive Israel as a bridegroom comes forth to meet the bride."[4] Thus, it is plausible that the Fourth Evangelist draws upon the rich Sinai nuptial imagery to present his account of Cana, whereat Jesus the messianic bridegroom manifests his glory (John 2:11), just as God had manifested his glory at Sinai as bridegroom to Israel.

The Chosen's portrayal of the Blessed Virgin Mary at the wedding of Cana likewise merits close attention against the background of Jewish Scripture and tradition. In the Old Testament, the mother of the Davidic king had a special title, the *Gebirah* or "Great Lady."[5] The queen mother did not just have a special title; she also had an official role in the kingdom. She was the main advisor to the king and also interceded on behalf of the people.[6] *The Chosen* vividly depicts Mary fulfilling this role of the *Gebirah*. In this episode, we see the great friendship that Mary has with Dinah, the mother of the bridegroom.[7] When the wine for the wedding runs out, Mary intercedes on behalf of Dinah and her son. Mary comes to Jesus and says, "They've run out of wine." Jesus's response here in *The Chosen* is a bit disappointing in terms of the Gospel of John. *The Chosen* has him say, "Why are you telling me this?" In the Gospel of John, however, Jesus says, "What is this to me and to you, woman?" (Greek: *Ti emoi kai soi, gynai*). Why is this important? Because Jesus's response, although a refusal, includes Mary in a more explicit manner.[8] There is an intimate connection between the work of Jesus and that of Mary. Recall the words of Simeon in the Gospel of Luke when the infant Jesus is presented in the temple: "Behold, this child is set for the fall and rising of many in Israel, and for a sign that is spoken against (and a sword will pierce through your own soul also)" (Luke 2:34–35). This connection between Mary and Jesus is strengthened by Jesus calling her "woman." Jesus calls his mother "woman" twice in the Gospel of John: here at Cana (2:4) and also at the cross (19:26). There is an implicit connection in both passages to that first *woman*, Eve (cf. Irenaeus, *Demonstration of the Apostolic Preaching* 1.3.33). Mary thus takes the role of the new Eve to Jesus as the new Adam. At this wedding where the messianic bridegroom is present, so is his bride, represented by his most faithful disciple, Mary, his mother, who represents all of us who are united to the messianic bridegroom.

In *The Chosen*, the scene continues with Jesus pulling his mother aside and saying, "Mother, my time has not yet come." This again accords well with John's Gospel. But there is an unstated assumption here. What does Jesus's "time" or "hour" (in John's language) have to do with providing wine? Again, the Old Testament suggests an answer.[9] The prophet Isaiah foretells a time when Israel will cry out for lack of wine:

> The wine mourns, the vine languishes, all the merry-hearted sigh. The mirth of the timbrels is stilled, the noise of the jubilant has ceased, the mirth of the lyre is stilled. No more do they drink wine with singing; strong drink is bitter to those who drink it. The city of chaos is broken down, every house is shut up so that none can enter. There is an outcry in the streets for lack of wine; all joy has reached its eventide; the gladness of the earth is banished.

> Desolation is left in the city, the gates are battered into ruins. For thus it shall be in the midst of the earth among the nations, as when an olive tree is beaten, as at the gleaning when the vintage is done. (Isa 24:7–13)

Israel has no wine and destruction is all around. But the prophecy does not end there. Later in Isaiah we read, "On this mountain the L ord of hosts will make for all peoples a feast of fat things, a feast of wine on the lees, of fat things full of marrow, of wine on the lees well refined. And he will destroy on this mountain the covering that is cast over all peoples, the veil that is spread over all nations. He will swallow up death for ever, and the Lord G od will wipe away tears from all faces, and the reproach of his people he will take away from all the earth; for the L ord has spoken" (Isa 25:6–8). Given this prophecy, it seems that Jesus in the Gospel of John implies that, if his hour had come, he was already planning on providing wine! This is also a fulfillment of the prophet Amos: "'In that day I will raise up the booth of David that is fallen and repair its breaches, and raise up its ruins, and rebuild it as in the days of old; that they may possess the remnant of Edom and all the nations who are called by my name,' says the L ord who does this. 'Behold, the days are coming,' says the L ord, 'when the plowman shall overtake the reaper and the treader of grapes him who sows the seed; the mountains shall drip sweet wine, and all the hills shall flow with it'" (Amos 9:11–13). Jesus's changing twenty to thirty gallons of water contained in six stones jars into wine is certainly a sign that will cause people to take notice.

Yet Jesus says that his time has not yet come. In response, in *The Chosen* we see Mary acting in her other role as the *Gebirah* when she counsels Jesus: "If not now, when?" It is at this point in the show where we find a connection with the teaser at the beginning of the episode when Jesus is found in the temple. Back then, Mary was the one who hesitated: "It is too early for all this." The twelve-year-old Jesus responds, "If not now, when?" Mary pleads, "Just help us get through all of this ... *with you*, please." Then there is a close-up on Mary's face. At the wedding at Cana, we see the same close-up on Mary's face as she says, "Please." Jesus sighs and smiles. Mary understands that Jesus will do it and turns to Ramah and Thomas: "Do whatever he tells you." This scene wonderfully brings to life the intimate connection of Jesus with his mother.

Then Jesus gets to work. What comes next is a brilliant combination of cinematography, storytelling, and theology. While Jesus prays over the six stone jars of ritual purification water, there is a juxtaposition of Jude Thaddeus talking about the permanence of stone masonry: "Once you make that first cut into the stone it can't be undone. It sets in motion a series of choices. What used to be a shapeless block of limestone or granite begins its long journey of transformation and it will never be the same." There follows a beautiful shot of Jesus reaching into the water jars and a close-up of his hand as it comes out of the jar and drips with red wine. This image is striking precisely because here at Cana, Jesus performs his first miracle, which begins the long journey to the cross. Things will never be the same. A transition takes place from the hidden life of Jesus to his public ministry. The red wine-soaked hand foreshadows the blood-soaked body that Jesus will later offer as a sacrifice on Calvary. It is through this self-offering on the cross that Jesus as the bridegroom Messiah will enable the messianic wine of his eucharistic blood to be given to his bride, the church (see John 6:53–56).

The Samaritan Woman at the Well (Season 1, Episode 8)

At the beginning of this episode, the patriarch Jacob is digging his well. Jacob is approached by a Canaanite who is concerned that the land is a bad place for a well and that Jacob has been cheated. Jacob tells him that he has faith in his God, a God that he has wrestled with, yet in fact has never seen. The Canaanite remarks that this is some god that he has chosen. Jacob responds, "*We* didn't choose him ... *he* chose us." Water then springs up from the land. This opening teaser sets us up perfectly, since Jesus will meet the Samaritan woman, Photina, at this very well and Jesus will describe himself as water that springs or wells up to eternal life.[10]

In *The Chosen*, by the time Jesus encounters Photina, her story has already been well established. She is an outcast, and her previous husband will not grant her a bill of divorce. Moreover, it is revealed that there is deep-seated animosity between Jews and Samaritans.[11] Jesus asks Photina for a drink and then reveals that he is the source of water that will "become in a person a spring of water welling up to eternal life." Photina thinks he is bluffing and challenges him to prove it. Jesus responds, "First go and call your husband and come back." Photina declares, "I don't have a husband." He counters, "Right, you have five and the man you are living with now is not your husband."

This exchange tracks perfectly with the Gospel of John. This also connects us back to the wedding at Cana in John 2, because while the Samaritan woman indeed had five husbands and is now living with one to whom she

The Voice of the Bridegroom

is not married, John wants us to see a deeper reality. The Samaritan woman represents the Samaritans as a whole. We see in 2 Kgs 17:24, 29, 33 that the Samaritan people are made up of five nations with their five local gods. These five gods are their Baals/husbands. The Samaritans have five Baals—that is, false gods—and the God that the Samaritan woman is with right now is not hers, that is, the Samaritans have not yet accepted Jesus as their bridegroom Messiah. For Jesus is not just the bridegroom Messiah of the Jews but of the Samaritans also—and of the Greeks and of all people! The setting of this scene is historically significant. In the Old Testament, a well was the very place a pious Hebrew man would go to find a bride. It is where Abraham's servant sought a wife for Isaac and where Jacob met Rachel. The bridegroom imagery of Cana thus overlaps with the woman at the well.

Photina nevertheless thinks Jesus is mocking her in *The Chosen*. She sarcastically says, "I see. You are a prophet. You are here to preach at me." Photina has come alone in order to escape condemnation. Here in both *The Chosen* and the Gospel of John, the conversation shifts to worship, a natural progression, since to accept Jesus as the bridegroom Messiah involves giving him due worship. But there is a problem. True worship is in the Jerusalem temple, where the Samaritans are not allowed. The Jesus of *The Chosen* tells her that he is here to break those barriers. The time is coming when neither on this mountain, Mount Gerizim, the place of the Samaritan temple, nor in Jerusalem will one worship the Father. Photina rightly asks, then, where she is supposed to go when she needs God. The Jesus of *The Chosen* says, "Anywhere. God is Spirit." This is an apt summary of the sentiment of Jesus in the Gospel of John.

Where the dialogue goes after this, however, invites critique in relation to the Gospel of John. Jesus says in *The Chosen*, "And the time is coming and is now here that it won't matter where you worship. But only that you do it in spirit and in truth." Then, the writers of *The Chosen* reveal their theological understanding of "in spirit and in truth": "Heart and mind... that is the kind of worshiper he is looking for." Later, before Photina goes off to share the good news of Jesus to the rest of the Samaritans, we get the following dialogue:

PHOTINA: "Spirit and truth?"
JESUS: "Spirit and truth."
PHOTINA: "It won't be all about mountains and temples...?"
JESUS (shaking his head): "Soon, just the heart."

To understand what worship in "spirit and truth" means in the Gospel of John, and why the above dialogue is problematic, we need to understand John's presentation of Jesus as the true temple.

The prologue of the Gospel of John hints at the theme of Jesus's identity as the new temple, thus alerting the reader to the unique role that Jesus plays in the new creation. Moving from the revelation in John 1:1 that the Logos is God to John 1:14, we see that the Logos has now taken on flesh (Greek: *sarx*) and that he "pitched his tent" or "tabernacled" (Greek: *eskēnōsen*) among us. In the Old Testament, the tabernacle and temple were the places where God dwells with men. To enter into the tabernacle/temple was to enter into the presence of God. Yet, now, in contrast to the stationary temple and like the moving tabernacle of the wilderness wandering, John informs the reader that God's presence is no longer confined to one static location, that is, the temple in Jerusalem, but can be accessed wherever Jesus is present. Further, John describes the effects of this tabernacling: "we have beheld his glory." In Ezek 43:2, the prophet foretold that when the eschatological temple arrives, the earth will shine with God's glory. What Ezekiel sees is an even greater instance of the presence of God's glory than was found in the original wilderness tabernacle (see Exod 40:34–35). As John continues his narrative, he brings into full relief the notion that the Second Temple, begun under Ezra and expanded by Herod the Great, is not the temple spoken of by Ezekiel.[12]

Jesus is both the fulfillment of the eschatological glory and of the eschatological temple.[13] This reality, only hinted at in John 1:14, is made explicit in John 2:21. After Jesus drives out the money changers from the temple and overturns their tables, "the Jews" ask Jesus by what sign he does these things. He responds in v. 19, "Destroy this temple, and in three days I will raise it up." While Jesus's audience is puzzled by this statement, John alerts his readers to the true meaning of Jesus's words in v. 21: "But he was speaking about the temple of his body" (ESVCE). The evangelist's comment reveals that there is a distinction between the cult that takes place in the earthly temple and the cult that belongs to the true temple of Jesus's body.

In the crucifixion scene of John 19, the evangelist brings to a climax his presentation of Jesus as the new temple. Mary Coloe points out that the blood and water flowing from Jesus's pierced side (John 19:34) evokes the eschatological temple of Ezek 47.[14] It is true that Ezekiel does not have blood flowing from his temple vision, but John has more than the Ezekiel temple in mind.

He also wants his readers to notice what those in Jerusalem at the time of Jesus's crucifixion would have noticed: that the blood and water flowing from Christ's side is reminiscent of the blood and water flowing out of the side of the Temple Mount as a result of the blood from the multitude of paschal lambs being slaughtered for the Passover, combined with water poured on the altar to wash it by the temple priests.[15] For John, this is of such magnitude that he interrupts his narrative to affirm the veracity of his testimony: "He who saw it has borne witness—his testimony is true, and he knows that he tells the truth—that you also may believe" (John 19:35). As Coloe points out, "A writer familiar with the Jerusalem Temple and its altar, who has already brought together architecture and anatomy, in speaking of Jesus' body as the Temple (2:21), may here be further exploiting the rich symbolism of Jewish sacrifice. Christians need no longer look to the blood and water in the *ḥeq* (cavity) of a pierced altar, for the blood and water have now been released from the side (*pleura*) of Jesus."[16] Now that Jesus has been lifted up on the cross and his identity as the true temple has been revealed, he will draw all men to himself (see John 12:32) so that they can partake of the new worship in the new temple and so have access to eternal life.

In John's Gospel, Jesus is not only designated as the new place of worship, but in his conversation with the Samaritan woman, he also reveals that worship will take on a new character: it will now be done in "spirit and truth." Jesus is not speaking here of a purely immaterial or unembodied worship devoid of ritual, buildings, priests, and the like but of a worship that is centered on Jesus as the new temple and experienced through the agency of the Holy Spirit.[17] In the words of J. P. Heil, "To worship in 'Spirit and truth' means to worship in close association with Jesus. He is the one upon whom the 'Spirit' descended and remains (1:32). God gives him the 'Spirit' without measure (3:34). He baptizes with the 'Spirit' (1:33), so that one may be reborn to divine life eternal by being baptized from water and the 'Spirit' (3:5), symbolized by the 'living water' Jesus offers (4:10). And Jesus is full of a gift of 'truth' (1:14), the gift of the 'truth' that came to be through him (1:17)."[18] "True worshipers" are those who have been reborn as children of God (1:12) through water and the Spirit. In this way, the true worship in Spirit and truth is a familial worship reserved for God's children.

With the gift of the Holy Spirit, one is re-created as a child of the Father and made fit for true worship in Spirit and truth. In John 14:6, Jesus reveals that he is the truth, along with the way and the life, and that no one comes to the Father, except through him.

The Chosen brilliantly captures one final dynamic in this scene. Jesus tells Photina that this invitation to true worship is for all: "It won't matter where you're from or what you've done." Photina hesitates. Jesus, then, asks directly, "Do you believe what I am telling you?" She answers, "Until the Messiah comes and explains everything and sorts this mess out, including me, I don't trust in anyone." Jesus tells her that she is wrong in thinking that she has never received anything from God. He reveals himself as the Messiah and tells her intimate knowledge about her husbands. Photina insists that Jesus has picked the wrong person. But Jesus has come to Samaria precisely in order to meet her. He has chosen *her*, just as God chose Jacob and the Israelites nearly two thousand years prior. Still, Photina insists, "I am rejected by others." She does not speak only on behalf of herself but for all of us sinners who are ever mindful of our sinful pasts. She speaks for all of us who feel unworthy of God's love. And the Jesus of *The Chosen* responds in a way wholly in line with the Gospel of John and the entirety of the Old and New Testaments: "I know. But not by the Messiah."

Conclusion

The climax of the encounter with the Samaritan woman is also the climax of season 1 of *The Chosen*. As for Mary Magdalene in the very first episode, so also for the Samaritan woman, for those at Cana, and for all of us who have encountered Christ. We were one way, and now we are completely different. And the thing that happened in between was Christ, the bridegroom Messiah.

11

The Chosen as a Contribution to the Debate over the Historical Jesus

A Child of the Third Quest

JAMES F. KEATING

The Chosen has accomplished something significant. It has given us a life of Jesus that has garnered very little opposition and considerable affirmation from a wide variety of Christian believers. This is no small achievement since I suspect every viewer comes to the show with a bundle of preconceptions—sometimes thought out, mostly not—of what Jesus and his apostles were like. Adding to the challenge, the creators have made some bold artistic choices. Not only have they invented interwoven backstories for the people who populate the Gospels, they have given us a very human Jesus—a man not very good at sports, who has complicated relationships with those around him, and most strikingly to me at least, visibly delights in the miracles his heavenly Father works through him. Yet this same Jesus is filled with the confidence of the Beloved Son. He speaks and acts with divine authority. This aspect of Jesus increases as the series progresses (through the first four seasons, as of this writing), without sacrificing his humanity. In other words, *The Chosen* gives us a Jesus both comfortably familiar and jarringly strange, one who resonates with believers and challenges them as well.

This calls to mind (albeit on a much smaller and less intense scale) the challenge that faced Peter Jackson in bringing *The Lord of the Rings* to the big screen. Ever since J. R. R. Tolkien published his tome, readers have employed their imaginations to recreate Middle-earth and its inhabitants. Jackson had to accomplish two things as a filmmaker. First, he had to fulfill his own potential as an artist and fashion something that matched his creative powers. Second, he had to be true to the source material of which he is merely one among millions of other beneficiaries. He was not the only person who had translated these words into images, but he was one who dared to speak for all. It is only through a union of creative genius and love of another's creation that he was able to pull it off. More remarkable than the movies themselves is the fact that they were widely accepted as an authentic second artistic creation by those devoted to the first.

The task before the makers of *The Chosen* is considerably more daunting. Christ is not Frodo. Far from a beloved character in a medievalist fantasy, he is the incarnate Son of God who walked the earth we still inhabit. The stories of his life recounted in the Gospels are not fiction but historical in nature. Both come to us in the form of words on the page, however, requiring readers and hearers to create images in their minds.[1] These mental images can be translated into works of human art accessible to others who likely have their own internal pictures of the same events. For centuries Christians have sought to capture the life of Christ in representational art, mosaics, frescoes, paintings, and sculptures. While these works often depict a scene from the Bible, they are artistic creations and not mere mirrors of the text. Interpretive choices must be made. The details that make up human interactions—facial expressions, body positions, background—need to be filled in. These details differ depending on the artist's technical skill, cultural location, and imaginative power.

Roman Catholics are convinced that artistic creations enhance the experience of hearing the Bible. A simple look at our church buildings confirms this. We commission artists to decorate walls, ceilings, and even floors with images, enveloping believers in art as they hear the word proclaimed and the sacraments celebrated. Art, it is believed, has the capacity to strengthen and inform the faith of believers by expanding their imaginations, drawing the individual believer and the community into the stories of Jesus, the lives of his most exemplary followers, and ultimately the cosmic history of salvation. John Paul II, in his 1999 "Letter to Artists," puts it this way: "Every genuine art form in its own way is a path to the inmost reality of man and of the world. It is therefore a wholly valid approach to the realm of faith, which gives human experience its ultimate meaning. That is why the Gospel fullness of truth was bound from the beginning to stir the interest of artists, who by their very nature are alert to every 'epiphany' of the inner beauty of things."[2]

Artistic creation and the Bible are not in competition but work together to carry the faith forward. In this sense, the Catholic Church holds that art is an essential aspect of its sacred tradition. The Bible, inspired by God himself, has a normative function, but its reception by the people of God is inseparable from the work of Christian artists. Later in the same letter, the pope writes, "Art remains a kind of bridge to religious experience. In so far as it seeks the beautiful, fruit of an imagination which rises above the everyday, art is by its nature a kind of appeal to the mystery. Even when they explore the darkest depths of the soul or the most unsettling aspects of evil, artists give voice in a way to the universal desire for redemption."[3] This is not to deny, of course, that art can be done badly or that artistic choices can sometimes detract from an authentic hearing of the biblical word. This potential, however, only highlights the potency of art in the work of the church.

The range of artistic choice and interpretation increases as one moves from static media to film—a fusion of animation and storytelling. Moving pictures possess an unsurpassed capacity to capture the details that constitute human interaction in time as well as space. While a text or painting can evoke motion through well-chosen phrases or shades of light and dark, film captures the action of real life. The before and after of the crucial moment must be filled in with the same level of detail. When dealing with the life of Jesus, these interpretations, it can be said, add a historical depth not found in the Gospels or in still depictions of biblical scenes. Indeed, the very possibility of a film about the life of Jesus highlights a simple but unsettling fact about the Gospels as a source for the Jesus of history. Even if everything recorded happened just the way claimed, we still would not have a historical Jesus.[4] The Jesus who lived in first-century Palestine is not, and cannot be, only what is said or depicted in the Four Gospels. Too much is left out for a fully human life. I refer not merely to the aspects of Jesus's life that are not recorded. "If these were to be described individually," John confesses, "I do not think the whole world would contain the books that would be written" (John 21:25).[5] Yet even this would not suffice to tell the story wholly. A complete account would include not only everything Jesus did or said but also the relationships he had. These relationships would, in turn, involve not just how Jesus related to others over time but how those others related to one another and each related to Jesus. It is of the nature of every human experience to belong to, and derive its meaning from, a larger and changing whole. The gospel writers sometimes allude to these larger wholes but never attempt to do justice to them.

A filmmaker, therefore, has no other choice than to place the biblical Jesus in a larger nexus of human relationships than the text of Scripture provides. To do anything less would be to undermine the doctrine of the incarnation, to turn Jesus into a stick figure neither fully human nor fully divine. What can be left out or only suggested in a painting must be fleshed out on film. *The Chosen* has taken up this challenge in a particularly robust way, filling in the gaps with speculative brio. The creators make no claim to be presenting history, as if this is what literally happened in exactly the way depicted, but neither are their stories mere flights of fancy.

I have heard it said that *The Chosen* belongs to the genre of fan fiction, an activity whereby fans of a particular work add layers to the narrative world of the original text. That is not a crazy thought, but I would offer two counters. First, the writers of *The Chosen* are clearly and happily bound to the basic structures of the biblical narrative, which they treat as historical truth. In this sense, it would be better to think of their art as a form of historical fiction, along the lines of a novel about Socrates or Abraham Lincoln. Artistic imagination is employed to bring out the truth history provides. As with all Christian artists, the desire is to lure believers and potential believers into a deeper consideration of what God has revealed through the biblical text. Second, the writers of *The Chosen* understand that, in the case of Jesus, the question of history can never be taken lightly. For Christians, the life of Jesus has revelatory significance. Christians have no other reason to believe what they do apart from what God has revealed in the life and work of Jesus of Nazareth. Their faith either rests on what God caused to happen in history, or it is the work of human artifice. Accordingly, it is striking that *The Chosen*'s writers do not seem particularly anxious about bringing fact and fiction into a single narrative. Should they be? I will explore that question by placing *The Chosen* within the ongoing discussion of what historians can tell us about Jesus.

The Chosen *as a Contribution to the Debate over the Historical Jesus*

The Quest for the Historical Jesus

Concern for the historical truth of Jesus belongs to the deep logic of Christian faith. Because God chose to reveal himself and his plan of salvation in the life of the incarnate Son, that life is the supreme norm not only for Christian behavior but also for what Christians think about God, creation, and humanity. It follows, therefore, that the events of Jesus's life matter—for the Christian, nothing matters more. This interest in history explains the very fact of the Gospels—the decision of early Christians to stabilize the oral traditions of what Jesus did and said in written form. Getting it right was of theological importance. Luke spells out this reasoning in the opening lines of his gospel (Luke 1:1–4). We also see it in Paul's desire to substantiate the fact of Jesus's resurrection by pointing his Corinthian readers to living witnesses: "After that, he appeared to more than five hundred brothers at once, most of whom are still living, though some have fallen asleep" (1 Cor 15:6). In subsequent centuries, patristic figures found it necessary to make arguments for the historical veracity of the Gospels to pagan and Jewish interlocutors.[6] Later, we find similar arguments made against Muslim critics, whose holy book has a different story to tell about the one called Isa. In each case, the defenders of the Bible were unable to rely solely upon claims of divine inspiration but compelled to concoct arguments independent of faith. Nonetheless, one notes a serene confidence on the part of the apologists regarding the probity of their arguments. Anxiety over the historical Jesus creeps in only with modernity. Only then is it suggested that one must set out on a quest to find him.

The change was brought about with the posthumous publication of the work of an obscure German academic, Hermann Samuel Reimarus (1694–1768). Reimarus was not the first to doubt the historical value of the Gospels, but he was the first to employ modern historiography to present an alternative account of who Jesus was. This new method differed in that it did not rely primarily on trusted eyewitnesses for what happened in the past but rather sought the most credible reconstruction of a historical event given all the available evidence. Firsthand testimonies can be considered, but they are taken as only part of a larger whole. Moreover, their credibility is scrutinized according to contemporary standards of what is possible. Reimarus's radical claim was that once modern methods are turned loose on the New

Testament, it becomes apparent that the Jesus of history was not the source of the gospel writers but their victim. Matthew, Mark, Luke, and John had hijacked a rationalist, Jewish preacher who vainly hoped to instigate a messianic uprising against Roman power and failed. The apostles, however, saw an opportunity. They stole Jesus's body out of the tomb and concocted stories of his postmortem appearances.[7] Their aim was to turn the executed Jesus into the resurrected Lord of a new religion with themselves as its leaders.

Some writers, such as the Hegelian biblical scholar David Friedrich Strauss (1808–1874), saw Reimarus's work as an opening to describe central gospel stories as mythic—a lower stage of reflection to be sublated by philosophy. For Strauss, Christianity as an idea was detachable from the historical character of the New Testament. Others, however, better understood the fundamentally historical nature of the Christian religion. Among these observers, some defended the gospel accounts by the traditional means of relying on the trustworthiness of the apostles, men who were not only firsthand witnesses to the events depicted but who followed the resurrected Son of God to their deaths. Surely, they, of all men, would not deceive. Still others recognized that such arguments no longer carried weight in a modern context. The discoveries of historical criticism made it difficult, if not impossible, to think of the Gospels as simply the apostolic witness translated into Koine Greek. The distance between the events and when scholars date the earliest of the Gospels is not only chronological (about thirty years) but theological and cultural, shaped by developments in early Christianity. Reimarus had opened a door that could not be easily closed. If Jesus was a figure of history, he could be studied like any other. Evidence from ancient testimonies could be sifted and weighed to reconstruct a historically credible portrait. It is this approach that constitutes the quest for the historical Jesus.

It is now standard to divide the quest into three stages.[8] The first was the work of Enlightenment thinkers, who argued that the Jesus of history was primarily a teacher of morality, more concerned with how we act than with what we believe. This was a transportable Jesus, one who belongs to no time and, thus, to all time. He was no longer a Jewish religious figure informed by the various and competing cultural forces of first-century Palestine but a transhistorical teacher concerned only with universal ethical principles. Albert Schweitzer famously put the lid on these efforts with a jarring image: "The study of the life of Jesus has had a curious history. It set out in a quest of the historical Jesus,

The Chosen *as a Contribution to the Debate over the Historical Jesus*

believing that when it had found him it could bring him straight into our time as a Teacher and Savior.... But he does not stay; he passes by our time and returns to his own. He returned to his own time not by any application of historical ingenuity, but by the same inevitable necessity by which the liberated pendulum returns to its original position."[9] In other words, the Jesus who lived two thousand years ago in a distant place and alien culture remains forever a stranger. This is not a possible position for serious Christian theology.

It is often thought that Schweitzer put the quest for the historical Jesus in deep freeze for nearly fifty years (1906–1953). Such a view, however, leaves out the many attempts by both Catholic and Protestant scholars to apply modern historiography to the Gospels, not to undermine them but rather to bolster them. Their goal was to show that the Jesus of history and the Jesus of the Gospels are the same. The examples are many, but perhaps the most energetic was the Swiss Capuchin, Hilarin Felder (1867–1951). His massive *Christ and the Critics* was an attempt to show that scientific history, rigorously applied, yielded not a merely human Jesus but the figure upheld by Christian orthodoxy. He assured his nervous readers that "every christological conception which regards Jesus as a mere man is, if historically considered, a fanciful monstrosity."[10] Felder and those like him are rarely included in histories of the quest, but this, I think, is a mistake. The essence of the quest is that the historical Jesus is somehow methodologically detachable from the Jesus of apostolic faith—the one we find in the Gospels—and this holds true whether the intention is to undermine Christian orthodox faith or to support it.

The Second Quest began as a rebellion of precocious students against their teacher. The teacher was Rudolf Bultmann, the titan of twentieth-century New Testament scholarship. Bultmann, like other scholars of his time, doubted the historical character even of the Gospel of Mark. It was, to be sure, the first written and thus the basis of the synoptic tradition, but careful analysis revealed it more indebted to early church dogma than historical memory.[11] Indeed, when all is said and done, there is little of historical certainty retrievable from the Gospels beyond that Jesus lived and that he died. Like Strauss before him, Bultmann saw the loss of historical confidence as positive. Without history to rely upon, one is compelled to confront Jesus's message, his kerygma, in its purest form—a moment of crisis that demands a decision for or against authentic existence. It is the existential power of Jesus's preaching that is decisive and not whether its details can be historically confirmed.[12]

Bultmann's best students, however, did not agree. They feared that a Jesus beyond the reach of history would be a docetic Jesus, one who only appeared to be human. In this sense, they agreed with Christian apologists throughout the ages that the historical defense of the New Testament has theological significance. In October of 1953, Ernst Käsemann announced a new quest for the historical Jesus in a speech entitled "The Problem of the Historical Jesus."[13] He accepted his teacher's argument that the synoptic tradition tells us more about early Christianity than the Jesus of history, but Käsemann rejected Bultmann's view that nothing important about Jesus could be retrieved. Such skepticism had the effect of allowing Jesus to become the plaything of ecclesiastical and political power, as had happened with the presentation of an Aryan Jesus by the German Christians in the 1930s. If Christianity was to have integrity, it could not rest solely on what the early Christians believed about him but rather on a solid historical foundation uncovered by the application of critical principles. As Käsemann rightly saw, the various strands of the synoptic tradition agreed "that the life history of Jesus was constitutive for faith, because the early and exalted Lord are identical." Things went wrong, however, when the students decided to employ their teacher's criterion of double dissimilarity, that is, the idea that the credibility of any testimony to Jesus increases to the extent that it differs from either first-century Judaism or early Christianity. In Käsemann's words, "It is unsafe to predicate authenticity of any passage where there is agreement with contemporary Judaism and/or the post-Easter community."[14]

The result is a Jesus made up of fragments, a collection of disconnected sayings and events that are neither particularly Jewish nor anticipate the emergence of Christianity. One of the distinctive marks of the Second Quest is the conviction that it is no longer possible to write a "life of Jesus."[15] Ironically, this quest yielded a decidedly unhistorical Jesus. What makes us historical is that we live within the flow of time, shaped by our time and place and shaping it in turn. We live within stories and make contributions to them. The Jesus of the Second Quest, however, seems to have popped in and popped out of existence. What is left is not a whole life, informed by a localized culture and a host of evolving human relationships but rather bits of sayings and actions deemed to have met a scientific standard. The historical Jesus provided in this manner might fit a description, such as an eschatological prophet, a cynic philosopher, or a Mediterranean Jewish peasant,[16] but it fails to present a personality who could set alight a new messianic movement that would spill out of Palestine and overtake the Roman world. The infamous Jesus Seminar, which blackballed around 80 percent of the Gospels, was simply the logical conclusion to this approach.[17] John P. Meier, one of the great figures of the next stage of the quest, referred to the Jesus of the Second Quest as more like the monster of the *Frankenstein* movies—an unsightly assemblage of parts— than a historical person.[18]

Happily, the quest moved beyond this phase, and we can speak of a Third Quest. There are many ways to describe this next phase, but I shall restrict myself to two. The first is to see Jesus as a figure standing between the end of Second Temple Judaism and the beginning of early Christianity. Thus, instead of ruling out anything that shows Jesus to be either a Jew of his time and place or the instigator of the forms of life that make up the church of the New Testament, the Third Quest seeks to locate Jesus in both. The scholars who belong to the Third Quest—for example, John P. Meier, Ben F. Meyer, E. P. Sanders, J. D. G. Dunn, and N. T. Wright—employ different methodologies and come to different conclusions but all agree that the Jesus of history was, in Meier's apt phrase, "a marginal Jew." That is, the historiographically reachable Jesus must be someone who makes sense within a first-century Palestinian context yet who also could make claims and behave in such ways that would lead to his rejection by Jewish leaders and to his death at the hands of the Romans.[19]

A second and related characteristic of the Third Quest is its rejection of the idea that one comes closer to the historical Jesus through breaking him into discreet parts to be assessed. Rather, the Jesus of history understood himself and can only be understood as part of a larger cultural and religious whole. As Wright puts it, "Within the Third Quest ... the task before the serious historian of Jesus is not in the first instance conceived as the reconstruction of traditions about Jesus, according to their place within the history of the early church, but the advancement of serious historical hypotheses—that is, the telling of large-scale narratives—about Jesus himself, and the examination of the *prima facie* relevant data to see how they fit."[20] In the hands of N. T. Wright, the most reliable pathways toward the historical Jesus are the theological stories that constituted the Judaism of his time and the new stories of what God has done in Jesus that make up biblical Christianity. While the historical Jesus did not fit neatly into either, the best place to look for him is at the intersection of Second Temple Judaism and the early church. For Wright in particular, this means interpreting the words and actions of Jesus within a much larger, and mostly implicit, nexus of beliefs and stories about creation, covenant, the power of sin and death, and the future reconciliation of all that exists with its Creator.

In sum, the historical Jesus is not, and cannot be, simply the Jesus presented in the Gospels but rather a human person fully involved in and shaped by a greater cultural whole. He will disrupt this whole and by disrupting it create a more capacious one capable of providing the framework for the beliefs and practices of early Christianity.

Conclusion

To be clear, I am not claiming any direct connection between the Third Quest and *The Chosen*, at least not on the need to find a historical Jesus as the basis for the Gospels. For the writers of *The Chosen*, the historical question is important but is handled within the life of Jesus. Matthew is shown to be a persnickety scribe who accompanied Jesus from the beginning of his public ministry. The apostle John is a special confidant of Jesus, receiving his material directly from his Lord. Luke's connection to Mary Magdalene in the postresurrection era is mentioned. I cannot say that I find these particularly convincing as an explanation for the synoptic tradition or the Fourth Gospel. At the same time, I do not consider them outlandish suggestions. Recent scholarship has revived the question of written apostolic testimonies as a primary source for the Gospels.[21] At the very least, there is no denying that one can approach the historical Jesus only through the impression he left on those who followed him.

A clearer convergence between *The Chosen* and the Third Quest is the Jewishness of Jesus. Nothing is more distinctive of the portrait of Jesus offered by *The Chosen* than his embeddedness in the world of first-century Jewish Palestine. Indeed, the writers have been especially creative in constructing a rich and complex tapestry of Roman and Jewish leaders, each affected by Jesus in highly personal and unexpected ways. The biblical accounts provide the guideposts, of course, as they have for every cinematic construal of the life of Jesus. Yet none, to my knowledge, has presented a Jesus so profoundly shaped by his Jewish faith and practice. He is at the margins, to be sure, but thoroughly Jewish. This is true, even if the Judaism presented is more continuous with later forms of talmudic Judaism than is probably justified historically.

The Chosen *as a Contribution to the Debate over the Historical Jesus*

More important for my purpose is the common conviction that historical human beings are inseparable from the various stories in which they participate. This is no less true in the ancient world than in the contemporary one, although the forms of sociality differ. The decision by the creators of *The Chosen* to produce a work of art that goes beyond the bare bones of the gospel to fill out the unrecorded dimensions of Jesus's life on earth ought to be understood not as merely supplementing history with fiction but as a religiously powerful choice to take Jesus's historical existence seriously. As a historical person, Jesus would have lived within interwoven matrixes of human relationship. There is much we do not know about these relations, but we know they existed and account for what we find in the Gospels. We do not know the name of Peter's wife, but we can be sure that Jesus did and would have been aware of her developing attitude about her husband leaving his profession to follow an itinerant preacher and possible Messiah. The narrative arc of Eden's character can make no claim to history, but it nevertheless reveals a necessary human aspect of Jesus's historical life. One can say something similar about many of the stories invented to fill out the reality of biblically attested events in Jesus's life. The Gospel of John tells us about a wedding feast attended by Jesus, his mother, and his disciples. The focus of the evangelist is the first of Jesus's signs, but just enough quotidian details are provided to give the reader the sense of an actual feast, with the bustle and the anxiety of the hosts. *The Chosen* goes further, of course, taking the occasion to introduce two main characters, Thomas and Ramah. Yet the basic idea is the same. One serves historical credibility with the details that make up a human life in a particular time and place and with a particular set of ever-changing social forms. Thus, as strange as it might sound, the decision of the creators of *The Chosen* to employ their artistic imaginations, as Christian arts have always done, to go beyond the gospel stories about Jesus and his followers, uphold and give credence to that most central and decisive of Christian beliefs: "And the Word became flesh and dwelt among us, full of grace and truth; we have beheld his glory, the glory as of the only Son from the Father" (John 1:14).

12

Matthew, Mark, Luke, and John

Portraying the Evangelists in *The Chosen*

PATRICK GRAY

Jesus movies always include the apostles in the cast of characters, but aside from Judas and sometimes Peter, rarely do individual apostles stand out from the group. *The Chosen* is an exception to this rule. The series is focused on the followers every bit as much as on Jesus. In this respect, it is not entirely unlike early Christian apocryphal writings, especially the many Acts that were written—Acts of Peter, John, Paul and Thecla, Thomas, even Pilate. Many of these stories imaginatively fill in gaps left by the biblical authors or purport to chronicle their later careers, after the resurrection when Jesus sends them out to evangelize the nations. Most of these stories were regarded as nothing more than pious entertainment. Some contained material deemed heretical, though much of it posed no doctrinal problems in the eyes of church authorities. Historians believe very little of this body of literature reveals anything new about what really happened in the ministry of Jesus or in the activities of his disciples after his death, even if it is a valuable witness to the theological controversies and to the popular imagination of the ancient church. This material does not usually make it into standard Jesus movies.

Another distinctive element of the show, related to the prominent role of the apostles, is that it includes moments dramatizing the process by which the story of Jesus was remembered by his followers and written down for posterity. This is atypical for obvious reasons: making a movie or TV show about writers can be a challenge because it is usually not very interesting to watch someone writing. Of the four evangelists, three have appeared in *The Chosen*—Matthew, Luke, and John—and there are scenes in which they are portrayed in their roles as authors, when we see them writing what will become the Gospels of Matthew, Luke, and John. (Mark has not appeared as of the end of season 4, but it would not be a surprise to see him in future seasons.)

This chapter (1) puts these vignettes into conversation with various ancient traditions about the evangelists specifically as authors, (2) considers the narrative effect of depicting the evangelists in the act of writing in *The Chosen*, and concludes by (3) contemplating the theological significance of these cinematically unique portrayals, which suggest not only who they thought Jesus was but also when and how they came to those convictions.

Ancient Traditions about the Evangelists as Authors

Many modern scholars question the belief that Matthew, Luke, and John were the actual authors of the texts that bear their names. In what follows, the traditional attributions of authorship will be used without entering into these debates, which are beyond the scope of this chapter.

Matthew

The earliest discussion of Matthew is by the church father Papias early in the second century. Papias says that he had "compiled" (*synetaxato*) Jesus's "sayings" (*ta logia*) in the "Hebrew dialect" and that "each interpreted as he was able" (see Eusebius, *Ecclesiastical History* 3.39.16). This leaves unclear whether Matthew wrote or just collected material, and whether this is meant to describe just the sayings or the entire gospel. Furthermore, it is not clear whether this is only a characterization of Matthew's literary style as Jewish or whether it means he also translated it into the Greek we now possess from either Hebrew or Aramaic. Origen (see Eusebius, *Ecclesiastical History* 6.25.4) states that his gospel was composed in Hebrew near Jerusalem for Hebrew Christians and translated into Greek.

Matthew's reputation as a writer takes off from there. Jerome, Epiphanius, and other early authors refer to various works that were attributed to Matthew and used by Jewish-Christian groups such as the Gospel of the Nazarenes, the Gospel of the Ebionites, and the Gospel of the Hebrews.[1] Later still is a seventh-century text called "The Book about the Origin of the Blessed Mary and the Childhood of the Savior." In this text, which scholars call the Gospel of Pseudo-Matthew, on their flight to Egypt the holy family is resting outside a cave when a number of dragons suddenly fly out and worship the baby Jesus. Another highlight features Mary asking for some fruit from a high tree, and the tree itself bends down so that she can reach it, an episode memorialized in the medieval "Cherry-Tree Carol." Had J. R. R. Tolkien been tasked with writing a gospel, one suspects that the result might resemble the Gospel of Pseudo-Matthew.

Luke

Little is known about one of the most important authors of the New Testament. The author of Luke also wrote the Acts of the Apostles, so whoever "Luke" was, he wrote approximately one-quarter of the New Testament. There is a Luke mentioned as a coworker of Paul in the letters and once called "the beloved physician" (Col 4:14; 2 Tim 4:11; Phlm 24), and some speculate that Paul is referring to Luke in 2 Cor 8:18 when he says he is "sending the brother who is famous among all the churches for his proclaiming the good news" (see Ambrose, *Commentary on Luke* 1.11; Origen, *Homilies on Luke* 1.6).[2] Others place Luke among the seventy sent out by Jesus in Luke 10 (Hippolytus, *On the End of the World* 49) or identify him as the unnamed pilgrim who encounters the risen Lord on the road to Emmaus in Luke 24. According to Tertullian, Paul was Luke's "inspirer," and he called the Gospel of Luke a "digest" of Paul's gospel (*Against Marcion* 4.5.3). Several early writers noted that Acts shifts gears a few times and speaks in the first person by noting that "we" traveled here or there around the Mediterranean. This is often cited as support for the idea that Luke's authorial activity was based on shoe leather reporting, so to speak, since he would have had opportunity to meet with eyewitnesses to the events he narrates.[3] In the opening verses of his gospel, Luke says that he is privy to information from eyewitnesses and that he has read other accounts of Jesus's life. To the chagrin of later scholars, he did not include footnotes or a bibliography.

Attempts to demonstrate that Luke was the author of the gospel and Acts have occasionally focused on the purported usage of medical terminology, though the prevalence of animal terms has led others to observe waggishly that if the author was a doctor, he must have been a veterinarian. The eminent scholar of Luke-Acts Henry J. Cadbury wrote his 1914 Harvard dissertation on this topic, and it was said that he earned his doctor's degree by depriving Luke of his.[4] Whatever his professional occupation, patristic writers understood Luke's calling as a chronicler of early Christian history in connection with the mission to the gentiles, a task for which he was highly qualified as an excellent Greek stylist (Jerome, *On Illustrious Men* 3.7). A third-century anti-Marcionite prologue states that Luke wrote his gospel for "the Greek believers, so that they would not be led astray by the lure of Jewish fables, or, seduced by the fables of the heretics and stupid solicitations, fall away from the truth."[5] As for other literary endeavors, Clement of Alexandria suggests that the Epistle to the Hebrews was written by Paul but translated into Greek by Luke (Eusebius, *Ecclesiastical History* 6.14).

Byzantine tradition regards Luke as the first painter of icons for having produced images of Mary as well as Peter and Paul. There are even ancient and medieval paintings of Luke in the act of painting the Virgin.[6] Perhaps we are to understand from these traditions that it was on such occasions when Mary and other prominent disciples sat for their portraits that Luke was able to conduct interviews that became the material for his gospel. According to other traditions, Luke is said to have illustrated a gospel book with a full cycle of miniatures.[7] From the beginning, then, Luke is seen as having given careful consideration to his audience's holistic experience of the gospel story.

John

The Gospel of John refers to an unnamed "disciple whom Jesus loved" (John 13:23; 18:15–16; 19:26–27; 20:2, 4, 8; 21:7, 20–24), who "bore witness to and wrote" its message (21:24). The Gospel of John itself, curiously, never names John as one of the Twelve. From an early date, however, Christian writers identified the "beloved disciple" as the son of Zebedee (e.g., Irenaeus, *Against Heresies* 3.1.1) and speculated that he refrained from naming himself out of humility. Irenaeus says he lived to an old age composing his gospel in Ephesus. Most patristic writers believe this John to be the same as the John who names himself as author of the book of Revelation on the island of Patmos (an association that has not yet been made in *The Chosen*). Yet there were also doubts about this. Dionysius of Alexandria believed that the author of Revelation was not John the evangelist but, rather, a different man also named John (Eusebius, *Ecclesiastical History* 7.25). Early traditions and iconography depict John dictating the book of Revelation to Prochorus, one of the first deacons of the church according to the Acts of the Apostles.[8] Iconography often pictures him with a scroll inscribed with the words *in principio erat Verbum* ("In the beginning was the Word"), the opening line of the Fourth Gospel.

Along with Luke, John is the only other evangelist to speak in first person. John supplies some information about his habits as a writer at the end of the gospel: "Jesus performed many other signs in the presence of his disciples, which are not recorded in this book. But these are written that you may believe that Jesus is the Messiah, the Son of God, and that by believing you may have life in his name" (John 20:30–31 NIV). He expands on this comment in John 21:25: "Jesus did many other things as well. If every one of them were written down, I suppose that even the whole world would not have room for the books that would be written." (In *The Chosen*, John gets the idea for this disclaimer from Mary.) Many readers are astonished to learn that an author with unparalleled access to Jesus would intentionally omit stories and sayings. Apparently others had the same reaction in the ancient church because several patristic writers address this very frustration. Gregory of Nyssa gives voice to a common response. According to Gregory (*Answer to Eunomius* [PG 59:481]), John is trying to discourage idle inquiry into superfluous matters. This censure didn't stop people from speculating, however. Much of the speculation focuses on what is sometimes called the Gospel of the Forty Days, the period between the resurrection and the ascension. Just as Jewish tradition holds that there was an Oral Torah given to Moses during his forty days on Mount Sinai alongside the Written Torah, many writers held that what Jesus taught the apostles during these forty days is an oral gospel, alongside the written Gospels. This, it is believed, included a collection of Old Testament passages that were regarded as messianic prophecies (cf. Luke 24:44–47) and other matters.

Two works attributed to John merit mention in this regard, the Apocryphon of John and the Book of the Secret Supper (*Cena secreta*), also known as the Questions of John (*Interrogatio Iohannis*).[9] In the Secret Supper, John essentially conducts an interview with Jesus about the fall of Satan, what happened before the creation of humans, and other esoteric matters. In the Apocryphon of John, Jesus transmits secret knowledge to a grief-stricken John, revealing among other things that he was the one who caused Adam to sin in the garden of Eden. While such questions do not necessarily fall into the category of idle or morbid curiosity, one can easily imagine Gregory of Nyssa shaking his head as he reads them.

The Evangelists in *The Chosen*

Among the most distinctive elements of *The Chosen* are those scenes where Matthew, Luke, and John are working on what will become the Gospels.

Matthew

In season 2, episode 8, Jesus is preparing for the Sermon on the Mount. Matthew takes notes as Jesus brainstorms and dictates. Matthew even offers feedback, much of it focusing on the hard sayings (e.g., simply lusting after a woman is committing adultery; it is better to gouge out an eye than to allow it to cause one to sin). Matthew suggests balancing out the harshness with some sweetness. Although he is merely acting as a scribe at this stage, Matthew is already contemplating how an audience will (mis)understand Jesus's figurative language. There is a humorous back and forth as Matthew asks Jesus what he means by saying his followers are "the salt of the earth." Jesus offers more straightforward explanations, to which Matthew replies, "Why not just say it like that?" Bemused, Jesus concludes, "Allow me a little poetry."

Eventually, Jesus revises the opening of his sermon in light of Matthew's comments, which implies that he recognizes that there is a rhetorical dimension even to revelatory or inspired speech. It is not necessarily a flash from on high. Jesus is shown to be working at it here rather than speaking off the cuff. In terms of authorship, Jesus is the author of this sermon, which will later be incorporated into Matthew's Gospel. At the same time, if we keep in mind various theological debates about the nature of inspiration, there is the suggestion that the human authors are not merely passive instruments or blank slates onto which God's word is inscribed.[10]

Luke

Luke appears in a flash-forward in the Christmas-special episode. Mary Magdalene pays a visit to Mother Mary. She asks Mary Magdalene about Luke and learns that he is in Rome with Paul. Mary says there is more she needs to tell him: "I didn't tell him everything." With a twinkle in her eye, she says she had "kept something to herself" but is now eager to share it. It is implied (and later confirmed) that she is thinking about the Magnificat (Luke 1:46–55) and that she was inspired by God when she uttered the poetic words of praise when she is hailed by her relative Elizabeth as the "mother of [her] Lord." "These felt like God's words as much as my own," she explains. Mary Magdalene writes it down as Mary dictates what she has had in her heart for decades. Without Mary Magdalene, the prophecy that "all generations shall call me blessed" might not otherwise have come to fulfillment. What Mary understood when she first received the news from Gabriel that she would have a child (Luke 1:26–38), moreover, is not the same as what she would come to understand when that child would grow up and die on the cross.

Mary Magdalene then travels to meet Luke in Rome. Luke says that he has finished writing his work but then asks, "Did [Mary] have something to add?" Does she ever! The idea that the Magnificat might have been an afterthought causes one to reread it in context. When the reader considers the whole of Luke's story, the Magnificat seems well integrated with the entire birth narrative and the characteristic themes of the entire gospel. Luke says he has been gathering historical accounts (cf. 1:1–4). The firsthand reflections of participants in the events he is chronicling would naturally influence the way Luke tells his story. The portentous tone of his question— "Did she have something to add?"—and Mary Magdalene's knowing look at the end of the episode again makes one wonder: Does *The Chosen*'s Luke go back and revise his whole work in light of Mary's bonus material, or does he simply squeeze it into the margin of the papyrus at the last minute before going to press?

John

There is a brief scene in season 1, episode 7 where we see John eavesdropping on Jesus's conversation with Nicodemus (cf. John 3) and writing down what he hears, but the main depiction of John as an author is in season 2, episode 1, where he appears in a flash-forward conducting interviews sometime after the death of Jesus and beginning his book.[11] He interviews Peter, Thomas, Mary, and others about their first encounters with Jesus. They are looking straight into the camera before we are shown that they are talking to John, in the style of a mockumentary like *This Is Spinal Tap* or *The Office*, only not as humorous.

A common theme in their answers is how they see now how they misunderstood many of Jesus's words and actions in the moment (cf. John 2:21–22). At one point, Mary Magdalene wishes she had not made a remark that may be prone to being misunderstood and asks for it to be edited out. John replies that he does not yet know what he will be including in his book.

As he turns from his interview material to the process of composition, John tells Mother Mary that he needs to write or else Jesus's words will be "lost to history." He says he will start "at the beginning," even earlier than his birth. When Mary asks whether he means his ancestry, John replies, "I think Matthew has that covered," a seeming reference to the obsessive attention to detail of *The Chosen*'s Matthew and how that trait might manifest itself in the form of a genealogy. Together they recall Jesus saying, "Heaven and earth will pass away, but my words will never pass away" (Matt 24:35), inferring that his words are eternal, without beginning or end (and by implication, that John himself is a vehicle for the fulfillment of this particular prophecy uttered by Jesus). This vignette is presented to explain how John gets the idea for his opening—"In the beginning was the Word" (Greek: *En archē ēn ho logos*). Mary and John's conversation is intertwined with a flashback of Jesus preparing to read from the first chapter of Genesis at a synagogue. John says to Jesus that the notion of divine reason expressed in Greek by the word *logos* ("Word") is similar to God's creative speech in the opening verses of the Bible. Jesus replies, "I like that. It's a favorite memory." For those who like their humor droll—and mingled with trinitarian overtones—this is the high point of the entire series.

Theological Significance of *The Chosen*'s Portrayals

The Gospels make no secret that they were written after the fact. Their readers already knew the story, in some form, before they encountered it in the written form produced by the evangelists. The same is the case for most viewers of *The Chosen*. There are no surprise endings in store. The series does not dwell extensively on the way in which Jesus's death was the primary impetus for the writing of the Gospels in the first place, though Dallas Jenkins and his collaborators are true to the sources in that they do not try to turn Jesus into a sage who simply dispenses wisdom in pithy sayings after the fashion of the Coptic Gospel of Thomas. In Jesus's lifetime, his followers saw him as special, no doubt, but even his closest followers had little inkling of just how cosmically significant his life and death and victory over death would be. The flash-forwards in the series, however, are a reminder that the fullness of this revelation was processed only after Jesus's death, and that it broke certain molds in terms of their expectations. The example of Mary sending the Magnificat to Luke via Mary Magdalene also seems to suggest that access to the earliest stages of the story is not necessarily the deepest or fullest understanding, and viewers get the impression that Mary understands the incarnation better as she ages and gets further from the events of Jesus's life. Where a story starts and where it ends, furthermore, has a lot to do with what that story means, and the flash-forwards with Luke and John are a reminder that the story that the evangelists are telling does not end with Jesus's death or even with his resurrection, just as it did not really begin with his birth.

Apart from the flash-forwards showing the evangelists reflecting and writing, most of the series takes place when Jesus's followers do not know what is coming. While the Gospels portray Jesus foretelling his death and resurrection (Matt 17:22–23; 20:17–19; Mark 9:9, 30–32; 10:33–34; Luke 18:31–34), the dismay and, later, elation of the disciples on Good Friday and Easter Sunday suggest that they either misunderstood or did not take any such predictions seriously. To see how the Gospels might be misread on this point, one might compare the ending of *The Greatest Story Ever Told* (1965). On the third day, Mary Magdalene literally wakes up, remembers Jesus's predictions of his resurrection, and runs to the tomb—as if it is Christmas morning and she wants to see what presents have been left under the tree. To the contrary, the earliest sources suggest that the disciples did not know what to expect and that they were confused and even frightened by what they would later proclaim as good news. (Many scholars believe that the original ending of the Gospel of Mark comes at 16:8, where the women who discover the empty tomb flee and "say nothing, for they were afraid.") The earliest christological reflection appears to have taken some time and did not necessarily arrive like a thunderbolt from heaven.

The earliest believers in Jesus as the Messiah were not passive recipients of divine revelation. Then as now, Christians have heard the good news and done their best to process it, variously embracing it with joy, resisting its implications, plumbing its mysteries, misunderstanding its significance, or asking "what if?" questions that spring from normal human curiosity. The ensemble cast of *The Chosen* makes this range of responses vicariously available to viewers. The characters they portray are not only the sources of the memories that are incorporated into the Gospels; they are also the audience for the story.

When it comes to the role of the audience in the story, the opening verses of Luke's Gospel provide a fitting conclusion. Luke (1:1–4) says that "many have undertaken to set down an orderly account of the events that have been fulfilled among us." He finishes his brief preface by stating his purpose. He is writing "so that you may know the truth concerning the things about which you have been instructed" (NRSV). Perhaps his intent to write an "orderly account" reflects some discontent with the way in which the story had previously been told. After all, there is little reason to produce such a substantial work if the job has already been done in a satisfactory manner.

Crucially, Luke says that he wants to provide *asphaleia* concerning the contents of the story. Many translations render this term "truth," which gives the misleading impression that Luke fears his readers have been deceived. He might have used another word, *alētheia*, that he uses elsewhere and more literally means "truth (as opposed to lies)," but instead he uses a word that means "certainty" or "confidence" or "firmness." If his aim is to provide certainty, then it follows that in Luke's estimation there is something about the way the story has previously been told that leaves audiences a little up in the air or in doubt. They do not always provide the certainty or conviction that readers need. How that story gets told, according to Luke, is almost as important as what the story contains. By renarrating Israel's history and bringing it up to the present—by telling the story in a certain way, and in a certain order, even—Luke seeks to reassure his readers that God has kept his promise that not only would Abraham and his progeny be blessed but that in him "all the families of the earth shall be blessed" (Gen 12:1–3). The makers of *The Chosen*, it seems very clear, have a very similar aim in mind.

Part Four

EMOTIONAL RESONANCE, WOMEN, *and* PERSONHOOD

13

"You Are Mine"

Jesus and the Emotional Resonance of *The Chosen*

JESSE D. STONE

The opening episode of *The Chosen* (S1E1) contains two important and now representative characteristics that viewers around the world have come to love and expect from the show. The first can be seen within the initial seven minutes of the episode. After the opening credits, we are introduced to Nicodemus and his wife, Zohara, as they are met en route to Capernaum by a small group of Roman soldiers led by the praetor, Quintus. In the brief exchange that follows, we hear mention of Pharisees, Sadducees, Essenes, and Zealots—the four schools mentioned by the ancient Jewish historian Josephus (*Antiquities* 18.1.2–6)—followed by conversations about God and taxes. Immediately, one gets the sense that we are being brought into a larger social and political world, a world that is like and unlike our own. This is the world sometimes concealed between the lines of the Four Gospels, or, perhaps more accurately, the one merely assumed by their authors. This first characteristic, the attempt by the show's creators at a plausible reconstruction of the world of Jesus and the apostles, has been a frequent subject of discussion since its debut.

The second characteristic feature of *The Chosen*, and the one arguably more common and dear to the experience of its viewers, comes at the end of the same episode with the first appearance of Jesus. The show returns to the place where it began in the cold open, with Mary Magdalene and with the words of the prophet Isaiah. But this time, we see Jesus speak the words of the prophet Isaiah over Mary as he frees her from the torment she carries. "Thus says the Lord who created you, and he who formed you: 'Fear not, for I have redeemed you. I have called you by name. You are mine.'"[1] In seeing this and seeing Mary's response, we can hardly help but be moved. This experience at the end of season 1, episode 1 is but a taste of what awaits those who press on and follow the story from here, and veteran viewers will know by now that it is best to watch the show with a box of tissues close at hand. I will refer to this second characteristic as the emotional resonance of the show.

I have encountered a fair number of fans of *The Chosen* who have appreciated the amount of work the writers and creators have done to bring the first-century world of the Gospels to life, even those like me who smile at the carefully concealed Easter eggs reserved for only the nerdiest of Bible nerds.[2] Nevertheless, I have yet to meet a viewer or fan of the show who does not have at least one moment from the series they can recall that moved them or resonated with them in this deeper sort of way, and it is that experience of resonance that I wish to reflect on in this brief chapter.

A Word about Our World

To say something about the experience of emotional resonance, I need to say something about what it means for us to be human—that is, to be the sort of creature capable of this kind of experience—and, more particularly, what it means for us to be human in our time. In his work of spiritual autobiography, Augustine (AD 354–430) addresses God in prayer with a famous line: "you have made us and drawn us to yourself, and our heart is unquiet until it rests in you."[3] This statement contains one of the most profound insights ever written about human interiority, whether spiritual or psychological. Humans are unique creatures because we are the ones, as Wordsworth put it, with "intimations of immortality." We are the ones with a creeping sense that we were made for more than what we see, hear, smell, taste, and touch as we wander and fumble about on this rock in space. Augustine provides a theological explanation for this: we were made for God. To know God, to love God, and to find rest in God. He also describes what happens to our lives when we separate ourselves from God. Our hearts become "unquiet" (*inquietum*), a word that might also be rendered "restless" or "anxious."

Augustine's ancient insight speaks to a profound need in our own time, when it is becoming less and less obvious to most people just how deeply they need what God alone can give. Today, as the work of the Canadian philosopher Charles Taylor has shown, we live in a secular age, where our lives are fixed between the competing cross pressures of faith and doubt.[4] Despite this growing secularization, divine revelation still calls to us from within and from without to remind us of what Augustine says. Internally, we wrestle with deep longings and hopes that cannot find satisfaction in the world, and externally, we inhabit a creation that is, in Gerard Manley Hopkins's phrase, "charged with the grandeur of God." Nevertheless, the pervasive cultural sense in our time remains that religious commitments to any transcendental reality are thoroughly doubtable and contestable. We imagine the world around us to be a self-enclosed, purely immanent space. There might exist as part of that immanent space a door that allows for interference from a transcendent exterior, with some supposing the door to be open and others supposing it closed. The point, however, is that it has become possible for us to conceive of the world, and our lives in the world, as inhabiting a system that has no relation to the transcendent. This is, according to Taylor, the uniqueness of what it means to be secular.[5]

What happens to humans when the world becomes secularized? Following Augustine's maxim, we can say our secular age has left us with our restless and anxious hearts and no consolation about where we might rest them. Add to this that the modern secular age is one in which our anxieties exponentially grow. Take one example. Of all the creatures that inhabit this earth, humans are the only ones, so far as we know, haunted by what we might call a *chronic anxiety*, an anxiety concerning the passage of time. Jesus recognized this worry two millennia ago (Matt 6:25–34), though it has arguably become more pronounced in the modern, postindustrial era of human history. Anxiety about time, in fact, is one of the major themes in T. S. Eliot's *Four Quartets*. In one of the most vivid and disturbing lines of the poem, Eliot describes the "strained, time-ridden faces" humans wear in the modern world as they are "distracted from distraction by distraction" while "filled with fancies and empty of meaning" ("Burnt Norton," *Four Quartets*, 100–102).[6] These words, over eighty years old now, could have been composed today.

In fact, today it is common to hear about a crisis of mental health, anxiety, and depression, especially among young people.[7] For example, OneHope's *Global Youth Culture* study, published in 2020, revealed the following about Gen Z's struggle with mental health.[8]

- Over 50 percent of Gen Z globally struggles with anxiety.
- Over 60 percent of teens globally reported struggling with loneliness.
- One in four teens globally reported suicidal thoughts.

It is important to note that the data for this study was gathered *prior to* the global COVID-19 crisis. So, while things were already very bad before the global crisis, they have continued to get worse. Explanations for this crisis among young people today abound, but one common factor that comes up frequently is the use of technology.[9]

How is it the case that, in a day when we have so many opportunities for connecting with others online, we have so many young people struggling with loneliness? How can it be that in a day where we have more time-saving devices than ever before, we feel as though we have less time available to us? The German sociologist Hartmut Rosa has proposed that part of the problem is the *acceleration* of modernity.[10] He tracks this acceleration along three lines: technical (or technological) acceleration, accelerated social change, and an accelerated pace of life.[11] These three relate to one another and propel each other, so that the acceleration of modernity continues at ever increasing rates. Technological acceleration makes more of the world available and accessible to us. Today, we carry the world's information around in our pockets. This technological acceleration leads to accelerated social changes, because our cultures and values are consistently being brought into conversation or conflict with other cultures and values that we encounter through the improved technologies that make more of the world available to us. Finally, these accelerated social changes contribute to an accelerated pace of life, where many of us are plagued not only by a fear of missing out on the changes occurring regularly but also by a compulsion to constantly adapt to the changes in order to keep our heads above water. This means that the gifts of the modern, accelerating age that promise us rest end up making our hearts more restless instead. What are we to do in response to this situation?

"You Are Mine"

Resonance in the Modern Age

In response to his diagnosis of the crises caused by modernity's acceleration, Rosa has latched on to the category of *resonance* to describe at least part of the antidote.[12] The acceleration of modernity makes more of the world available, accessible, and attainable to us, but it also makes our experience of the world increasingly one of *alienation*, where human relationships to the world are indifferent or hostile.[13] In other words, we are no longer deeply impacted by the world around us, and this breakdown in the human relationality results in depression, burnout, increased anxiety, and despair. The opposite of this alienation, according to Rosa, is resonance.

Resonance is defined by Rosa as "a kind of relationship to the world formed through af←fect and e→motion, intrinsic interest, and perceived self-efficacy, in which subject and world are mutually affected and transformed." He uses the image of a vibrating wire connecting the human subject to the world to illustrate a "bidirectional oscillation" in which "the subject is affected, that is, touched and moved, by some segment of the world, at the same time responding with an accommodating, outwardly directed emotional movement." These bidirectional oscillations are illustrated with arrows and labeled as "af←fect" and "e→motion."[14]

Rosa conceptualizes the human experience of resonance across three axes: horizontal, diagonal, and vertical. Each axis represents a different dimension of connection that contributes to human fulfillment and meaning. The horizontal axis pertains to the way individuals relate to one another through family, friendships, and community. The diagonal axis concerns how humans relate to objects and social institutions, like schools, sports, and work. Finally, the vertical axis deals with human relationships with transcendent (or seemingly transcendent) things like religion, nature, art, and history. What we want as humans is to experience life in such a way that our relationships along all three of these axes are resonant ones.

From a North African theologian (Augustine) through a Canadian philosopher (Taylor) to a German sociologist (Rosa), we have explored some of the complexities of being human in the twenty-first century. From Augustine, we gain an important first principle of theological anthropology, namely, humans are made for God, and separation from God leaves the most inward and central part of our selves in a state of restlessness. Charles

Taylor gives us an account of our secular age, helping us to see how it has become possible for us to conceive of human life and the world around us without any reference to the transcendent, and thus without any reference to the one who made us and who can give rest to our restless hearts. Finally, through the work of Hartmut Rosa, we come to appreciate how modernity's acceleration exponentially increases our heart's anxieties, which lead us into a crisis of burnout, depression, and other mental health problems. Additionally, we gain from Rosa a thick philosophical and sociological description of the subject of resonance, which provides some insight into that for which our restless hearts long. In what remains, I would like to apply some of these observations to *The Chosen*, focusing especially on the experience of resonance for viewers of the show and adding some of my own theological reflections along the way.

Resonance in *The Chosen*

Because *The Chosen* is a multiseason streaming show, it is first and foremost an artistic work. Its chief architect is its writer/director, Dallas Jenkins, but the show as a whole is the product of a creative collaboration involving writers, producers, actors, and a substantial crew managing everything from costumes to sets and props. As a show, *The Chosen* brings together two modes of artistic expression, image and narrative, both of which have immense power to generate resonant experiences. Images are powerful because one of our most primal ways of engaging the world is visually. After all, we see the world long before we learn to think rationally about it or speak about it. Our visual capacities give us some of our first clues that there is, in fact, something else besides us in the world.

Narrative, on the other hand, is a more heightened way of engaging with life because it requires us to connect our lives or the lives of others to things outside ourselves in a coherent and structured way. One of the most unique things about humans is that we are storytelling creatures. In fact, we are not only storytelling creatures, but we are also story-shaped creatures. Stories have a special capacity to deeply impact our lives. According to Rosa, it is their ability to communicate stories that gives film a particular potency in creating experiences of resonance.

The strong degree to which *stories* are capable of generating in us not only emotional and psychological but even sensorimotor resonance can be seen in any cinema, as the spectators, following along with what they see on the screen, clench their fists, pull at their hair, laugh and cry, hold their breath; their pulses quicken, their skin tingles, etc. And the situation is not terribly different in the case of reading or listening to stories. We can see that the "firing of our mirror neurons" (at least in a metaphorical sense) here largely eludes our conscious direction and control by the fact that all of the same effects occur (and with no less intensity) *even when we are completely aware that the stories being told are pure fiction*.[15]

To be sure, the subject matter of *The Chosen* is the life of Jesus of Nazareth and his followers, a life recorded for us in the Four Gospels, books that Christians believe not only tell us the truth about Jesus but books that are believed to be inspired as the word of God. All of this serves to raise the stakes for the show, at least for the many committed Christians who watch it. Nevertheless, while the show does aim to be true to Jesus and the events from his life as they are portrayed in the Gospels, it also aims to be a good and beautiful show that entertains and engages its audience. This is what has led the creators of *The Chosen* to add fictitious material to the story being told, even if one might call some of it plausible fiction. In fact, these fictitious additions have been used by the show's creators to deliver some of the most profound truths. Because of this, they can generate experiences of resonance. Four examples from *The Chosen* illustrate the phenomenon Rosa describes.

Jesus and the Children

The episode "Jesus Loves the Little Children" (S1E3) does not aim to tell a story from the Gospels. The entire episode is fictitious, and yet it is often cited as a fan favorite because of the emotional response it generates. Why? I would suggest that there are several reasons. One is that the relationship depicted between Jesus and the children is a deeply resonant one. We can recall Rosa's category of horizontal resonance here, where resonant human relationships are mutual experiences of affect and emotion. The relationship between the children and Jesus is one where they are all impacted by him, and he is impacted by them. They take joy in his company, and he takes joy in theirs. It is a beautiful sight.[16]

We even see Jesus moved emotionally as he listens to the children recite the Shema prayer from Deut 6:4–5. Additionally, seeing children inhabit this kind of resonant relationship to their world provides all of us with a reminder of the innocent lives we once enjoyed before we jumped aboard the ever-accelerating train of the modern age. In many ways, we long to return to the innocence of childhood, a time when our hearts were not as restless as they are today.

However, the most important feature of this episode that contributes to its popularity and generation of resonance among viewers is that, in it, we are witnessing a way of relating to God that all of us are invited to have. By the grace of salvation, we can be adopted as God's children. We can call upon him as "Abba, Father" (Rom 8:15; Gal 4:6). His love for us makes us his children (1 John 3:1). Just as Jesus wants to spend time with Abigail, Joshua, and their friends, he wants to spend time with us. Just as he takes joy in their company, he takes delight in us. And just as he shows patience at their questions and offers them wisdom, he is patient toward us and offers his wisdom freely to us. This, I suggest, is what creates resonance in viewers.

The Curious Case of Nicodemus

Nicodemus is a standout from season 1. His character arc is one of the strongest in the season, despite the fact that the Gospel of John tells us very little about him. We know he is a member of the Sanhedrin (John 3:1; 7:50), that he is a teacher (3:10), and that he will assist Joseph of Arimathea with the burial of Jesus after his crucifixion (19:39). Throughout the season, we get to experience Nicodemus's authority as a member of the Sanhedrin and his reputation as a great teacher. We also get to witness what is arguably the most famous conversation between two characters in all the Four Gospels (John 3:1–21).

What is so interesting and puzzling about the character of Nicodemus in the Gospel of John is the ambiguity that surrounds him following this conversation. We have no indication of how he ultimately responds to what Jesus tells him in John 3. His appearance in John 7:50–52 continues to hold him in an ambiguous space, as he seems to speak on behalf of Jesus to the other Jewish rulers, but he does so in a timid, indirect way, making no mention of his own personal interactions with Jesus. The show depicts this ambiguous, even tragic story of Nicodemus most powerfully in the final episode of season 1, "I Am He" (S1E8). As Jesus and his disciples prepare to leave Capernaum, they find a bag with money, which Jesus knows was left there by Nicodemus, who is watching the group in secret around a nearby building. Jesus looks up the road with sadness, saying, "You came so close," before departing with the disciples. We then see Nicodemus weeping as he struggles with his inability to do what he knows he must. Nicodemus here serves as a stand-in for many who cannot bring themselves to pay the cost of discipleship to Jesus. When we see a scene like this, we are moved, not because we feel what Nicodemus feels as he weeps (though that might be the case) but because we feel what anyone should when they see someone in Nicodemus's position: compassion.

Mary Magdalene's Repentance

Another resonant moment comes from the episode "Unlawful" (S2E6), where Mary Magdalene is shown falling back into sinful patterns of behavior associated with her way of life before she knew Jesus. This moment generated some criticism from viewers of a peculiar theological persuasion, who believed it was wrong to suggest that a disciple of Jesus could backslide in such a dramatic way.[17] Again, the entire subplot in this episode is fictitious, and yet it is true to life. Most of us who have lived long enough know what it is like to struggle with sin and failure, even massive failure. We know the self-hatred, the condemnation, the guilt, and the shame that accompany our sin-sick souls as we wander away from light into darkness. And we know how powerful the medicine of divine mercy is.

Mary Magdalene returns to Jesus and repents for falling back into sin. Jesus tells Mary to look him in the eye. She struggles but manages to look as she hears Jesus say, "I forgive you." Anyone who has experienced the grace of forgiveness, whether through a priest, pastor, family member, or friend, knows that it is one thing to believe you are forgiven, but it is something else to have another person look you in the eye and pronounce forgiveness over you. What *The Chosen* does in this scene is help us imagine that sort of experience with Jesus himself, and that creates a moment of resonance.

Little James and the Question of Miracles

A final example, and one of the most memorable moments from season 3, comes in the episode "Two by Two" (S3E2). After Jesus sends out the twelve apostles to proclaim the kingdom of God (Matt 10:1–15; Mark 6:7–13;

Luke 9:1–6), Little James approaches Jesus for a conversation outside Simon and Eden's home in Capernaum. Again, this conversation is entirely fictitious and yet deeply true at the same time. Astounded at the notion that Jesus has given him the power to do miracles and heal others, Little James struggles to reconcile this information with his own disability. He says to Jesus, "I just find that difficult to imagine with my condition, which you haven't healed." Little James wants to be healed, and he knows by now that Jesus has the power to heal him. "Why haven't you?" he asks.

What proceeds is a deeply moving, pastoral conversation about the problem of pain, the goodness of God, and the fellowship in suffering that those who are closest to Christ will experience. Most of us, at some point in our lives, will wrestle with these and other difficult questions. We might spend weeks, months, or years wrestling with unanswered prayers for deliverance from sufferings we face. What this conversation in *The Chosen* helps us to do is to imagine bringing these requests to Jesus in a concrete way. We can picture more easily, with the help of Jonathan Roumie's acting, how Jesus looks upon us with compassion and love, even as he explains the deeper more mysterious purpose that might underlie our ongoing struggle with suffering. It does not make the suffering easier, as Little James knows and says openly, but it helps nonetheless.

Of course, it is not only the fictitious moments created by the writers that generate this kind of resonance. I have used these only as examples, but numerous other moments in *The Chosen* that adapt and portray stories from the Gospels could be included here as well, such as Jesus calling Simon (S1E4), the healing of the woman with the issue of blood (S3E5), the beheading of John the Baptizer (S4E1), and the raising of Lazarus (S4E7). What all these stories share in common is their ability to generate experiences of resonance among viewers, and the common factor in all of them that gives them this capacity is the role of Jesus in the story.

Conclusion

It seems fitting here to follow the example of season 1, episode 1 and conclude where we began, with Mary Magdalene's first encounter with Jesus. What is it that makes this moment resonate in the sense I have described? Mary finds healing when she hears the Word of God, but it is not the Scripture that heals her. She had spent her life clinging to the prophet's words, God's words, as they were written on a small sheet of papyrus, and they did not deliver her from her bondage. But now, at the end of the episode, something is different. This time, when the Word of God comes to Mary, it comes with flesh and blood and voice. It approaches her with a compassionate gaze, a tender smile, and a warm embrace. The Word comes to Mary, in other words, as it comes to us all, through the gentle and lowly incarnate one, the one who loves us and who was crucified for us.

The Word, which was with God and was God (John 1:1), became flesh and dwelt among us (1:14). God assumed a human nature with a human face, and because of that, it is possible for us to see God reflected, even if imperfectly, through the face of another. We see the face of Christ reflect imperfectly off the face of Jonathan Roumie as he looks with compassion, not only at Mary but at us, too. As we watch him lovingly embrace Mary, or Little James, or Nicodemus, Jesus embraces not only them but us as well.

God assumed a human nature with a human voice, and because of that, it is possible for us to hear the voice of God reverberate, even if imperfectly, through the voice of another as they speak his words. We hear the voice of God reverberate imperfectly through Jonathan Roumie as he says, "You are mine," not just to Mary but to us. He says, "I forgive you," not just to Mary but to us. And he says, "Follow me," not just to Simon, or Matthew, or Nathaniel, or Zee, but to us.

The psalmist says, "The voice of the Lord is powerful; the voice of the Lord is majestic" (Ps 29:4). His voice calls from beyond the secular frame into the rushed and frantic modern world to reach our restless hearts. That voice, when we at last remember its sound, gives us a taste of the rest our hearts have forgotten, the rest that awaits us when we see the one who made us, no longer imperfectly, but face-to-face.

14

Jesus as Personalist

Recognizing the Other in *The Chosen*

DEBORAH SAVAGE

I have no recollection of what finally led me to begin watching *The Chosen*. I do remember hearing about it—and feeling a certain pressure to join the growing number of people who were already tuning in. I began to feel left out of a conversation. But I was used to that since, aside from Turner Classic Movies, I am generally not a big fan of television. At least at first, I assumed that was all it was.

Frankly, I was a bit skeptical. I think I may have seen almost every film, show, or made-for-TV movie about Jesus that has ever been made. Many I loved. Some have become annual must-see events for our family. But I was hesitant: did I really have time for what was probably just another one of those sentimental Jesus movies, especially one that requires I turn it on every week? One with seasons for heaven's sake? Were these people even faithful Christians—or just good actors, covering the story for its entertainment value?

I don't remember the moment I watched the first episode. I do remember that I was soon moving hungrily through the first three seasons. When I got to the end of season 3 and found there was no place to click "next episode," I was genuinely upset. I was overjoyed when I learned that more seasons were on the way.

In the interest of full disclosure, I am Catholic and a theologian. I teach theology at a Catholic university. And so, unsurprisingly, my orthodoxy radar was on full alert, at least at some level, especially after I learned (forgive me) that the creator of the series wasn't Catholic. While there were certainly moments when the producers took some liberties with the narrative, such concerns gradually faded into the background as I was drawn more and more into the story, portrayed so movingly by actors who seemed to be the very embodiment of their characters. Each scene conveyed a palpable sense of the reality that the mysterious and transformative events of the gospel were lived through by actual, *concretely existing* persons. The story was alive in some unusual way that I could not fully articulate. What made *The Chosen* different?

In what follows, I will suggest one possible answer to that question. It can be summarized as follows: regardless of whether the creators of the series intended it, regardless of whether the actor who plays Jesus meant it explicitly, the Jesus portrayed in *The Chosen* is, without question and as I will argue below, a personalist. Indeed, once grasped, one cannot *unsee* the personalism hidden in every episode. The Jesus we encounter here embodies in every way what has been referred to as the "apostolate of being."[1] This term was coined by two well-known personalists, the Catholic philosophers, Dietrich and Alice Von Hildebrand. It refers to a stance toward others that intentionally, yet wordlessly, attracts others through one's own capacity for inner peace and joy. This apostolate is embedded in the words of *The Chosen's* Jesus, but above all it is discernible in his gaze.

Let me state clearly that I am in no way making the claim that those involved *intended* this explicitly. But when, for example, in the last episode of season 1, Jesus says to Eden, the wife of Simon (before he is renamed Peter by Jesus)—at the exact moment she needs to hear it the most—"*I see you*," the elusive thread that lay hidden just beyond my ken suddenly appeared. It was at that moment that I recognized what I had been trying to grasp since the first episode. For in his gaze, we see that what is communicated to Eden is surely what Jesus himself would have meant to convey: a profound recognition that she *exists*—and is a *person*, the only creature on earth that God willed for his own sake—a *someone*, not a some*thing*. Jonathan Roumie's Jesus is a *personalist*.[2]

In this chapter, I hope to demonstrate that this may be the key to the impact of *The Chosen*. My proposal is meant to suggest an explanation for the genius of the series. It also has the potential to illuminate the way forward for the church's efforts at evangelization. For in watching just that one encounter between Jesus and Eden, I realized that what brought me back again and again to episode after episode was my own inner longing to be *seen* and known—to be *seen* in my totality, right down to the bedrock of my being. My working hypothesis will be that *The Chosen*, with its portrayal of Jesus, somehow puts us all in touch with our own unspoken wish to be *seen and known* by the only one who truly understands and loves us for who we are, flaws and all.

But first, a caveat. It must be crystal clear as we proceed that the personalism we wish to understand here cannot be reduced to a meaningful gaze or mere sympathy for the other. These very human capacities—even when sincere—can easily descend into a kind of sentimentality, or turn into a sort of false compassion, or even be replaced by the sorts of techniques taught in workshops on good listening skills. We cannot permit it to serve as a stand-in for the deadly subjectivism that threatens to derail the search for truth in contemporary culture. These approaches cannot possibly explain the profound impact *The Chosen* has had on so many. Clearly, there is something more at work in the series than mere technique or some version of the "I'm OK. You're OK" mentality popularized by 1960s self-help books.

The task here is to arrive at a fuller account of the vision of the human person at work in the theory of personalism and to consider how that understanding might inform our own interactions with those we encounter. This is more than a philosophical investigation. The premise at work is that the Jesus portrayed in *The Chosen* sees those he encounters through this lens and that this is what explains the enormous appeal of the series for those who wish to follow Jesus. My interest is in the intersection of the personal and the philosophical as it emerges in a life open to grace.

Since no other thinker embodies this convergence more completely, or more publicly, than Pope John Paul II, I am relying on the theory of personalism particular to him—*not* as pope but as the philosopher known as Karol Wojtyła. I will show that his account, and the witness he bore to it in his own person, points us toward the intellectual scaffolding needed to both account for the impact of *The Chosen* and to learn from it.

What Is Personalism?

It would be impossible to reduce the many strands of personalism to a single definition. But they all share a common theme: a self-conscious intellectual commitment to the centrality of the person, whether divine or human, as the primary locus of meaning.³ This profound recognition of the primacy of the person requires a conscious encounter with the reality of their personal *existence*—and of one's own—as the locus not only of existence but of action.⁴ This is radically true of Wojtyła's brand of personalism. In what follows, I sketch his general framework and then return to two scenes in *The Chosen* as a reference point for exploring two key insights that inform his particular understanding of the person.

Perhaps the easiest way to enter into what Karol Wojtyła means by the term "personalism" is to consider the analogy offered by existentialist philosopher Gabriel Marcel. Imagine you are walking with a companion through your favorite nature preserve, and you notice a flower you don't recognize. If you are a naturalist, even an amateur one, you will certainly stop to look. And you will likely ask, "What is this flower?" You are fortunate in that your friend is a botanist and is happy to give a detailed response. He tells you to which botanical family the flower belongs, describes its genus and species, and so on. That is, he gives you a scientific answer. And unless you have picked the last living example of this particular flower, his answer is couched in terms of the many members of the species to which this one flower belongs.

But, Marcel points out, we still have not really answered the question "What is *this* flower?" Because the answer our friend gave us completely disregards its singularity: Yes, you insist, but what about *this* flower? What has actually happened, says Marcel, "is as though my question had been interpreted as follows—'to what thing other than itself, can this flower itself be reduced?'"⁵ The original question "What is *this* flower?" has been sidestepped, virtually ignored. We may have satisfied ourselves that we now know its genus and species; that is, we now know how to categorize it. But that is not the same thing as penetrating to the inner meaning of the single flower I am presently holding in my hand.

Now, you may be saying to yourself, "Who actually cares about the 'inner meaning' of a flower? In fact, is there such a thing?" Fair enough. The significance of Marcel's analysis becomes dramatically clear, however, when we consider its analogous application to our main pursuit: an account of the human person.

Let's say you and your companion are now walking down the street on your way home and you encounter a person you have never seen before. The stranger has stopped you to ask for directions. Without hesitation, you direct him to his destination. Why wouldn't you? You have every reason to assume that he has asked a rational question and will comprehend your answer. You are vaguely aware that you are standing in front of a member of the species *human*. After all, this person has all the characteristics and features found in virtually all the members of that species. Even if he happens to be missing a limb or is blind, you are still quite certain they are a fellow human being.

But let's say you decide to ask again, "What is *this* person?" Your botanist friend might find it more difficult to satisfy you with a simple answer. If he considers himself a materialist, he might be quite content with describing the person in terms of his genus and species, thus reducing him to his basic DNA, his material existence. No doubt, you would hear all about atoms colliding in space, firing neurons, synapses, brain studies, and so forth. He may even take you all the way back to the origins of the materialist theory about the cosmos in the thought of the sixth-century BC philosopher Democritus. But you might find that answer unsatisfying. Surely there is more to the human person than mere matter.

So, let's say your companion is not a confirmed materialist—but a philosopher who has studied the thought of Aristotle or maybe even that of Thomas Aquinas. In that case, you most certainly would get a full account of the theory of hylomorphism and the principle that distinguishes the entire human species from the rest of creation: the singularly human power of reason. You would hear about the union of the body and the soul, the fact that man clearly possesses a rational soul—and that he possesses intellect, will and freedom, features of the species *human* that cannot be predicated of any other creature. This response might give you some measure of relief. But you are wiser now. You smell a rat. You would recognize immediately that both of these answers are still accounts of the human person given in terms of the many members of the species to which this particular individual belongs. Just like with the flower, even the metaphysical account, while it certainly seems more reasonable, does not and cannot account for the unique instantiation of the species *human* standing in front of you at this moment. And the stakes are a bit higher now. We are seeking a fuller account of a particular human being.

Wait a second, you say to yourself, all that might be true. Clearly, I am talking to a human being. He possesses all those attributes. But there is nothing *generic* about him. In fact, now that you think about it, there is no one in the whole human race who is like my botanist friend, or my mother, or me. Nor is there anyone else like the man standing in front of me, patiently awaiting my assistance. He is a *someone*, not a *something*, and you know it.

Here we come to the point. Wojtyła's personalism applies Marcel's very apt analysis to his vision of the human being. He spotlights the "human being as an individual existent first and a member of the human species second."[6] That is, he sees the person *first* in his unique and unrepeatable reality. He is pointing out something we all know intuitively: that the defining note of the *person* is his *uniqueness*. Indeed, each person is irreplaceable and absolutely irreducible to simply another member of the species *human*.[7] Each and every human person is made in the image of the triune God who thus possesses an inexhaustible dignity and worth. He can never be used as a means to an end. For he "is a good towards which the only proper and adequate attitude is love."[8] The human person is "the only creature on earth that God willed for his own sake"—a *someone* not a *something*—who cannot "fully find himself except through a sincere gift of himself."[9]

Karol Wojtyła fully affirms the metaphysical analysis of Thomas Aquinas. In fact, his entire project is grounded in it. But, he argues, while it has laid out the metaphysical terrain for the Catholic understanding of the person, Aquinas simply does not go far enough to account for the lived experience of human action that is, in every instance, the act of a concretely existing *person*.[10] Wojtyła extends his own analysis to embrace not only his existence as a member of a species but the inner dynamism of the person *in act*.[11]

THE APOSTOLATE OF BEING

The enormous personal appeal of John Paul II is a matter of historical record. Especially after his death in 2005, it was evident that his appeal transcended religious, doctrinal, and cultural boundaries, as well as age and gender gaps. Many have reported that in his presence, whether as part of a large crowd or in a private audience, they felt as though they had been personally acknowledged, deeply affirmed, and called to a new level of holiness. Countless individuals who have had even brief meetings with John Paul II mention his eyes and the way his gaze made them feel as if they were seeing Christ. Skepticism in the face of such stories is understandable. Whatever one's view on the pa-

pacy or the legacy of this one pope, such widespread evidence of his personal impact nonetheless begs for some kind of explanation.

John Paul II was no ordinary philosopher. He seems to have embodied the personalism we wish to understand and to have furnished proof that it can be lived. His life reveals that the true thrust of philosophical reflection is not toward more and more comprehensive abstractions but toward a more complete embodiment of the truth embedded in them. My argument is that the Jesus portrayed in *The Chosen* embodies this vision of the person and that it appears in the words he is given to say and, most visibly, in his gaze—even if this is not the conscious intention of Dallas Jenkins and his collaborators. When Jonathan Roumie's Jesus looks upon the other, he seems to not only *possess* holiness; rather, he *transmits* it and invites others into a relationship of self-giving love.

Two Illustrative Scenes from *The Chosen*

Several scenes from *The Chosen* illuminate the significance of two key elements that inform Karol Wojtyła's personalism. They reflect ideas that can be associated with the influence of two particular thinkers: the primacy of existence in the existential Thomism of Etienne Gilson, and the meaning of faith in Saint John of the Cross. Taken together, certain insights that Wojtyła gleaned from their bodies of work help us to see more deeply into the Jesus portrayed in *The Chosen*.

But let's sharpen our question: If the character of Jesus portrayed by Jonathan Roumie in *The Chosen* is a personalist, what would he *see* when he looks at the other? What would inform that vision? What would he grasp about the person that lies out of sight to the naked eye?

The Priority of Existence: Simon's Wife

The interaction between Jesus and Simon's wife, Eden (S1E8), was the scene that first awakened me to what I perceived as the personalist thread in the series. It is worth noting that this is found nowhere in Scripture. We only infer that Peter has a wife because Jesus heals his mother-in-law (Matt 8:14; Mark 1:29). Still, the story here makes sense, and perhaps we can surmise that the fact that it is *not* found in Scripture reveals an express intention of the producers.

As the scene opens, we find Eden in her home, bowed down by worries. Her mother is gravely ill. Simon is about to go on his first journey as a disciple, leaving her alone. She is troubled. But when Jesus unexpectedly appears at her door, she puts this aside and turns toward him immediately, offering him something to drink. But he is not there to be served; he is there to serve. He knows that Simon's sacrifice is hers as well. Her face lights up when she learns that she "has a role to play in all this, too." But, yes, it will be difficult. Ruefully, he acknowledges that he cannot make it any easier for her. He takes a step closer: "But—I *see* you." There is a pause. "Do you understand?" he asks.

This question is actually meant for the audience. Can we understand what it would mean to be *seen* by Jesus? Is it not the case that we long for it? To be seen in our totality? To experience the relief of being completely understood and loved.

The first insight requires that we grasp one simple principle that lies hidden in the personalism of Karol Wojtyła, namely, the priority given to existence in the thought of Etienne Gilson. From Gilson, Wojtyła learns that the context for the metaphysics of being in Thomas Aquinas is *not* Aristotle's notion of being as an existing substance but the moment in the book of Exodus when God reveals his identity to Moses as "I Am Who I Am" (Exod 3:14).[12] For Aquinas, being means existence; it is an *act*, not a form; its function is to confer existence on the already formed essence that receives it.[13]

In Aquinas, being and good are convertible.[14] Everything is a good insofar as it exists, a goodness derived from, and proportional to, the goodness of existence that is God. And in Wojtyła's account, this good is not only known through metaphysical analysis; in the first place, it is known through human experience. As was said earlier, Wojtyła spotlights the "human being as an individual existent first and a member of the human species second."[15] That is, he sees the person *first* in his unique and unrepeatable reality. Wojtyła understands that the Thomist tradition contains a fundamental truth about human personhood. The human person, held in existence by God at every moment of his or her life, is a good precisely because he or she *exists*. In other words, the starting place in grasping the significance of any living person is not in the first instance *who* he is but *that* he is. In his encounters with the other, Wojtyła's first step is to affirm the fact of the other's existence. He affirms the other, he loves him, because the other exists and therefore represents a good that is created and held in existence by a God who loves him every minute of every day.

Augustine tells us that we cannot love that which we do not know, and so we have concluded that love of another must follow the process of getting to know that person. But Wojtyła understood that the universal love demanded of us is based on the knowledge that *who you are*, that is, your essence, is secondary to *that you are*, that is, the fact of your existence. When Wojtyła looked at someone, he would have been armed with the conviction that every person, no matter who they are, is held in existence by a God who loves them. We "exist and move and have our being" (Acts 17:28) in virtue of an unceasing embrace from above, without which we would all cease to exist (see Col 1:17; Heb 1:3).

This principle is at work throughout the series. It appears immediately in the encounter with Mary Magdalene (s1E1), in the initial confrontation with each of the disciples, in the conversation with Jairus (s1E8), and in the beautifully told conversion of Nicodemus (which culminates in s1E7). The priority given to existence can be discerned in every encounter with the other in *The Chosen*. It is visible in the gaze with which Roumie's Jesus looks at others. He *sees* them. And in that look, they see themselves.

Faith as the Metaphysical Indwelling of the Divine Substance: The Hemorrhaging Woman

The encounter between Jesus and the hemorrhaging woman is certainly one of the most moving passages in the Gospels (Matt 9:20–22; Mark 5:24–34; Luke 8:43–48). The highly charged atmosphere of this scene in season 3, episode 4 is palpable. The exchange between Jesus and the woman has an inexpressible depth; it is completely believable.

When the woman first appears, she is attempting to eke out a living washing other people's dirty laundry. She is an outcast, abandoned by her family, barred from entering the synagogue, ostracized by the community. Her condition renders her ritually impure without any real expectation of a cure. Yet she has not given up hope. She has heard testimony of a holy man and healer whom she feels certain can help her. She meets Nathaniel and Thaddeus on the road and follows them to the edge of town in season 3, episode 5 where she hopes to have her chance. But a frantic crowd has formed as more and more of Jesus's followers

Jesus as Personalist

hear of his presence in the square. He is in a hurry, on his way to the house of Jairus whose daughter is gravely ill. It seems impossible to get through the dense throng as people crush each other in their eagerness to reach him. Her escorts advise her to wait for a better time. Tomorrow perhaps? She turns back toward the square, looking for a way through the thrashing crowd. Suddenly a man who knows her to be unclean recognizes her and announces it to those nearby. She pleads with him. Again, she is advised to retreat. But she knows this may be her only opportunity. "Just one thread," she repeats, "just the fringe, one thread." The tumult seems to reach a fever pitch as she launches herself into the crowd and reaches out to grab "just the fringe" of his garment. In the moment she succeeds, Jesus stops, visibly shaken, as though his breath were taken away.

"Who touched me?" Jesus asks, looking around. "Who touched me?" he repeats to his incredulous disciples. What can this mean in the midst of the crowd pressing all around them? Jesus insists, "I felt the power go out of me. Whoever touched me ... come forward!" The woman is in a state of amazement; she has been cured. Fearfully she admits that it was she who touched him. "It was me," she whispers. "But just the fringe, only on the edge. I promise you, you are not unclean." Jesus, clearly moved, responds with the words she only now realizes she has long waited to hear: "My daughter ..." The ensuing exchange is one of the most compelling in the series. One can read its unmistakable meaning in both Jesus's look and in his words. He recognizes her and claims her as his own. But he also corrects her: "It was not my piece of clothing that healed you. ... it was your faith." He sends her on her way saying, "Go now and be at peace. Your faith has made you well."

This concluding statement captures a second key insight that enriches Karol Wojtyła's personalism, one arrived at through meditation on the meaning of faith in Saint John of the Cross. Wojtyła's studies led him to see the need to reconcile an apparent tension between a faith expressed in dogmatic terms (usually couched in the language of Scholasticism like that used by Thomas Aquinas) and a faith grounded in mystical experience (such as that described by Saint John of the Cross). Rather than oppose these two viewpoints, Wojtyła's effort is to reconcile them. In Saint John of the Cross, Wojtyła finds a writer who reveals a hidden aspect of the Thomist tradition: "a capacity to speak to the dynamism of human existence and the *experience* of faith."[16]

For Aquinas, faith is a virtue of the intellect inasmuch as the will moves it to assent. The act of faith proceeds from both the will and the intellect.[17]

But for Saint John of the Cross, faith is an experience in which the intellect is obscured and must ultimately give up trying to know God according to the natural mode of knowledge, that is, as an object. In his account, faith is that which makes a personal encounter with God possible; it is the means "proper to the intellect for uniting the soul with God in love." Yet this unity is not one in which the intellect is able to grasp fully the divine essence. Knowledge of God is not available to us through the senses like other objects of human knowledge.[18] For to know God is not to know an object. To know God is to know a person. As a person, God can be known only in a reciprocal relationship of mutual self-giving: the human person dwells within God's person, and God dwells within the human person, without merging or obscuring their differences.[19] The intellect knows God through participation in God's own being.

Through Saint John of the Cross, Wojtyła comes to understand that faith is more than intellectual assent to dogmatic formulations. He learns that it is participation in God's own life. It is a gift. It is the "metaphysical indwelling of the divine substance."[20] Every person we encounter is (at least potentially) a vessel containing the "metaphysical indwelling of the divine substance." With Saint John of the Cross, Wojtyła understands faith to be a personal encounter with God, indeed a participation in the very life of God. This encounter is not peripheral or ancillary to human experience but central to it. Thus, it is not only for mystics but accessible to all those who seek it. It is essential to the mystery of every human person. For Wojtyła, grasping the metaphysical reality that each person is simultaneously inhabited by God and lives in God, a God that is not an object but a person, meant that he was called to affirm the reality of human dignity without hesitation or retreat.[21]

The power that went out of Jesus and flooded the hemorrhaging woman with its healing grace found space in her, in virtue of her utter emptiness. But her emptiness was not a void. Her faith in the saving power of the Christ (in another manner of speaking) was evidence that she was already a vessel of the metaphysical indwelling of the divine substance. Her entire being was open for the reciprocal exchange of self-giving love that took place between her and Jesus.

"*You* have blessed *me* today," he says in departing from her.

Wojtyła's investigation of the thought of Gilson and Saint John of the Cross led him to conclude that defining the meaning of human personhood must begin with the recognition of a mystery, that human persons are irreducible, unknowable, and incommunicable, and can be known at all only through a reciprocal relationship of mutual, self-giving love.

Conclusion

If the Jesus portrayed in *The Chosen* is a personalist, it means that he looks at every person—Jew or gentile, Roman or Greek—as a person held in existence by God at every moment of the day. And this means that he is called to love each of them *as God loves them*, all the while hoping that they will use their freedom as a means for returning to the Father. On this reading, he would know that every person, at least potentially, is a vessel of the metaphysical indwelling of the divine substance and that this possibility prepares them to receive the grace that the Father already wants to give them.

The Jesus portrayed in *The Chosen* reminds us that there are no ordinary people, that none of us have ever spoken to "a mere mortal."[22] The series bears witness to this reality in every scene. And it puts all of us in touch with our own longing to be *seen* by Jesus, to be embraced by him, and to be loved as a child of God.

15

Counting Sheep with Jesus

The Significance of the Individual in *The Chosen*

ROBERT K. GARCIA

In this chapter, I explore how the life and teachings of Jesus, especially as imagined in *The Chosen*, provide credible and compelling support for the following idea:

> VIP: Each person has irreplaceable and infinite value.

As its acronym aptly reminds us, VIP implies that each human being is a *very important person*. My aim is to motivate two theses concerning VIP. To begin, however, I set the stage by showing why VIP is a vexed idea and that this, in turn, creates an urgent need. I then turn to my theses, which together suggest that this need is met by the life and teaching of Jesus, especially as imagined by the show.

VIP is vexed because, even though it is widely accepted, it is also increasingly undermined by various forces. On the one hand, VIP enjoys widespread—though not universal—acceptance in both popular culture and international politics. In popular culture, VIP is commonly taken for granted or treated as a truism—as if both its meaning and truth were obvious. To see this, I invite you to do a Google image search for "I am unique" or "I am irreplaceable." In a more serious vein, some of our most important proclamations explicitly appeal to something akin to VIP. Consider the opening statement in the preamble to the United Nations' "Universal Declaration of Human Rights": "Recognition of the inherent dignity and of the equal and inalienable rights of all members of the human family is the foundation of freedom, justice and peace in the world."[1] To be sure, the preamble's claim is not as strong as VIP. After all, *equal and inherent* value is not quite the same as *infinite and irreplaceable* value. Nonetheless, the preamble makes a bold claim about the value of persons. More importantly, if VIP were true, then we would have a *basis* for accepting the preamble. But this raises an important question: On what grounds do we accept VIP or the preamble? Can we have any rational confidence that either is true? In our current context, these questions are not easy to answer.

On the other hand, VIP is increasingly undermined by what John Crosby calls "depersonalizing forces."[2] Some of these forces are ideological—prevailing attitudes or philosophies that undercut the credibility of VIP. One such attitude is skepticism or cynicism about lofty valuations of human beings: *Infinite value? Irreplaceable? Don't flatter yourself. Why think VIP is anything more than wishful thinking or a useful fiction?* Another ideological undercutter is philosophical naturalism, according to which a person is entirely physical or determined by what is physical. On such a view, it can be hard to see how persons *could* have value, much less *irreplaceable* or *infinite* value.

Compounding the ideological ones, there are also *concrete* depersonalizing forces. These are systemic factors or patterns of behavior that treat persons as if VIP were false. One example is racism. As Martin Luther King Jr. observed, the "stinging darts" of racism create a "degenerating sense of 'nobodiness.'"[3] Another example is sexual violence. According to Andrea Dworkin, "rape signifies that the individual victim and all women have no dignity, no power, no individuality, no real safety. Rape signifies that the individual victim and all women are interchangeable, 'all the same in the dark.'"[4] Dworkin's point can be generalized to many cases of sexual violence in which the victim is treated as if they are interchangeable—replaceable and not individually unique or valuable.

Depersonalizing forces put VIP in jeopardy. This creates an urgent need for a basis or rationale for VIP that is both credible and compelling: credible to resist *ideological* depersonalizing forces and compelling to resist *concrete* depersonalizing forces. In other words, we need a basis for VIP that does more than give us a reason to *think* that VIP is true. We also need a basis that will empower and move us to *act* on the truth of VIP.

In the rest of this chapter, my aim is to show how this urgent need is met by the life and teaching of Jesus, especially as imagined by *The Chosen*. More specifically, I offer support for two main theses:

1. As depicted in the Gospels, the life and teachings of Jesus provide credible and compelling support for VIP.
2. By using its artistic license to imagine and supplement the gospel stories, *The Chosen* enhances the ways in which the life and teaching of Jesus provide support for VIP.

In the next three sections, I offer three sources of support for VIP from the life and teaching of Jesus and show how these sources are creatively imagined in the show.

As a caveat, it is important to note that support for an idea may come in varying strengths. One line of support might be very strong or compelling, whereas another might be weaker but still significant. As we will see, this is true of the support for VIP. The first source offers significant but not decisive support for VIP, whereas the second and third offer stronger support. It is for the reader to judge whether the support they offer is *decisive*!

Jesus, Kinds, and Photina

Here is the first source of support: In the Gospels, we are faced with a Jesus who refuses to reduce a person to a *kind*. A kind is a general category to which more than one thing can belong. Or, to put it differently, a kind is a shareable feature that more than one thing can have. There are numerous kinds—such as *banker*, *baker*, *saint*, and *sinner*—and any given person might belong to (or have) any number of them.

There is nothing bad about kinds or about belonging to a kind. In fact, to be human is to belong to a kind. However, if you were *reducible* to one or more kinds, then you would not be unique in any significant way. Consider: If a person were reducible to a kind (or kinds), then her significance would be entirely determined by her being the kind (or kinds) of thing(s) that she is. But, by definition, kinds are not unique features—they are features that someone else can have. Thus, if a person were reducible to a kind, then everything of significance about her would be something that could be true about someone else. She would have no *unique* significance. Consider me, for example. Here are some of the kinds I belong to: *Puerto Rican*, *male*, and *philosopher*. If I were reducible to those kinds, then my significance would be limited to those facts about me. But, of course, there are or could be other persons who belong to any or all of those kinds. Thus, if I were reducible to those kinds then I would have no unique significance.

I would now like to suggest that the above reductionism is hard to square with the way that Jesus loves individuals in the Gospels, especially as imagined in *The Chosen*. In Luke 7, we read that one of the Pharisees invites Jesus to dinner. However, a scandal ensues when an uninvited woman arrives and anoints Jesus. Below is the passage. As you read, pay attention to the language used to talk about the woman.

> A woman . . . who lived a sinful life learned that Jesus was eating at the Pharisee's house, so she came there with an alabaster jar of perfume. As she stood behind him at his feet weeping, she began to wet his feet with her tears. Then she wiped them with her hair, kissed them and poured perfume on them. When the Pharisee who had invited him saw this, he said to himself, "If this man were a prophet, he would know who is touching him and what kind of woman she is—that she is a sinner."
>
> [In response, Jesus tells a story about forgiving debts.]
>
> Then he turned toward the woman and said to Simon, "Do you see this woman? . . . You did not give me a kiss, but this woman, from the time I entered, has not stopped kissing my feet. You did not put oil on my head, but she has poured perfume on my feet. Therefore, I tell you, her many sins have been forgiven." (Luke 7:35–47 NIV)

Notice that Jesus and the Pharisee use different language in talking about the woman. The Pharisee's language reduces her to a *kind*: "what kind of woman she is—that she is a sinner."[5] In contrast, although Jesus does not deny that she has sinned, he does not reduce her to a sinner. In fact, his language demands that attention be paid to her individuality: "Do you see this woman?" Jesus's question suggests that the Pharisee was seeing only a kind of person—a sinner—but was not actually seeing *her*.

This passage provides strong evidence that, in the eyes of Jesus, a person is not reducible to the specific kind, *sinner*. Strictly speaking, of course, it does not follow that a person is not reducible to some *other* kind or collection of kinds. Nevertheless, it is significant that Jesus insists that we see her *as* an individual. By my lights, his insistence is hard to square with the idea that she is reducible to *some* kind of thing. Rather, his insistence suggests that her significance cannot be entirely understood in terms of her being a certain kind of person, no matter what kind we are talking about. No matter what *such and such* she happens to be—whether being a woman or a Jew or a sinner—she is not *merely* a *such and such*. In other words, Jesus's insistence suggests that, although you belong to many kinds, you cannot be reduced to any or all of them—there is more to you than the shareable or general kinds to which you belong. There is something about you that is not shareable or general. You are, in other words, *unique*.

Jesus's love and attentiveness for the individual is creatively imagined in a plausible and compelling way in *The Chosen*. To see this, consider how the show depicts the woman at the well from John 4:1–42. Although the woman is not named in the gospel, the show follows an old tradition and gives her the name Photina. In season 1, episode 8, "I Am He," we see her in two poignant scenes. First, we see her in the marketplace where she has a painful encounter with a seller:

SELLER: We don't serve your kind here.
PHOTINA: And what kind is that?
SELLER: You know what you are.

Notice the seller's reductive language and blindness. He does not see or recognize *her* but sees her only as a *kind* of person—and it is clear that the kind to which she is reduced is *sinner*.

Second, we see Photina arrive at the well where Jesus has been waiting for her. Eventually, they talk about thirst, water, and her marital status, at which point Jesus proceeds to name her previous husbands. The following dialogue ensues:

PHOTINA: Why are you doing this?
JESUS: I have not revealed myself to the public as the Messiah. You are the first. It would be good if you believed me.

PHOTINA: You picked the wrong person.

JESUS: I came to Samaria just to meet you. Do you think it's an accident that I'm here in the middle of the day?

There are several things to note about how *The Chosen* imagines this exchange. As with the woman in Luke 7, Jesus does not deny that she is a sinner. And, unlike the seller, Jesus does not reduce her to a kind. In fact, his words reveal that she has value and significance that cannot be reduced to or destroyed by her being a sinner. However, whereas the gospel story clearly implies that Jesus sees her as a person with value, *The Chosen* creatively expands on the gospel to make the point explicit: "I came to Samaria just to meet you."

This last line is not found in John's Gospel, yet I am guessing that most viewers, like me, did not balk at it. Presumably, this is because we find this creative expansion to be quite plausible given how Jesus is depicted in the Gospels. But notice that the plausible expansion has a profound implication—that Photina is worth all the considerable time and effort it cost Jesus to come to Samaria and wait for her at the well. Consider the opportunity costs. Jesus could have gone out of his way to meet any number of other people—people of power, influence, wealth, and so on. And Jesus could have used his time in any number of other ways, to maximize his productivity. The implication is that *Photina has a priceless value*, one that cannot be compared to the value of time or effort or expense, and a value that is not determined or diminished by her belonging to a certain kind—whether saint or sinner, rich or poor.

Before moving to a second source of support for VIP, I need to tip my hat to a nineteenth-century author, Phillips Brooks, for showing me that Jesus resisted attempts to reduce persons—especially women—to a kind.[6] Nowadays, Brooks (1835–1893) is best known for his song, "Oh Little Town of Bethlehem." In his day, however, Brooks was a champion of the idea that the "central power of Christ's ministry" was "the intense value which the Saviour always set upon the souls for which He lived and died. It shines in everything He says and does. It looks out from His eyes when they are happiest and when they are saddest. It trembles in the most loving consolations, and thunders in the most passionate rebukes which come from His lips. It is the inspiration at once of His pity and His indignation. And it has made the few persons on whom it chanced to fall . . . luminous forever with its light."[7]

Robert K. Garcia

Jesus, Sheep, and Jesse

The second source of support for VIP is Jesus's explicit teachings on the value of each person. Two teachings are especially relevant. The first concerns the value of each person relative to the value of material things. In Mark 8:36–37, Jesus asks a rhetorical question: "For what does it benefit a person to gain the whole world, and forfeit his soul? For what could a person give in exchange for his soul?" (NASB). According to Dallas Willard, in asking this question, Jesus is encouraging the listener to consider the value of her soul relative to the value of things in the world. The implied point is that, *if you were able to exchange your soul for everything in the world, you would have gotten cheated.*[8] So, think about all the highly valuable stuff in the world, from land, to gold, to diamonds. You are worth more than the sum total of all of that. But Jesus is making a much stronger point. It isn't simply that you are worth more than the sum total of what our world *actually* contains. Our world might have contained a lot more gold or diamonds than it actually does. For example, presumably (!) our world does not contain a diamond the size of our solar system. But even if our world were to contain a trillion such diamonds, you would still be worth more than the sum total of what the world contained. Thus, Jesus's point is that *no amount of valuable things can equal the value of your soul.* Your soul, in other words, is priceless; you have infinite value.

Whereas that first teaching concerned your value relative to the value of material things, the second instruction concerns your value relative to the value of other persons. Consider Jesus's teaching in Luke 15:4–7:

> What man among you, if he has a hundred sheep and has lost one of them, does not leave the other ninety-nine in the open pasture and go after the one that is lost, until he finds it? And when he has found it, he puts it on his shoulders, rejoicing. And when he comes home, he calls together his friends and his neighbors, saying to them, 'Rejoice with me, because I have found my sheep that was lost!' I tell you that in the same way, there will be more joy in heaven over one sinner who repents than over ninety-nine righteous people who have no need of repentance. (NASB)

Many hearing this would have been familiar with the story of Abraham pleading for Sodom (Gen 18:16–33). Faced with God's plan to destroy the city,

Abraham boldly asked God a series of "what if" questions: *Will you destroy the city if there are fifty righteous people in it? What if there are forty-five? Or forty? Or thirty? Or twenty? Or ten?* To each scenario, God gave the same reply: "I will not destroy it." Inspired by Abraham's pleading, someone could have asked Jesus a similar series of questions about his story of the lost sheep: *What if the shepherd had a thousand sheep? Would he still bother to go after the lost one? What if he had a million? Or a billion? Or a trillion?* Plausibly, to each scenario, Jesus would have given the same reply: "He will go after the lost one." If it is plausible to think that Jesus would offer such a reply, then the implication of that reply is also plausible, namely, that the value of each sheep cannot be diminished or replaced by the value of other sheep, no matter how many other sheep there might be. Of course, Jesus isn't making a point about the value of sheep but of persons. His point is that *your value cannot be diminished by how many other people there are; you have a priceless and irreplaceable value.*

To see how *The Chosen* conveys these teachings, consider how it imagines the paralytic at the pool of Bethesda. We learn about him in John 5:2–9:

> Now in Jerusalem, by the Sheep Gate, there is a pool which in Hebrew is called Bethesda, having five porticoes. In these porticoes lay a multitude of those who were sick, blind, limping, or paralyzed. Now a man was there who had been ill for thirty-eight years. Jesus, upon seeing this man lying there and knowing that he had already been in that condition for a long time, said to him, "Do you want to get well?" The sick man answered Him, "Sir, I have no man to put me into the pool when the water is stirred up, but while I am coming, another steps down before me." Jesus said to him, "Get up, pick up your pallet and walk." Immediately the man became well, and picked up his pallet and began to walk. (NASB)

In season 2, episode 5, "Spirit," *The Chosen* gives the paralytic the name Jesse and casts him as the brother of Simon the Zealot. The brothers are close throughout their childhood, during which time Simon looks after Jesse. But when Simon becomes a young man, he chooses to abandon Jesse to become a Zealot. As someone entirely dependent on the charity of others, Jesse had no economic or social value. No doubt, in the eyes of many he had very little worth, if any. Sadly, Simon's choice to become a Zealot suggests that he, too, did not esteem his brother's worth very highly. To the viewer, his choice indicates that he valued the Zealot cause against Roman oppression more than he valued his brother. In doing so, the show uses its creative license to emphasize that the value given to Jesse by society—and even by his own brother—was very low. In the show, this is in sharp contrast to the value given to Jesse by Jesus.

In remarkable contrast to Simon, Jesus goes out of his way to seek out Jesse. And when he finds Jesse, he doesn't simply fix his problem, much less treat him with contempt. Jesus does not take Jesse's woes as evidence of low worth. Rather, by asking "Do you want to be healed?" Jesus engages with Jesse in a way that preserves Jesse's dignity. Indeed, Brooks takes Jesus's question to reveal his profound reverence for human persons: "There is never a touch of contempt in His dealing with distress. When . . . by the Pool of Bethesda, He probes the intention and desire of the sick man's soul . . . do you not feel the infinite and exquisite reverence which is in His touch and His voice for the human nature to which His word is spoken, or on which His hand is laid?"[9] By contrasting these different attitudes about the value of Jesse and highlighting Jesus's "infinite and exquisite reverence" for each person, the show underscores the profound value that Jesus ascribes to Jesse. He has a value that is not only priceless but also is not dependent on his socioeconomic standing or contributions. Moreover, by healing him, Jesus does not restore or increase Jesse's value. Rather, Jesus heals him *because* of his value and to *demonstrate* his value to both Jesse and those looking on. In sum, by creatively and plausibly expanding on the gospel account, the show highlights the ways in which Jesus affirmed the irreplaceable value of each person.

Jesus, Kinship, and Veronica

The third source of support for VIP is Jesus's teaching on the fatherhood of God. At the heart of this teaching is a revolutionary invitation: to see God as your intimate Father and yourself as God's beloved child—indeed, as someone with the *irreplaceable and infinite value* of a beloved child. To see this, we first need to consider three things: Jesus's invitation to see ourselves as God's children; how this invitation is rooted in our being created in the image of God; and how the latter implies that *every* person is a child of God. We will then consider why being a child of God involves having irreplaceable and infinite value.

The fatherhood of God is a striking and central theme of the entire New Testament. It has been powerfully explored by Virgilio Elizondo in his book, *Galilean Journey: The Mexican-American Promise*.[10] According to Elizondo, Jesus encouraged us to see God and ourselves in a revolutionary way: "It is clear from the gospels that Jesus exhibited an intimacy with God that was totally unheard of even to the Jewish people. This intimacy with God was at the very core of the uniqueness of Jesus. It is especially evident in the way he referred to God his Father, and taught his followers to imitate him in doing so."[11] In the Judaism of Jesus's day, describing God as a Father was not unprecedented. However, when such descriptions occur in the Old Testament, God is typically said to be the father of groups, rather than individuals. Predominantly, God is called the father of the nation or people of Israel. And in other cases, God is called the father of certain kings, such as David and Solomon, or certain groups, such as the fatherless.[12]

It is striking, then, when Jesus invokes the fatherhood of God in a personal and intimate way. First, Jesus "broke with all Jewish custom" by invoking the fatherhood of God in a *personal* way: he referred to God as *my* Father, and moreover, he did so not in Hebrew but in Aramaic, the ordinary language of the people. Second, Jesus invoked the fatherhood of God in an *intimate* way: "*Abba!* It was the very familiar term used by young children, and by adults, in addressing their own fathers. *Abba* is a very childlike expression, comparable with the English 'Dad' or 'Daddy', or with the Mexican-American *Papacito* or *Diosito*." Jesus's invocation of God's fatherhood was not only personal and intimate, it was also invitational. As Elizondo notes, Jesus does not merely talk about "my" Father. Jesus also says that God is "our" Father (Matt 6:9–13) and "your" Father (Matt 6:4, where the "your" is singular). In doing so, Jesus was inviting us to follow his example and, by implication, to see each person as a beloved child of God. Elizondo suggests that this implication "reveals a new anthropology."[13] I would suggest, however, that the revealed anthropology was not so much new as ancient.

Jesus's invitation to see ourselves as God's children is rooted in one of the oldest biblical teachings—that human beings are created in the image of God. In the first chapter of Genesis, we read, "Then God said, 'Let Us make mankind in Our image, according to Our likeness; and let them rule over the fish of the sea and over the birds of the sky and over the livestock and over all the earth, and over every crawling thing that crawls on the earth.' So God created man in His own image, in the image of God He created him; male and female He created them" (Gen 1:26–27 NASB). The exact meaning and implications of this text are a matter of long-standing debate. Recently, however, Catherine McDowell has convincingly shown that "to be created in God's image is to be God's kin, specifically, 'son,' with all the responsibilities and privileges sonship entails."[14] She offers several arguments in support of this claim, but here it will suffice to summarize only one of them.

Following M. G. Kline,[15] McDowell observes that the key terms in Gen 1:26–27, "image" and "likeness," recur in Gen 5—but there they describe the father-son relationship between Adam and Seth: "On the day when God created man, He made him in the likeness of God. He created them male and female, and He blessed them and named them 'mankind' on the day when they were created. When Adam had lived 130 years, he fathered a son in his own likeness, according to his image, and named him Seth" (Gen 5:1–3 NASB). Notice that this passage directly juxtaposes two uses of "likeness": first, "likeness" describes the relationship between God and Adam, and second, it describes the relationship between Adam and Seth.[16] This indicates that "image" and "likeness" are kinship terms and imply a filial relationship. Thus, according to McDowell, the use of these terms in Gen 1:26–27 "must be understood in light of these same terms in Genesis 5:1–3, where they describe the father-son relationship between Adam and Seth."[17] In other words, when "image" and "likeness" are used in Gen 1 to describe the relationship between God and humanity, the implication is that *we are God's kin*: "To be created in the image of God is to be created as a 'son' of God the Father."[18]

McDowell notes, however, that the filial relationship between God and humanity is importantly different from the filial relationship between Adam and Seth.[19] In describing the relationship between Adam and Seth in Gen 5, the key terms are used *literally*, to describe a genealogy. In describing the relationship between God and humanity in Gen 1, the key terms are used *metaphorically*. Their metaphoric use has two crucial implications. First, the use of the terms in Gen 1 does not imply that human beings are (literally) divine. Second, the use of the terms in Gen 1 is not limited to males (literal "sons") but applies to both males and females. McDowell underscores the importance of this implication: "By defining both male and female as created in the image and according to the likeness of God, and, hence, applying the metaphor of sonship to both male and female, Genesis 1 makes a most remarkable statement: *At creation, male and female shared equally in the status of 'son' as it was defined in the biblical world.*"[20] In other words, "all human beings are royal children of God."[21] All are made in God's image, which means that all are God's kin. This indicates that kinship with God is not a special status enjoyed only by certain persons, such as the faithful. After all, even the prodigal son *was a son*; his prodigality did not destroy his sonship (see Luke 15:11–32).

Let's take stock. We've seen that Jesus's invitation to see ourselves as God's children is rooted in our being created in the image of God, and this, in turn, implies that every person is a child of God. We can now consider why a child of God has irreplaceable value.

By encouraging us to invoke God as our intimate Father, Jesus is indicating that God sees you the way that a perfect Father sees his child. God, in other words, *values* you the way that a perfect parent values their child. But how *does* a perfect parent see and value their child? Arguably, in the eyes of a perfect parent, a child is irreplaceable and priceless. The implication, then, is that in the eyes of God, each of his children is irreplaceably and infinitely valuable. But, of course, God is not mistaken in what he sees. If in God's eyes you have irreplaceable and infinite value, then you *do* have irreplaceable and infinite value. Thus, in teaching us to take God to be our Father, Jesus is indirectly teaching us that each of us is irreplaceably and infinitely valuable. Henry Churchill King put the point succinctly: "Christianity's great revolutionary conception is the conviction that every man is a child of God, and therefore of priceless value, always an end in himself and never to be used merely as a means."[22]

Before considering how God's fatherhood is imagined in *The Chosen*, it might be good to address a worry: Isn't the current point, *that I'm a child of God*, in tension with the previous point, *that I'm not reducible to a kind*? After all, I'm not the only child of God. So isn't *being a child of God* a *kind*? Yes, being a child of God is a kind—we are all God's children. However, you are not reducible to *being a child of God*. You are not merely *a* child of God. You are *this* child of God. In other words, you are a child of God in a *unique* way, and by definition, the *way in which you are unique* is not a kind. Thus, although there is some subtlety here, there is no inherent tension between the two points.[23]

In *The Chosen*, Jesus's revolutionary invitation to see yourself as God's beloved child is imagined in a powerful and plausible way. To illustrate, consider how the show imagines the woman with the issue of blood. Her story is found in each of the Synoptic Gospels. Here is the account from Luke 8:43–48:

And a woman who had suffered a chronic flow of blood for twelve years, and could not be healed by anyone, came up behind Him and touched the fringe of His cloak, and immediately her bleeding stopped. And Jesus said, "Who is the one who touched Me?" And while they were all denying it, Peter said, "Master, the people are crowding and pressing in on You." But Jesus said, "Someone did touch Me, for I was aware that power had left Me." Now when the woman saw that she had not escaped notice, she came trembling and fell down before Him, and admitted in the presence of all the people the reason why she had touched Him, and how she had been immediately healed. And He said to her, "Daughter, your faith has made you well; go in peace." (NASB)[24]

In season 3, episode 5, "Clean Part 2," the woman is given the name "Veronica," and her conversation with Jesus is expanded in a way that emphasizes her status as a child of God. In each of the Synoptics, the story ends with Jesus addressing the woman in a striking way—as "daughter." In the show, however, this address is personalized and then emphasized:

JESUS: "My daughter"
VERONICA: "I am no one's daughter anymore."
JESUS: "Look up. Yes, you are."

As with Jesse the paralytic, Jesus does not take Veronica's plight and societal status to indicate lesser worth. The clear implication of "my daughter" is that she has *always* been a daughter—*God's* beloved daughter. And in the show, to a woman who presumably feels dejected and worthless, Jesus says, "Look up." This exhortation suggests that her value merits a posture of not only hope but *dignity*. Moreover, it illustrates how *The Chosen* imagines the gospel story in a way that amplifies Jesus's invitation to see yourself as a beloved child of God.

Conclusion

We began this chapter by considering the vexed status of VIP. Although it is a widely accepted and important view about human persons, it is also in jeopardy due to depersonalizing forces. VIP urgently needs credible and compelling support. We considered three sources of supports for VIP from the life and teaching of Jesus, especially as imagined in *The Chosen*. First, we saw that Jesus refuses to reduce a person to the kind, sinner. This suggests that, although you may belong to many kinds, you cannot be reduced to any or all of them: you are unique. Second, we saw that Jesus teaches that no amount of material things can equal the value of your soul and, moreover, that your value cannot be diminished by how many other people there are: you have a priceless and irreplaceable value. Finally, we saw that Jesus invites you to see God as your Father and yourself as God's child: you have the infinite and irreplaceable value of a beloved child.

Together, these considerations motivate my two main theses. As depicted in the Gospels, the life and teaching of Jesus provide credible and compelling support for VIP. And by using its artistic license to imagine and supplement the gospel stories, *The Chosen* enhances the ways in which the life and teaching of Jesus provide support for VIP. By doing so, *The Chosen* helps us to see that Jesus meets one of our deepest and most urgent needs: to know that we matter in a very important way, that every one of us is a unique and irreplaceable member of God's family.

16

"Behold the Handmaid(s) of the Lord"

The Chosen's Amplification of Women's Voices in Scripture

GAYE STRATHEARN

One of the most endearing aspects of Dallas Jenkins's film adaptation of the ministry of Jesus of Nazareth in *The Chosen* is its conscious effort to highlight the role of the women. In a discussion between Jenkins and four of the major female actors in the series he noted, "The one thing we want to do is to spotlight women . . . and the importance of women in this story because . . . it seems like there were key moments in [Jesus's] ministry where he specifically chose women to be a vital part of it." He stated further that "for me, honestly, one of the top five things that I've really enjoyed about [*The Chosen*] is exploring the role of women in that time and in the ministry and how it's unique and how it actually made Jesus's ministry stand out."[1] Likewise, scholars who are interested in women and their place in the Bible have long championed the need to identify, recover, highlight, and promote women's voices in our study of, and sermonizing from, the Bible.[2] Thus, for both scholars and filmmakers, the question is not whether women's voices are important for a modern audience but how one goes about helping them access those voices.

This crucial focus of Jenkins and his team on women's voices is, however, impacted by two major issues: first, because of the limited information provided in the Gospels, they needed to create extended storylines that deal

"Behold the Handmaid(s) of the Lord"

with women; and second, there are positives, but also some challenges, that come when adapting female biblical individuals and their stories into modern media. The creators of *The Chosen* must have wrestled with these issues as they made decisions about the visual portrayals of women and events in those scripts. Of course, these issues are not unique to film adaptations of the biblical texts, but they do play an important role in the tension between scriptural texts and film adaptations using the word of God as a source. I will first briefly address both of these issues because they will influence our discussion of *The Chosen*'s portrayal of the women. I will then discuss the portrayal of Mary Magdalene as an example of the creative ways that the series portrays women, particularly in the first three seasons of the series.

The Silence of Women's Voices in Biblical Texts

Scholars have long wrestled with the limited portrayal of women in both the Hebrew Bible and the Christian Testament. Even though there are women present throughout Scripture, they are generally not there telling their own stories. They are certainly mentioned in the stories centered on men, but the women rarely have a voice. Thus, the stories tell us more about what men think about women than representing the voices of women themselves.[3] The book of Ruth is a case in point. Even though the book is named after Ruth and describes the efforts of Naomi and Ruth "to proactively become self-sufficient in their pressing time of need, their story takes place in a patriarchal society, and their efforts are only fully realized as they join forces with Boaz."[4]

In this way, I am addressing not the absence of women from Scripture but their relative silence. Speaking specifically of the Hebrew Bible, but voicing concerns that also exist in the Christian Testament, Judith Plaskow argues that women "can be present and silent simultaneously." They are silent when "they are not the subjects and molders of their own experiences." Furthermore, silence exists when women's "perceptions and questions have not given form to scripture, shaped the direction of Jewish law, or found expression in liturgy."[5] Instead the texts treat them as outsiders to the story whenever "the language and thought-forms of culture do not express *their* meanings."[6]

The modern reader is confronted with a notion of silence early in the opening chapter of Genesis that culminates with the creation of humanity. "Then

God said, 'Let us make man [Hebrew: *adam*] in our image, after our likeness. And let them have dominion over the fish of the sea and over the birds of the heavens and over the livestock and over all the earth and over every creeping thing that creeps on the earth.' So God created man [*adam*] in his own image, in the image of God he created him; male [*zakar*] and female [*neqebah*] he created them" (Gen 1:26–27 ESV).[7] This description is primarily narrated in androcentric language: both God and humans are described with male pronouns, and it only secondarily acknowledges that "man" includes a plurality of both men and women.[8] On the assumption that androcentric language implies that, in Plaskow's words, women are not "the subjects and molders of their own experiences," one might argue that female silence is a facet of the text from the very beginning of the Hebrew Bible.

This androcentric approach is not unique to the creation story but continues throughout the biblical narrative as evidenced by two of its defining themes.

First, the relationship between God and the Israelite people is defined by the covenant of Abraham, Isaac, and Jacob, even though the covenantal promise of seed could never have been realized independent of Sarah, Rebekah, Leah, Zilpah, Rachel, and Bilhah.[9] Second, the covenantal promise given to Abraham was that God would "establish my covenant between me and you and your offspring [*zera*, not "sons"] after you throughout their generations for an everlasting covenant, to be God to you and to your offspring after you" (Gen 17:7). Jacob had thirteen children, twelve sons and a daughter, Dinah (Gen 29:31–30:24; 35:18). But the Bible speaks only of the twelve (male) tribes of Israel (Gen 49:28; Exod 24:4; Matt 19:28; Luke 22:30). The covenantal land is divided among twelve tribes (Josh 13–14).[10] The promised covenant blessing of restoration of land is reserved for the twelve tribes of Israel (Ezek 47:13).

The silence of women's voices is certainly not unique to the ancient biblical texts. It is a historical reality that modern readers, including scholars and filmmakers, must confront when dealing with many ancient texts. Nevertheless, this silence creates challenges for modern readers—particularly female readers—who want to feel connected to the Scripture story. Although Plaskow sees the silence as "an invitation to experiment and explore," she also recognizes that such exploration can occur "only after we have examined its terrain and begun to face its implications."[11]

Are Plaskow's concerns also warranted in the gospel accounts in the Christian Testament? Certainly, women are included as followers of Jesus. They were present at his birth, they traveled with him, they were recipients of his miracles, they were present at the cross and the garden tomb. They financially provided for his traveling ministry. We assume that they were part of the multitudes who heard him teach the Sermon on the Mount/Plain, where they are promised that "your reward will be great, and you will be sons [Greek: *huioi*] of the Most High" (Luke 6:35). The silence is not because they are not present in the Gospels. It is because we rarely experience the women telling *their own* stories; we rarely hear *their* voices. To be sure, there are a few occasions when the Gospels feature women speaking in first person such as Mary's Magnificat and Mary Magdalene at the garden tomb, but mostly the canonical text talks *about* women. Perhaps one reason why *The Chosen* creates so much dialogue for the women (and men) in their series is to help them have a voice.

One way that scholars have sought to better understand the place of women in the Christian Bible is to see what light archaeology and social science methodologies can bring to help us understand women's lives, their contributions to family and its finances, and to village life in first-century Palestine.[12] These approaches help us find answers to important questions for understanding the various roles that women played in earliest Christianity, questions such as the following: What was life like for a woman in first-century Galilee and Jerusalem? What was it about Jesus's teachings that was so attractive to women? Would women have understood his teachings in the same way that men did? Why is it significant that Jesus included women in his ministry? As Amy-Jill Levine and Marc Zvi Brettler remind us, "the answers we receive, the interpretations we develop, are all dependent on the questions we ask, the experiences we bring, and the preferences we have."[13]

Modern Media Adaptations of Jesus's Ministry

How can modern readers and filmmakers address these limitations regarding the place of women in the story of Jesus? Making a concerted effort to understand the Gospels in their original historical settings will help us understand how the earliest audiences might have understood them. Yet we modern readers also come to the biblical text with our own questions and needs, in the hope that it can also speak to us and not just to the ancient audience. Otherwise, the biblical text is little more than an ancient artifact. The creators of *The Chosen* are interested in trying to bridge the gap separating the ancient world and the modern world of readers.

How do *The Chosen* scriptwriters tackle the issue of the limited textual information about women in gospel accounts? They do so from several different angles, usually through the use of fictional narratives. First, they acknowledge the disparity between the status and roles of men and women in the biblical world. For example, in season 2, episode 3, while sitting around a campfire, Big James asks his fellow Jesus followers, "If someone had told you growing up that you would be a student of the Messiah, that you would be close to him, would help him on his mission, what would you have thought?" One of the women in the group, Ramah, replies, "I would have said, 'Sorry. I'm a girl. Ask my brother.'" But there is also an acknowledgment that women can overcome some of the gender inequities about learning Torah, despite their lack of formal opportunities. In a subtle, yet poignant moment, in season 1, episode 3, Jesus befriends and teaches a small group of boys and girls. When he asks them, "What does the Lord say in the law of Moses about justice and vengeance?" a young girl named Abigail answers his question by quoting Scripture, "Vengeance is mine" (Deut 32:35). Jesus praises her answer and says, "Boys, pay attention. She doesn't even go to Torah class." When Abigail attempts to answer another question soon afterward, however, Jesus says, "Let's see if someone who studies this at school is learning."

Second, they make a conscious effort to highlight the female stories. Naturally, the story of Jesus's mother Mary, with Gabriel's Annunciation, and her visit to Elizabeth (Luke 1:26–45) is portrayed, although the series surprisingly does not start here but instead portrays these events through flashbacks in latter episodes (e.g., season 2 Christmas episode; S4E1).[14] Other important expansions upon the biblical text in the first four seasons include the Samaritan woman at the well (John 4), the women followers in Jesus's travel party in Galilee (Luke 8:1–3), the woman who suffered with a discharge of blood (Matt 9:20–22; Mark 5:24–34; Luke 8:43–48), and the story of Mary and Martha (Luke 10:38–42).

These expansions are a third way that the scriptwriters have chosen to highlight women. It is a practice that is known in the ancient world when they were faced with gaps in scriptural accounts. Ancient readers created storylines to fill the vacuum. For example, we have limited information about Jesus's childhood except for Luke's account of his family's trips to the Jerusalem temple when he was a newborn (Luke 2:21–39) and then again when he was twelve years old (Luke 2:41–50), along with two general statements about his physical and spiritual development: "And the child grew and became strong, filled with wisdom" (Luke 2:40); "Jesus increased in wisdom and in stature and in favor with God and man" (Luke 2:52).

This scant information about the early life of Jesus must have raised questions even for the early readers of the biblical texts. Such gaps in the texts concerning the biography of Jesus led many ancient authors to supply missing details. The writing of nonbiblical texts such as the Protevangelium of James and the Infancy Gospel of Thomas appear to have been produced, at least in part, to respond to this need. The same may be said for other Christian non-canonical texts that developed over time to fill in the gap in the opening verses of Acts when Jesus is said to have "presented himself alive to them after his suffering by many proofs, appearing to them during forty days and speaking about the kingdom of God" (Acts 1:3). Questions about what Jesus may have taught during those forty days gave rise to a genre of texts that claim to be the secret teachings that Jesus gave to select individuals and groups after his resurrection (e.g., Apocryphon of John, Apocryphon of James, Epistle of the Apostles, and Gospel of Mary).

This practice resembles the approach of *The Chosen* in its expansions on the canonical gospels' descriptions of individuals, including their portrayal of women. In his chapter in the present volume, Douglas Huffman describes this practice as relying on "historical plausibility," meaning that from what we know about history, it is reasonable that something like this could have happened. Certainly, there is some historical plausibility in their efforts to portray the love that Jesus's mother had for her son. In the Synoptic Gospels, there is little mention of Mary outside of Luke's and Matthew's birth narratives. *The Chosen*, however, portrays her as an occasional visitor to the traveling group. On one such occasion, Mary joins the group, helps them prepare a meal, and then sits around the fire with them (S2E3). Jesus's students are naturally interested in her account of the Annunciation and the birth, but there is also a very tender moment when Jesus comes back to his tent after a long period of healing. He is exhausted, and while the others look on, his mother withdraws from the group and lovingly ministers to her son. There is nothing in the canonical accounts that depicts such a scene, but it seems reasonable that a mother would care for her son in such a fashion.

The creators of *The Chosen* have also engaged in more imaginative ways to portray the participation of women in Jesus's ministry. Some are simple, like giving names for many of the nameless women, but more substantial effort goes into creating storylines for many of the female characters.[15] A case in point is the creation of a storyline for Simon's wife. We know that she existed because the gospel accounts speak of Jesus healing Simon's mother-in-law (Matt 8:14–15; Mark 1:29–31; Luke 4:38–39), but she is nowhere else mentioned in the gospel accounts. The scriptwriters not only gave her a name—Eden—they also gave her a seat at the table as a follower of Jesus and provided an avenue for us to see her, and hopefully for the viewers to see something of themselves in her experience.

Eden is portrayed as a believer in Jesus, even before Simon was, and is excited when he finally recognizes Jesus as the Messiah. For me, one of the most powerful scenes in the first three seasons takes place in season 1, episode 8 as Jesus and his students prepare to go out on their first journey. Simon is concerned about leaving Eden for an extended period and for her ability to take care of her sick mother by herself. Recognizing the hardship that she will experience, Jesus comes to their home seeking a personal encounter with Eden before they leave.

> JESUS: "You saw it first, you know."
>
> EDEN: "What do you mean?"
>
> JESUS: "What I see in Simon. You were the first person to notice when no one else did—that connects us."
>
> EDEN: "My mother said I was drawn to his wildness and that I would regret it. I wonder what she'll say now?" . . . [Peter and Andrew enter and Jesus directs them to go sit with the mother-in-law].
>
> JESUS: "I told Simon to make sacrifices and to leave things behind in order to follow me. You are one flesh with Simon. He cannot make sacrifices that are not also yours. You have a role to play in all of this."
>
> EDEN: "Do I?"
>
> JESUS: "You will know in time. I can't make everything about this easier for you."
>
> EDEN: "That wouldn't be our people's way."
>
> JESUS: "No, it has not been, nor will it continue to be. But I see you! You understand? I know it is not easy to be home when your husband is out doing all of this. Even when you are excited about it, and proud of him. So,

"Behold the Handmaid(s) of the Lord"

I wouldn't ask you to do this without taking care of a few things." [Jesus then heals her mother].

This is a situation where a transcription of the dialogue cannot do justice to the power of this cinematic scene. But it serves as a poignant reminder that Jesus *sees* this particular woman and, by extension, that he also recognizes the sacrifices that other women also make.

Mary Magdalene

Perhaps the most prominent female character in *The Chosen* is Mary Magdalene. Her first mention in the canonical gospels comes in Luke 8, which describes Jesus's traveling entourage in Galilee. The group includes "the twelve ... and also some women who had been healed of evil spirits and infirmities: Mary, called Magdalene, from whom seven devils had gone out, and Joanna, the wife of Chuza, Herod's household manager, and Susanna, *and many others*, who provided for them out of their means" (vv. 2–3, emphasis added).

These verses become the foundational passage for *The Chosen*'s amplified stories of Mary Magdalene and Joanna.[16] Luke's description of Jesus's Galilean ministry after his baptism and temptations begins at Luke 4:14, four chapters before Mary Magdalene is introduced. The other gospels do not introduce her at all until the crucifixion scene (Matt 27:56; Mark 15:40; John 19:25). Therefore, it is surprising that she is one of the major characters introduced in the very first episode of the series.[17] This choice signals the intentionality of the series creators to make good on their goal to highlight the importance of women in Jesus's ministry.

Her early introduction in the series also provides a platform for several important storylines that run throughout the first four seasons and, one would assume, throughout the rest of the seasons as well. It prepares the audience for the major role that Mary will play in the series as an integral part of Jesus's traveling party from the very beginning of his ministry. It could be argued that her character receives an even greater focus in season 1, episode 1 than the corresponding male characters (Simon, Andrew, and Matthew) because, when Jesus eventually makes his first appearance in the episode, it is to Mary rather than to the men. This scene introduces what will undoubtedly be an important *inclusio* for the entire series that begins and ends with Jesus appearing to Mary first before he appears to any of the other disciples. John's Gospel alone focuses on Mary Magdalene's experience on resurrection morning (John 20:1–18), and one assumes that this will be an important focus in wrapping up the series.[18]

Mary's storyline in the opening episode is shaped by Luke's statement in Luke 8:2 that Jesus healed Mary Magdalene "from whom seven demons had gone out," but it is significantly expanded beyond the canonical description by latter traditions that developed around Mary Magdalene. These traditions often linked and conflated Mary's story with other stories of women anointing Jesus: Mary of Bethany, who anoints his feet and dries them with her hair (John 12:3);[19] and the woman who washes his feet and about whom he declares, "Her sins, which are many, are forgiven" (Luke 7:36–50). By the sixth century CE, the conflation of these stories resulted in the portrayal of Mary Magdalene as "the repentant whore," although no New Testament text describes her as a prostitute.[20] Thus, when Jesus appears to Mary in the first episode, she is described as someone who lives in "the red district" of Capernaum and is portrayed as being in a period of crisis, racked with guilt over things that she has done under the influence of the evil spirits and devoid of hope for a normal life. Not even the great teacher from Jerusalem, Nicodemus, could excise her demons—but Jesus can, and does.

Jesus's healing of Mary sets the scene for important themes in the developing storyline. First, Jesus's act of healing Mary Magdalene contrasts with the powerlessness of Nicodemus, as a representative of the Jerusalem religious elite. Encountering the healed Mary after his failure becomes the backstory for why Nicodemus eventually seeks out Jesus in John 2:23–3:21 and declares, "Rabbi, we know that you are a teacher come from God, *for no one can do these signs that you do unless God is with him*" (v. 2, emphasis added). *The Chosen*'s portrayal here differs from John's account, which links Nicodemus's fascination with Jesus to the miracles performed in Jerusalem at the first of three Passovers mentioned in John's Gospel.

Second, the early introduction of Mary prepares the audience for the prominent role that Mary will serve in the series as a central figure among the disciples that Jesus gathers together. She is portrayed as a student in every sense of the word. In season 2, episode 2, there is an interesting dialogue between Mary Magdalene and Ramah, one of the other female students traveling with Jesus.

"Behold the Handmaid(s) of the Lord"

MARY: "Wasn't it exciting yesterday when the men began quoting prophecy?"
RAMAH: "And ahhh, a little intimidating."
MARY: "Yes. We need to catch up."
RAMAH: "Okay. How? I can't read."
MARY: "I'll teach you how to read and write."

This conversation raises the question of when and how Mary learned to read and write.[21] No explanation is provided, and the fact that she can do both is surprising. Although the ability to determine how widespread literacy was in antiquity is notoriously difficult to assess, William V. Harris asserts that "the classical world, even at its most advanced, was so lacking in the characteristics which produce extensive literacy that we must suppose that the majority of people were always illiterate."[22] Even with such a low estimate of literacy rates, he argues that the rate for women would have been significantly lower than that of men.[23] In the land of Israel during the time of Jesus, Meir Bar-Ilan argues that the average literacy rate was around 3 percent.[24] This statistic is consistent with the oral nature of ancient Israelite society.[25] Jewish schools in Greco-Roman Palestine were rare and were not generally geared to teaching "practical writing skills" but "to prepare boys for the task of reading Torah in public," with no provision for the education of girls.[26] If women did enjoy any level of literacy, then they almost universally came from elite families in urban areas. But Mary Magdalene came from Magdala, a small fishing village in rural Galilee. This is not to say that women knew nothing about Jewish religious life or even Scripture, however; they could have learned them through hearing the stories and scriptural passages recited or read aloud in their homes and in the synagogues.

The primary purpose of Mary teaching Ramah to read and write is so that they (and Matthew) could study the Scriptures like the other male disciples and not just rely on other people's interpretations. The incongruity of women studying Torah, which was restricted to men, is highlighted in season 2, episode 2 when Ramah tells Thomas that she plans to study Torah with Mary and Matthew. Thomas laughs:

THOMAS: "Matthew doesn't know anything about Torah."
RAMAH: "How do you know what Matthew knows?"
MARY: "That's the point."

THOMAS: "You don't read."

RAMAH: "I wasn't sent to Hebrew school like you. So that's exactly what I'll learn from Mary first. It's not like we're trying to be teachers or anything. We just want to learn more." ...

THOMAS: "Anything you need to know, you can always ask me. I'd be happy to answer any questions. You know that, right?"

RAMAH: "Of course."

THOMAS: "Good."[27]

Thomas's attitude about men being the only purveyors of Scripture did not satisfy either Mary or Ramah. They wanted to know Scripture for themselves—and so they began studying.[28]

Conclusion

The Chosen's depiction of women represents a praiseworthy and essential effort to acknowledge and elevate the roles women held in Jesus's ministry. Under the direction of Dallas Jenkins, the series consciously aims to spotlight oft-neglected contributions of key named figures like Mother Mary, Mary Magdalene, Joanna, and the sisters, Mary and Martha, while also highlighting unnamed women who feature so prominently in the Gospels, like the Samaritan woman and the woman with the issue of blood. These disciples play vital roles in the Gospels, and these portrayals allow modern audiences, particularly women, to form meaningful connections with the biblical narrative.

Nevertheless, this depiction also underscores two significant challenges: the relative silence of women's voices in biblical texts even when they are present, and the complexities involved in adapting these texts for contemporary media. Despite these challenges, there exist opportunities to highlight women's stories through careful exegesis and creative elaboration, all while attempting to stay anchored to historical context. *The Chosen* addresses these issues by recognizing the gaps and imaginatively filling them with historically plausible narratives. This involves assigning names and backstories to otherwise unnamed women, like Simon's wife, Eden, and depicting their active involvement in Jesus's ministry. These creative choices provide a fuller and more relatable portrayal of biblical women, underscoring their importance

"Behold the Handmaid(s) of the Lord"

and the sacrifices they made. As contemporary readers and filmmakers continue to examine the roles of women in biblical stories, it is vital to balance creative expansions with a grounded understanding of historical and cultural contexts. This balance ensures that the portrayal of women in the Bible remains authentic and resonant, aiding modern viewers, particularly women, in feeling connected to the sacred narrative. In the end, *The Chosen*'s focus on women's voices serves as a crucial reminder of their relatively silent but significant presence and influence in the biblical story.

17

Meaning and Calling

A Rhetorical Analysis of Jesus's Interactions with Women in *The Chosen*

JOY E. A. QUALLS

The stranger places his hands on the desperate woman's hand. She rebuffs him, but the demons that torture her threaten yet again. While the bar keeper calls her Lilith, the name of an ancient Hebrew female demon, she turns to go. As she walks away, the stranger calls her Mary. He calls her by name. He redeems her and calls her his own. As she weeps in the arms of the stranger, the audience of *The Chosen* envisions what it may have been like when Jesus of Nazareth delivered Mary Magdalene from seven demons and called her as a disciple (S1E1).

The Chosen is the latest of many attempts to present the narrative of the life and work of Jesus and his followers to a popular audience. Like most such productions, the series condenses some timelines and locations and adds some backstories, relationships, and specific characters. According to the Gospels, Jesus had strong relationships with women, and *The Chosen* fleshes out many of these relationships. While the overarching narrative of the series is focused on the ministry of Jesus, it is not until the very end of the first episode that the main character makes his first appearance. When he finally appears, it is to a woman, Mary Magdalene, that he brings healing and salvation.

Women not explicitly included in the Gospels are also added to the cast of characters. For example, Matthew reports that Simon Peter had a mother-

Meaning and Calling

in-law whom Jesus heals of sickness (Matt 8:14–15), but we know nothing of Simon's wife. In *The Chosen*, the character of Eden fills in this gap. Throughout the first season, the audience is given glimpses into the tensions of a husband and a wife trying to make a life in Roman-occupied Israel. Eden is depicted as a godly woman who rebukes her husband for trying to take things in his own hands and reminds him that he answers to God first. When Simon encounters Jesus and is called to follow him, Eden recognizes him as the Messiah simply by her husband's testimony (s1E2). Jesus himself appears at the home of Simon and Eden where he calls out her faith and acknowledges the sacrifices of the families of those who are called to be disciples (s1E8). In his interaction with Eden, Jesus specifically says to her, "I see you," which is an allusion to the biblical story of Hagar referenced earlier in the episode (s1E8). Hagar, the slave woman of Abraham's wife Sarah, is the first recorded person in Scripture to name God *El Roi*, the God who sees (Gen 16:13). In the imagined interaction of *The Chosen*, Jesus sees Eden and the circumstances of her life. He is, for Eden, the God who sees. The allusion to Hagar may be missed by many viewers, but for those familiar with Scripture, the teaser about Hagar earlier in the program will tie the overarching story of God to the focused story of the Gospels.

In this chapter, my focus will be on the ways in which the series represents the relationship between Jesus and the women in his life and ministry. Drawing on previous research on religious rhetoric, I will analyze not only the ways in which Jesus's relationships convey his identity as Messiah but also the implications of his identity for the women in their lives and culture. Like all such enterprises, the show's creators exercise considerable artistic license. Close attention to their storytelling technique not only reveals how they foster meaning-making for the audience but also enhances our understanding of how Jesus's interactions with women elevated their position, redeemed their lives, and brought them into the kingdom of God.

Dramatistic Theory and Analysis

I employ two areas of rhetorical theory to analyze the meaning and message of *The Chosen* in how Jesus interacts with women. Dramatism is a category of rhetorical analysis that focuses specifically on narrative and the relationship between the drama of real life and the stories we tell. As rhetorical critic Kenneth Burke once noted, life is not *like* a drama; life *is* a drama.

Aristotle defined rhetoric as the art of discovering all the available means of persuasion in a given situation (*Rhetoric* 1355b). Burke expands Aristotle's definition to encompass the broader category of "symbolic action" and shifts the focus of rhetoric from persuasion, highlighting the psychological component of rhetoric by concentrating on the analysis of motive. By starting with humans as they react symbolically to their environment, Burke arrives at the basic function of rhetoric: "the use of words by human agents to form attitudes or actions in other human agents."[1] In other words, rhetorical action is one person trying to get another person to behave, feel, or think differently. Rhetorical practice is part of the human drama generated by language.

In his dramatistic theory, Burke describes human society as a dramatic process that includes the elements of hierarchy, acceptance and rejection, and the experiences of guilt, purification, and redemption. Hierarchy generates the structure of society. Power endows people with authority. Authority, in turn, establishes relationships among people that reflect the power they possess. As people accept their roles and the hierarchical structure, bureaucracy is formed, and with it comes order in society.[2] Burke's theory of rhetoric is rooted in humanity's propensity to accept or reject their situation and their attempts to symbolize these reactions. Language enables people to accept or reject their position within the hierarchy or even the hierarchy itself. According to Bernard L. Brock, "Acceptance results in satisfaction and order, whereas rejection results in alienation and disorder."[3]

The concepts of guilt, purification, and redemption complete the dramatic process and represent the effects of the acceptance and rejection of hierarchy. When hierarchy is rejected, guilt is felt. In every social institution—in the realms of family, religion, or politics—hierarchy emerges, and when two of these hierarchies conflict, one will be rejected. Because humans cannot prevent this conflict, Burke believes that we are saddled with perpetual guilt.[4] Guilt then sets off a psychological reaction: it reduces social connections and makes people feel fragmented, so they strive for redemption from guilt. Purification, according to Burke, comes through mortification or victimization, or both. Mortification is an act of self-sacrifice that relieves guilt, while victimization purges guilt through the use of a scapegoat. The process of purification must equal the degree of guilt if one is to receive redemption.[5]

With a concept he calls identification or consubstantiality, Burke argues that interests or perceived interests join one person with another.[6] Speakers, whose attitudes are reflected in their language, will accept some ideas, people, and institutions, and reject others; the audience will to some extent both agree and disagree. To the extent that audiences accept and reject the same ideas, people, and institutions, identification occurs. Identification is the critic's key to understanding the speakers' attitudes and the dramatic process.[7]

In answering the question, "What are people doing and why are they doing it?" Burke introduces what he calls the dramatistic pentad as a means of understanding the many layers of symbolic action. For the purposes of this chapter, a simple explanation of the pentad is found in the answers to five questions (and accompanying labels): what took place in thought or deed (*act*), when or where was it done (*scene*), who did it (*agent*), how did they do it (*agency*), and why did they do it (*purpose*)? These terms are key to assigning human motives because motives, as Burke states, "arise out of them and terminate in them."[8] The pentad—*act, scene, agent, agency,* and *purpose*—along with the notions of identification and the inherently dramatic nature of society provides a vocabulary and theoretical structure that allows the critic to describe humans as they respond to their world.

Walter Fisher formalizes Kenneth Burke's philosophical dramatism in a way that is helpful for analyzing a cinematic account like *The Chosen*. Fisher makes the case that storytelling epitomizes human nature. According to Fisher, all forms of human communication that appeal to our reason are rooted in story. No communication is purely didactic or merely descriptive. Narrative, as defined by Fisher, is symbolic actions (words and/or deeds) that have sequence and meaning for those who live, create, and interpret them.[9] Fisher proposes a shift from the rational world paradigm to a narrative paradigm where people are storytellers who make decisions based on good reason. Our history, biography, culture, and character determine what we consider good reasons.[10] The world, according to Fisher, is a set of stories from which we choose and thus constantly recreate our lives. Fisher proposes the twin tests of coherence and fidelity to determine narrative rationality.[11]

Narrative coherence asks whether the story hangs together. Narrative fidelity asks whether the story rings true and is humane. Narratives are laden with values, and these values set apart the logic of good reasons. Fisher argues that people tend to prefer narratives that fit with what they view as truthful and humane. The storyteller should seek to speak to an ideal audience that identifies the human values that a good story embodies. Therefore, we judge a story to have coherence and fidelity when we believe shared values between the storyteller and the audience can influence belief and actions.[12] Building on Burke's elements of the drama, a good narrative includes intriguing words/actions, a background setting, interesting characters, stimulating means by which events occur, and a sense of direction for the story.

There are several steps to completing a full dramatistic analysis of a narrative. In my application of these rhetorical theories to *The Chosen*, I will focus on two elements from each.

First, analyzing the storytelling as a rhetorical argument requires that we determine coherence and fidelity in order to explore the purpose of the narrative. Thus, we must identify the features of the narrative to discover how the purpose is accomplished. What work does the narrative appear designed to perform in the world? What strategies are selected to accomplish that purpose?

Second, I will investigate the motivation of the rhetorical action. By examining the pentadic elements of the drama, it is possible to determine which element emerges as dominant (i.e., *act, scene, agent, agency,* or *purpose*). This helps us understand how the storyteller tries to persuade the audience to accept his or her view of reality as true. The storyteller's worldview is revealed when one element of the pentad is stressed over the others, which gives clues into the storyteller's motivation. Realism, situational determinism, idealism, pragmatism, and mysticism are all motivations employed by storytellers to aid in the sharing of worldview and values, which in turn assists in persuasion via rhetorical action.

Narrative Elements of *The Chosen* and Analysis

While the multiple facets of *The Chosen* are ripe for dramatistic analysis, I have chosen to focus specifically on the portrayal of Jesus's relationship with the female characters in the program to highlight an important element of Jesus's life and teaching. First-century Roman-occupied Israel was a culture steeped in masculinity and dominated by male authority, with both Roman and Jewish cultures emphasizing female submission and enacting strict rules about male-female interaction. This created a setting in which women were often denied personal agency, autonomy, or cultural authority. The audience of *The Chosen* sees this addressed in several different ways throughout the series. For example, when we meet Photina, the woman at the well, we learn that a woman cannot write a certificate of divorce; only a husband can do that (S1E8).

That women could become Jesus's disciples is especially noteworthy. In season 2, the teachers of the law express surprise and concern that Jesus was seen eating with women of ill repute (S2E6). The greater shock seems to be that the women were engaging the rabbi as his disciples. One female disciple is even a gentile (an Ethiopian woman) (S2E6). Women were not allowed to be educated in the Torah as young men, if they were educated at all. They were not allowed into certain spaces in the temple. They were not allowed to serve as teachers. Yet, as portrayed in *The Chosen*, Mary Magdalene and Ramah learn together along with Matthew in the instruction of Torah, and Mary is even called a teacher by Ramah (S2E6). In the first season, Mary hosts a Shabbat dinner where Little James and Thaddeus appear as her guests. They encourage Mary to do the reading as it is her home. When Jesus suddenly shows up at her door, she offers him the place of the rabbi in the reading, but he defers to her. The scene shifts back and forth with another Shabbat feast led by Nicodemus, a chief rabbi. It was Nicodemus himself who could not rid Mary of the demons who plagued her. When explaining her healing, Mary states, "I was one way, and now I am different. The only difference is him" (S1E2). The contrast of Mary to Nicodemus in the Shabbat scene is striking—a woman acting (with permission) outside her role and the religious leader who could not leave his place of position to be a disciple of the healer.

The choice to highlight the women named in Scripture as well as include other female characters is a distinct rhetorical selection that emphasizes something conspicuous in the overarching narrative of *The Chosen*. The pentadic elements of the narrative (see above) provide a helpful rubric according to which we can arrive at a thicker description of specific examples viewers encounter in the series.

Narrative Analysis: Pentadic Elements

There are five pentadic elements of the narrative, which are uncovered in the rhetorical choices made in the writing and producing of the program.[13] (1) The *act*: the life and ministry of Jesus, about which specific examples are given in the analysis below. (2) The *scene*: first-century Roman-occupied Israel including Capernaum, Galilee, Jerusalem, Nazareth, among other communities and wilderness spaces. Specific homes and locations play some significant role, but all are set in these physical spaces during a specific time in history. (3) The *agent*: While other characters contribute to the act, the narrative is ultimately about the person of Jesus of Nazareth, called the Christ, and he is central to the rhetorical action of the story. (4) *Agency*: the verbal calling of disciples but also the process of discipleship that the characters experience. Agency may also include Jesus's interactions with nondisciples who nonetheless play significant roles in the story. We can acknowledge some peripheral or adjacent rhetorical actions of Jesus that also demonstrate his unique engagement with women. (5) *Purpose*: It slowly becomes more apparent within the story that the purpose of Jesus's life and ministry is to establish himself as the Messiah, the Savior.

Jesus's redemptive purpose includes rescue from the results of sin that created specific constraints on the lives of the women included in the narrative. In the case of this narrowly focused analysis, the women within the story are the immediate audience for the rhetorical action in the program. While there are several women included in the narrative, I want to highlight Mary Magdalene; Eden, the wife of Simon Peter; Tamar, the Ethiopian woman; Mary, the mother of Jesus; and Ramah, the winemaker's daughter betrothed to Thomas. Other women who are significant in the life and ministry of Jesus but who have limited roles in *The Chosen* include the little girl (Abigail) at Jesus's camp, Salome (James and John's mother), Photina (the woman at the well), Joanna (the wife of an official in Herod's court), Veronica (the woman with the issue of blood), Jairus's daughter, and Pilate's wife Claudia. My analysis is necessarily limited to the seasons that have been released at the time of writing (seasons 1 through 3) and not from studying the scripts or the subsequent novelizations of the show.

Narrative Summary: Some Women's Storylines

"A woman of valor! Who can find?" (s1E2). This refrain, exclaimed by the male members of the household at the start of the Shabbat meal, is a powerful example of the ways in which women are characterized in *The Chosen*. This opening line to a poem from Prov 31 is traditionally spoken over the woman of the house to begin the weekly Sabbath by the man of the home.[14] In many

Jewish households, the practice continues to the present day. The inclusion of this phrase ties the narrative to several key elements: the practice of Judaism, a culture of honor, and the role of women in the story. It would be easy to gloss over this proclamation if one is not aware of the significance of this Scripture and its use in Jewish tradition, but its inclusion in *The Chosen* is a reminder of the importance of women to the story of Jesus. Who is the *eshet khayil* (Hebrew for "woman of valor"),[15] and what does her story say about the narrative arc of the series as a whole?

Two women of valor featured prominently in *The Chosen* are named Mary: Mary Magdalene and Mary, the mother of Jesus.

(1) Mary Magdalene is the most prominent of the female disciples of Jesus. His reputation is marked by her presence and the presence of the other women. When the religious leaders are questioning who this man could be, it is repeated that he has many female disciples. It is often noted that he is found to be in the company of women of ill repute like Mary of Magdala (S2E6).[16] Mary is healed and restored as the opening storyline in season 1 and has a significant character arc throughout the story (see Luke 8:2). Jesus heals Mary, but he also elevates her. He allows her to lead the Shabbat dinner. He encourages her efforts at learning Torah rather than allow her to be seen as ignorant. He speaks to her and looks directly into her eyes as he elevates her from a life of death to full life as a disciple. When others see her as Lilith the demoniac, Jesus specifically reminds them that her name is, and always has been, Mary. This is important as an element of her interaction with him because Mary's beloved and now deceased father had spoken over her a Scripture from the prophet Isaiah that joined her name with her status in God's eyes: "Fear Not! For I have redeemed you! I have called you by name!" (S1E1; cf. Isa 43:1). God himself in the person of Jesus calls her name and requires that others acknowledge her identity as well.

Whereas Mary's restoration dominates her storyline, it is her wrestling with the fullness of her new life that makes her such a compelling figure. She is constantly present throughout the series, learning to read Torah and helping Ramah and the other women as well as Matthew (S2E6). She is never far from scenes with the male disciples and is physically present even when not specifically addressed. As a result, her temporary return to her old life is even more dramatic. When the disciples are confronted with another demoniac (Legion), the trauma of that encounter triggers something in Mary that sends her into a shame spiral and a return to the familiar patterns of her former life (S2E5). But her absence is felt by the group of disciples, so Simon Peter and Matthew set off to find her. Upon her return, the other women clean her up and cover her hair (a sign of modesty and dignity) before taking her to Jesus. It is here that another powerful encounter takes place. Jesus welcomes Mary back to the company of disciples and tells her that all he wants from her is her heart. A key moment in their interaction is that he commands her to look at him in the eye. Shame has no place in their relationship. He forgives her and proclaims that it is over before once again embracing her (S2E6).

(2) The other Mary, Jesus's mother, is also a significant female figure in *The Chosen*, their unique relationship forged from the very beginning of the narrative. Mary says she cannot remember life before knowing her son (S2E1). The audience is allowed to see what it means that she has pondered the meaning of her son's life in her heart through the ways she speaks about him and with him (cf. Luke 2:19, 51). The juxtaposition of a young mother who—fully aware that he was the Son of God!—knew her baby needed her to comfort him, to raise him, and to love him alongside the grown woman with a son who is nearing the revelation of his identity and purpose is striking. Furthermore, Jesus does not speak to his mother in the way he speaks to his disciples. He tells her he is tired; he honors her worries about him; he recognizes her knowledge of the timeline of his ministry (S2E3). She also wants to elevate him in the water-to-wine miracle at the wedding of Cana (S1E5). And when he is about to deliver the Sermon on the Mount, it is his mother who wants to adorn his garment and comes with the other women to offer a scarf of color to establish his role and give import to his words (S2E8).

Jesus's conversations with his mother are personal and familial. "What are you thinking about?" she asks. When Jesus answers that he is thinking about his father, she jokes with him, "Which one?" They reminisce and speak of missing Joseph as they walk out this part of life together without him (S2E8). She speaks with pride, as a mother does. Jesus knows who he is, and she does as well. In later episodes, they also speak of his brothers who are not yet comfortable with his public ministry. They share stories of the disciples, and Mary notes that her favorites are, of course, the women (S3E3)! In each of their conversations, clear and deep love and respect are manifest. But the occasional tinge of sadness appears. Mary knows better than anyone what is coming in the life of her son. She wants to protect him as his mother, but she also wants him to do the will of God and stands firm in creating the space for Jesus to fulfill his purpose.

Several other storylines demonstrate the significance of Jesus's relationship with women. With Photina, more popularly known as the woman at the well (John 4:1–45), we receive insight into her life prior to her encounter with Jesus. As a Samaritan and a woman who has been divorced multiple times, she is an outcast. When she encounters Jesus, he is direct in his communication but does not avoid contact with her. Photina challenges him and speaks directly in response to his questions. Jesus does not condemn or ignore her. In fact, he reveals who he is for the first time publicly. He then tells her the entire story of her life. It is here that she recognizes him and is redeemed. She sets out back to her home and people with an enthusiasm that is palpable. The male disciples are surprised it is here that Jesus has revealed who he is and does not keep his identity secret. This woman, rejected by everyone, is not rejected by the Messiah, and she cannot contain her excitement at her newfound role as a messenger of the gospel (S1E8).

Later, we are presented with one of the most striking stories in the life of Jesus, and again, it is a juxtaposition of two things happening at the same time that demonstrate significance in the narrative. The story is set up through an encounter with Simon's wife, Eden, where we meet Veronica, a woman who suffers from severe bleeding that makes her ritually unclean. Ironically, she is presented as a washer woman who takes in laundry as a means of provision. The rags she washes are likened to her life that, despite many attempts, cannot be made whole or clean. Yet she has heard of the healer from Nazareth, and if she can just get to him, she believes he will be the key to her wholeness and restoration. We bear witness to the flow of her blood and the ways people reject and fear her. But when she pushes through the crowd, collapses, and grasps at the hem of Jesus's garment, he is physically reactive. Stating that power has gone out from him, he asks who touched him. The crowd around Jesus is large, and there is a lot of physical contact, but this encounter is different. She responds that it was she who touched him—but just his hem—so she has not made him ritually unclean. This woman knows the law, perhaps better than most, given her circumstances. Once again, Jesus commands a woman he is addressing to "look up!" He calls her, "My daughter!" When she demurs, he corrects her: she is a daughter of the Most High. It was not his garment that healed her but rather her faith, her belief that Jesus could heal her that makes her clean. But it is in Jesus's response to her healing that he also tells her that she has blessed him in that moment. He then touches her on the face.

Veronica suffered for twelve years with a malady that made her an outcast, but her story is presented in tandem with that of another young woman, the twelve-year-old daughter of Jairus, an administrator in the local synagogue (see Matt 9:18–26; Mark 5:21–43; Luke 8:40–56). When his daughter falls ill, Jairus knows Jesus can restore his child to health. It is on the way to Jairus's home that Jesus is confronted by Veronica, and as a result of that delay, they are too late, and the little girl has died. Where Veronica was unclean in life, Jairus's daughter is now unclean because of death. Yet Jesus is not turned away by either situation. Again, he commands, "Do not be afraid!" and speaks directly to the little girl, "Little lamb . . . arise!" She is not dead but sleeping, he says. As the episode concludes, we resume the story of Veronica, who is cleansing herself in the sea with Tamar and Mary Magdalene caring for her (S3E5).

While these examples are just a portion of the narrative structure that highlights the stories of women in *The Chosen*, they are indicative of many such interactions featured throughout the first several seasons. Female characters seem to have a special intuition about who Jesus is and how he can uniquely change their lives and stations. Both with characters we know from Scripture and those invented for the series, there is a special relationship that differs from that of the male characters and how they engage the person of Jesus. Even Joanna (S3E1) and Pilate's wife (S3E6), both Roman women whose lives intersect with Jesus in a more indirect manner, are portrayed as having heightened curiosity about the man from Nazareth. Many other women mentioned in the Gospels have appeared only briefly (e.g., Mary and Martha), if at all (Anna the prophetess, the Canaanite woman with the demon-possessed daughter, the widow of Nain), in the first three seasons, and one suspects they may receive attention later in the series.

Revealing Motive through Coherence and Fidelity

In examining these characters' interactions with Jesus and engaging in pentadic analysis of each element of the narrative, it becomes clear that the *agent*, Jesus, is the central figure upon whom the drama is dependent. However, the second element that stands out is that of the *purpose*. Rhetoric that centers on purpose is focused on the question of "Why?" What is the goal of this rhetorical action? Throughout the first three seasons of *The Chosen*, we see that profound rhetorical engagement is the purpose of Jesus's interaction with everyone he encounters. Yes, he is the dominant figure for whom the entire narrative is dependent, but it is the purpose of his life and ministry that impels him to engage with such significant outcomes, particularly with the marginalized and the outcast. According to Burke's dramatistic theory, rhetoric that centers around *purpose* has an implied mysticism. Taken together with the emphasis on the *agent*, which demonstrates an idealism, we see why the rhetoric of *The Chosen* is so powerful. There is an idealism and a mysticism to this story that sets up a powerful mechanism by which those who are engaged in the rhetorical act cannot help but be changed and transformed. In this transformation, they become part of the grand narrative that elevates them beyond their culture, their station, and their humanity to something more. As the audience, we too are transformed and desire to know more and to have our own encounters with this man Jesus and engage him in the realization of his purposes. In Burke's terms, the motive of the creators of *The Chosen* is to enable us to see ourselves in the lives and relationships these characters have with Jesus, especially the women.

Does *The Chosen* also rise to meet the tests of an effective story? Narrative coherence is demonstrated repeatedly, even outside of the framework of the scriptural accounts because the plausible fictional components do not contradict the textual details or the theological constraints of Scripture. At one point, when the women are discussing their learning of Torah with the male disciples, it is Ramah who exclaims to Thomas that they are not trying to be teachers; they just want to learn about who the Scriptures say this Messiah is (S2E2)! While there is much debate among various Christian denominations about the role of women as teachers and leaders, there is no dispute that women are to come to salvation through a relationship with Jesus just as men are. Such rhetorical moments perhaps hint at the theological boundaries of the program, but they also allow the audience to find that the narrative rings true and is, in Burke's terms, humane to the audience.

Narrative fidelity is also manifest in the ways in which the story holds together. The constant juxtapositions of characters, timelines, and scriptural texts make the narrative believable. Even in the narrative of those characters for whom we know nothing from the Bible, their place in the story of

The Chosen adds to its believability. We see this especially in the way Eden's story arc is highlighted next to the story of her husband, Simon Peter, walking on the water. As both are separately immersed in dark waters, what it is that they both need is Jesus himself. We know the story of Simon, but the subplot with Eden—the loss of a child, the required faith and trust to move to a place of healing—resonates through the example of both the husband and the wife. Their immersion in water and their coming out are expressions of dependence on the Savior to heal them (S3E8).

· Conclusion

While *The Chosen* is presented as historical fiction, the powerful ways in which the writers engage the audience in rhetorical action allows the narrative to demonstrate idealism and a mysticism that invites the audience into the story of Jesus in a more meaningful way. Specifically, by portraying Jesus's relationship to women as one that is deep and personal while also elevating their status and position beyond their ordinary circumstances enables the audience to also think differently about those who are marginalized and often discounted. It demonstrates the upside-down nature of the kingdom of God that is not constrained by the culture or the era of time. *The Chosen* accomplishes this through an insightful narrative that does not shy away from the challenges of women in this time and place, but also does not conflict with what viewers know from the Bible about the person and ministry of Jesus.

Notes

CHAPTER 1

1. Quoted in Thomas Bonifield, "Harsh Criticism of 'The Chosen' Draws Emotional Response from Dallas Jenkins," *Christian Film Blog*, May 29, 2021, https://tinyurl.com/4ffzzfkv.

2. This statement occurs in the novelization of the first season of the television show by Jerry B. Jenkins, *The Chosen: I Have Called You by Name*, book 1 (Savage, MN: BroadStreet, 2021), 7. A shorter such note is found among the unnumbered introductory pages of the novelizations of the second and third seasons: "*The Chosen* was created by lovers of and believers in the Bible as Jesus Christ. Our deepest desire is that you delve into the New Testament Gospels for yourself and discover Jesus."

3. While I am utilizing "authenticity" and "accuracy" as roughly synonymous, I am aware that some people make nuanced distinctions between these terms. See, for example, Laura Saxton, "A True Story: Defining Accuracy and Authenticity in Historical Fiction," *Rethinking History* 24 (2020): 127–44. Saxton defines "accuracy" as the extent to which a story is consistent with the facts in evidence and "authenticity" as the impression of accuracy as assessed by the audience. Thus, for Saxton, "authenticity" is closer to what I mean by "plausibility."

4. See Michael John Petty, "This Is What Sets 'The Chosen' Apart from Other Faith-Based Projects," *Collider*, October 14, 2023, https://tinyurl.com/ynbyvuu6; Rusty Wright, "Why Is The Chosen, a Show about Jesus, So Popular?," *Washington*

Examiner, January 11, 2022, https://tinyurl.com/yj2ne2mt; and Brett McCracken, "4 Reasons Why 'The Chosen' Works," *The Gospel Coalition*, May 23, 2020, https://tinyurl.com/2wxn485f.

5. Differentiating between "true," "true-ish," "false-ish," "false," and "unknown," the *Information Is Beautiful* website (https://tinyurl.com/kzj6pvt7) has published an infographic that visually displays a scene-by-scene assessment of how faithful select Hollywood films are to their true-life source material. *The Chosen* is not among the examples.

6. Furthermore, there is little complaint that *The Chosen* is being subtitled and even dubbed in other modern-day languages. As of January 2024, season 1 of *The Chosen* had been dubbed in twelve languages and had available subtitles in another sixty-two languages. The goal is to have the whole show available in six hundred languages (one hundred dubbed and another five hundred with subtitles), and the Come and See Foundation (www.comeandseefoundation.org) is raising funds to make this possible.

7. Regarding the legitimacy of translating the Bible from its original languages of Hebrew and Aramaic in the Old Testament and Greek in the New Testament, see Jonathan Downie, "Your Bible Translation Is Imperfect. It's Also a Miracle: We've Forgotten That Translation Was God's Idea from the Start," *Christianity Today* 63 (September 2019): 58–62.

8. A recent study indicates that audiences evaluate a story as more plausible when the label "based on true events" is attached to an atypical storyline; conversely, when the storyline is considered typical, the truth-based label does little to increase its plausibility; see Francesa Valsesia, Kristin Diehl, and Joseph C. Nunes, "Based on a True Story: Making People Believe the Unbelievable," *Journal of Experimental Social Psychology* 71 (2017): 105–10.

9. The modern BC/AD (BCE/CE) calendar system was constructed in AD 525 by Dionysius Exiguus of Scythia Minor (a.k.a., "Dionysius the Humble" or "Dennis the Short") but was not widely used until after AD 800. Unfortunately, Dionysius's system assumes that Jesus was born after Herod the Great's death, which is dated in his system to 4 BC. But Matt 1–2 clearly indicates that Herod the Great was alive when Jesus was born, and that he ordered children two years old and younger to be killed in an attempt to destroy Jesus. Thus—allowing for the same two-year window that Herod did (see Matt 2:16)—Jesus's birth must be dated as occurring sometime between 6 and 4 BC. Given that there was no year 0, Dionysius's system is off by three to five years. Sadly, by the time Dionysius's error was recognized in the early 1600s, it was too late to correct the system.

10. For a brief but helpful discussion of these dating matters, see Mark L. Strauss, *Four Portraits, One Jesus: An Introduction to Jesus and the Gospels*, 2nd ed. (Grand Rapids: Zondervan Academic, 2019), 492–96.

11. While generally chronological, the Gospels are largely collections of Jesus stories with differing outlines and none claiming a strict chronology of events. Thus, we are not always certain about the precise chronological order of the various episodes. The Gospel of John has the most deictic indicators of order, that is, those little words that designate sequence (e.g., "He did this, and afterward he did that"; "Then the next day he went there"; etc.). But as discovered by those who have tried to produce harmonies of the Gospels, following the Gospel of John does not solve all the problems, as it does not have all the same stories as the Synoptic Gospels. In fact, apart from the resurrection, there is only one miracle story that all four gospels have in common: the feeding of the five thousand. Utilizing the CSB English translation and creating a forty-day reading experience, *The Chosen* has produced its own harmony of the Gospels: Steve Laube, Amanda Jenkins, and Dallas Jenkins, *The Chosen Presents: A Blended Harmony of the Gospels* (Savage, MN: BroadStreet, 2022).

12. In fact, timeline compression is so common in storytelling that the film industry celebrates when a TV show creates an episode that is one long take, that is, that is filmed without any breaks at all and where, for example, twenty minutes in the filming of the show takes exactly twenty minutes to watch.

13. Never mind that the real location of Cana is uncertain today. For another travel example, in S3E1 of *The Chosen*, Andrew travels from Capernaum to visit John the Baptist imprisoned at Machaerus and then returns—a roundtrip journey of something like 180 miles—but viewers might miss the fact that a week or ten days passes when they see Andrew back on the scene with the other disciples just a few minutes later in the episode.

14. To be sure, protestors are correct when they point out that the New Testament does not say Matthew was autistic. As far as I know, the concept of autism was not formulated until early in the twentieth century by the German psychiatrist Eugen Bleuler, who is also responsible for the concept of schizophrenia. See Bonnie Evans, "How Autism Became Autism," *History of the Human Sciences* 26 (2013): 3–31. But of course, it is rather implausible to suggest that such conditions as autism and schizophrenia did not exist until after the terms were invented.

15. No one wonders whether the "you" of the New Testament letters were real people in the first century with names even as the inclusive "we"/"us" of Paul's letters

included himself and his sometimes explicitly named amanuensis (e.g., Timothy in Col 1:1–12), and sometimes also his original audience (e.g., the Colossian believers in Col 1:13–14). And yet I suspect that Paul himself would invite any reader of his letters to identify themselves as part of the "you" of his comments no matter what language they speak or what century they live in.

16. All quotations of Scripture in this chapter are from the ESV.

17. In fact, from one point of view, it seems a bit counterintuitive to suggest that only imperfect people can prepare sermons and that a perfect person could not prepare a sermon. If a perfect person like Jesus could take six days to prepare the universe as a member of the Trinity in creation (see John 1:1–3; Col 1:16), why couldn't he take a few hours to prepare a sermon?

18. Faydra Shapiro, "Why This Jew Is Binge-Watching 'The Chosen' (and Maybe You Should Too)," *Pittsburgh Jewish Chronicle*, May 25, 2023, https://tinyurl.com/4ncw35hv; see also Mira Fox, "Hit Christian TV Show 'The Chosen' Is All about Jesus. So Why Is It So Jewish?," *Forward*, April 7, 2023, https://tinyurl.com/3c8rh4fs.

Chapter 2

1. See, for example, Melissa Camacho, "Parents' Guide to *The Chosen*," *Common Sense Media*, https://tinyurl.com/pajaxfkw; Peter T. Chattaway, "Review: *The Chosen: Season One* (Dir. Dallas Jenkins, 2019)," *FilmChat*, last modified August 25, 2022, https://tinyurl.com/5xdvambp; and Chris DeVille, "Christian America's Must-See TV Show," *Atlantic*, last modified June 28, 2021, https://tinyurl.com/5yse25p3.

2. Maurice F. Wiles, *The Spiritual Gospel: The Interpretation of the Fourth Gospel in the Early Church* (Cambridge: Cambridge University Press, 1960), esp. 41–64. On ancient Christian artwork, see Robin M. Jensen, *Understanding Early Christian Art*, 2nd ed. (New York: Routledge, 2024). Perhaps the most interesting expansion on the text of John's Gospel can be found in the noncanonical Gospel of Nicodemus (sometimes called the Acts of Pilate), which was enormously popular in the Middle Ages.

3. Unfortunately, Origen's comments on this passage are not extant, so I refer neither to him nor to the earlier work of Heracleon, whose gnostic commentary Origen discusses.

4. Craig R. Koester, "Messianic Exegesis and the Call of Nathanael (John 1.45–51)," *Journal for the Study of the New Testament* 39 (1990): 23–34, suggests that John

intends Jesus's comment to evoke Old Testament texts about fig trees, especially those with messianic import.

5. Biblical quotations in this chapter follow the ESV. Most commentators, ancient and modern, have taken Nathanael's statement at face value, but John K. Stafford, "The Call of Nathanael: John 1:49; A Rhetorical-Theological Study," *Perichoresis* 11 (2013): 199–210, suggests that Nathanael may have actually been sarcastic in this moment, growing out of his disbelief in Nazareth as the source of something good and responding to Jesus's apparent use of Old Testament eschatological language. According to Stafford, Jesus accepts Nathanael's confession as truth, and then the author of the gospel uses this rhetorically as "the apposition of limited human understanding and transcendent knowledge, yet claimed by and for Jesus in the Gospel" (203–4).

6. See Chris H. Knights, "Nathanael and Thomas: Two Objectors, Two Confessors—Reading John 20:24–29 and John 1:44–51 in Parallel," *Expository Times* 125 (2014): 328–32, on the parallels between Nathanael's and Thomas's sudden confessions of Jesus's lordship.

7. See *Tractate* 7 on John's Gospel in Augustine of Hippo, *Homilies on the Gospel of John 1–40*, ed. Allan D. Fitzgerald, trans. Edmund Hill, The Works of Saint Augustine: A Translation for the 21st Century III/12 (Hyde Park, NY: New City, 2009), esp. 163–67. The literature on spiritual/figural readings in the early church is voluminous; two excellent starting points are Frances M. Young, *Biblical Exegesis and the Formation of Christian Culture* (Cambridge: Cambridge University Press, 1997), esp. part 3; and John J. O'Keefe and R. R. Reno, *Sanctified Vision: An Introduction to Early Christian Interpretation of the Bible* (Baltimore: Johns Hopkins University Press, 2005), esp. chs. 4–5.

8. Theodore of Mopsuestia, *Commentary on the Gospel of John*, ed. Joel C. Elowsky, trans. Marco Conti, Ancient Christian Texts (Downers Grove, IL: IVP Academic, 2010), 25.

9. Cyril of Alexandria, *Commentary on John*, vol. 1, ed. Joel C. Elowsky, trans. David R. Maxwell, Ancient Christian Texts (Downers Grove, IL: IVP Academic, 2013), 88.

10. Moshe bar Kepha, *Der Kommentar des Moses bar Kepha*, part 2, *Übersetzung, Joh 1,1–10,21*, trans. Lorenz Schlimme (Wiesbaden: Harrassowitz, 1978), 151; John Chrysostom, *Commentary on Saint John, the Apostle and Evangelist, Homilies 1–47*, trans. Thomas Aquinas Goggin, Fathers of the Church 33 (Washington, DC: Catholic University of America Press, 1957), 198, in his homily 20; Nonnus of Nisibis,

Commentary on the Gospel of Saint John, trans. Robert W. Thomson, Writings from the Islamic World (Atlanta: SBL Press, 2014), 35.

11. Chrysostom, *Commentary on Saint John*, 198.

12. Nonnus, *Commentary*, 35.

13. Johan Hofstra, "Some Remarkable Passages in Isho'dad of Merw's Commentary on the Gospel of St. John," *Parole de l'Orient* 35 (2010): 12–18.

14. Isho'dad of Merw, *Commentary on the Gospel of John*, 2 vols., ed. and trans. Johan D. Hofstra, CSCO Scriptores Syri 259–60 (Leuven: Peeters, 2019), 2:26.

15. As commentators, ancient and modern, have noted, Nathanael's confession of faith does not mean that he gains a high position among the apostles (cf. the story of Simon Peter's confession in Matt 16). In fact, it is unclear whether Nathanael eventually becomes one of the Twelve at all; Augustine, *Tractate* 7.17, assumes that Nathanael does not become part of the Twelve but that this is intentional on Jesus's part to show that he chose lowlier people, "thereby to put the world to shame" (in Augustine, *Homilies*, 160). Traditionally, Nathanael has been conflated with Bartholomew, since the latter's name appears with Philip's in the New Testament lists (Matt 10:2–4; Mark 3:14–19; Luke 6:13–16), and since "Bartholomew" looks like a version of an Aramaic patronymic (something like "bar Tolmai"). Isho'dad is familiar with this identification; the beginning of his comment on Nathanael and the fig tree reads, "They hand down that Nathanael—that is to say, Bar Tolmi. . . ." (Hofstra, "Some Remarkable Passages," 13). For more on this question, see C. E. Hill, "The Identity of John's Nathanael," *Journal for the Study of the New Testament* 67 (1997): 45–61.

16. Nathanael's frankness is a theme that the screenwriters exploit in the episodes after this one, as is Nazareth's poor reputation.

17. This characterization continues into future seasons. In all, pejorative comments about Nazareth are made in S1E2, S1E5, S2E2, S2E5, S2E7, S2E8, S3E8, S4E1, S4E7, and S4E8.

18. Cyril, *Commentary*, 88.

19. Bede the Venerable, *Homilies on the Gospels, Book One: Advent to Lent*, trans. Lawrence T. Martin and David Hurst, Cistercian Studies 110 (Athens, OH: Cistercian, 1991), 170. His comment that Nazareth has a great name does not refer to any fame on the part of the village, but rather that he connects "Nazareth" with the Latin word *nazareus* (a word for "flower") and then links it with texts such as Song 2:1 and Isa 11:1 (the latter with a Latin text that diverges from the Vulgate, which uses the more common *flos*).

20. *Tractate* 7.15 in Augustine, *Homilies*, 159.

21. Chrysostom, *Commentary on Saint John*, 196. Other writers from the Syrian tradition give a similar interpretation—for example, Nonnus, *Commentary*, 33.

22. Ephrem the Syrian, *Saint Ephrem's Commentary on Tatian's Diatessaron: An English Translation of Chester Beatty Syriac MS 709 with Introduction and Notes*, trans. Carmel McCarthy, Journal of Semitic Studies Supplement 2 (Oxford: Oxford University Press, 1993), 93; Moshe bar Kepha, *Kommentar*, 147.

23. Theodore, *Commentary*, 24.

24. Cyril, *Commentary*, 88.

25. Augustine is the exception here in that he understands Nathanael's sinfulness as one of the matters about which Jesus is "giving testimony" (see *Tractate* 7.16–22 in *Homilies*, 159–65).

26. Ephrem, *Saint Ephrem's Commentary*, 93; cf. Moshe bar Kepha, *Kommentar*, 147–49. On whether Nathanael may actually have been a scribe himself, see Tjitze Baarda, "Nathanael, 'the Scribe of Israel': John 1,47 in Ephraem's Commentary on the Diatessaron," *Ephemerides Theologicae Lovanienses* 71 (1995): 321–36.

27. For example, Theodore of Mopsuestia, *Commentary*, 25, and Nonnus, *Commentary*, 34.

28. Cyril, *Commentary*, 88–89. Similarly, Bede (*Homilies, Book One*, 171) suggests that Nathanael is not questioning but affirming the possibility of the Christ's coming from Nazareth: Nathanael "did not delay devoting himself to the one who had been proclaimed to him," and as a result, Jesus responded quickly in order "to satisfy his desire with good things" and "repaid" him with praise.

29. Chrysostom, *Commentary on Saint John*, 198.

30. Here I will focus on the angels ascending and descending. For more on the "greater things" of which Jesus speaks, see William R. G. Loader, "John 1:50–51 and the 'Greater Things' of Johannine Christology," *Anfänge der Christologie: Festschrift für Ferdinand Hahn zum 65. Geburtstag*, ed. Cilliers Breytenbach and Henning Paulsen (Göttingen: Vandenhoeck & Ruprecht, 1991), 255–74.

31. Nonnus, *Commentary*, 35. See also Moshe bar Kepha, *Kommentar*, 155; Chrysostom, *Commentary on Saint John*, 203; Theodore, *Commentary*, 26.

32. Moshe bar Kepha (*Kommentar*, 155–56) pointed to times angels are specifically mentioned in Jesus's life in the Gospels. Theodore (*Commentary*, 26) suggested angels were present in Jesus's passion events. Chrysostom (*Commentary on Saint John*, 203) added Jesus's crucifixion to the list of angelic events, even though one of the gospel texts describes angels being present at the cross. Perhaps Chrysostom had in mind the words from Ps 91:11–12 (that God "will command his angels concerning

you; on their hands they will bear you up, so that you will not dash your foot against a stone"), Jesus's own statement in Matt 26:53 (that he had at his disposal legions of angels, ready to save him from his tribulation), or the brief note in Luke 22:43 (that an angel was with him on the Mount of Olives, ministering to him).

33. For example, Augustine (*Tractate* 7.22–23 in Augustine, *Homilies*, 165–67) saw the angels (literally, "messengers") as preachers exalting Christ's divinity ("ascending") and humbling themselves ("descending"). Similarly, for Bede (*Homilies, Book One*, 174) the ascension of the angels occurs when people preach about Jesus's divinity, and their descent when they teach about his humanity. Step'anos Siwnets'i (an Armenian contemporary of Bede) took "ascending" to mean going to the heavenly storehouse to acquire wisdom, and "descending" to mean coming "back down" in order to share that wisdom with others; cf. Step'anos Siwnets'i, *The Four Evangelists*, trans. Michael B. Papazian (New York: SIS, 2014), 289.

34. Unlike some modern historical-critical methodologies, modern literary approaches have more in common with the ancient interpreters under discussion here, particularly for their attention to the text's creative elements; see, for example, Marianne Meye Thompson, *John: A Commentary* (Louisville: Westminster John Knox, 2015).

35. O'Keefe and Reno, *Sanctified Vision*, 12.

36. Bede, *Homilies, Book One*, 168. This view of the intentionality of scriptural language and syntax goes back at least as far as Origen. Young (*Biblical Exegesis*, 22) expresses Origen's thinking as follows: "Those who desire to devote themselves to study should not let a single letter pass without examination and enquiry. If you cannot see how it fits, you should not imagine that it has no purpose."

37. James L. Papandrea, *Reading the Early Church Fathers: From the Didache to Nicaea* (New York: Paulist, 2012), 126.

Chapter 3

1. Bertrand Russell, *The Problems of Philosophy* (New York: Oxford University Press, 1912), 155.
2. Brie Gertler, "In Defense of Mind-Body Dualism," in *Reason and Responsibility: Readings in Some Basic Problems of Philosophy*, ed. Joel Feinberg and Russ Shafer-Landau, 13th ed. (Belmont, CA: Thomson/Wadsworth 2007), 303–15.
3. Gertler, "In Defense of Mind-Body Dualism," 305.
4. Alvin Plantinga, *God, Freedom, and Evil* (Grand Rapids: Eerdmans, 1977), 28.

5. J. L. Mackie, "Evil and Omnipotence," *Mind* 64 (1955): 200–212.

6. There are exceptions, but they are rare. One recent exception is James P. Sterba, *Is a Good God Logically Possible?* (London: Palgrave Macmillan, 2019). For an extended discussion of this topic, see Dolores G. Morris, *Believing Philosophy: A Guide to Becoming a Christian Philosopher* (Grand Rapids: Zondervan Academic, 2021), chs. 9–11.

7. See Daniel Howard-Snyder, ed., *The Evidential Argument from Evil* (Bloomington: Indiana University Press, 1996).

8. Charity Anderson, "Divine Hiddenness, Defeated Evidence," *Royal Institute of Philosophy Supplement* 81 (2017): 120.

9. Most notably, see a book-length defense of the argument in J. L. Schellenberg, *The Hiddenness Argument: Philosophy's New Challenge to Belief in God* (Oxford: Oxford University Press, 2015).

10. For example, Michael C. Rea, *The Hiddenness of God* (Oxford: Oxford University Press, 2018); Charity Anderson, "Divine Hiddenness: An Evidential Argument," *Philosophical Perspectives* 35 (2021): 5–22.

11. Rea, *Hiddenness of God*, 90.

12. To be precise, the standard argument does not rule out every kind of hiddenness. Schellenberg (*Hiddenness Argument*, 17) grants that God's *ways* might be hidden from us. Because, as I will note, the various ways in which God seems hidden all contribute to the kind of hiddenness with which Schellenberg is concerned, I am taking the liberty of speaking loosely here.

13. In this verse, God is hiding himself from the wicked. Elsewhere, Job laments his inability to find God (Job 23:3), as does the psalmist (Ps 13:1).

14. All quotations of Scripture in this chapter are from the NIV.

15. Theists who respond to the problems of evil and hiddenness by appealing to our limited understanding of God's ways are called—for reasons I don't quite understand—*skeptical theists*. See, for example, Stephen J. Wykstra, "Rowe's Noseeum Arguments from Evil," in *The Evidential Argument from Evil*, ed. Daniel Howard-Snyder (Bloomington: Indiana University Press, 1996), 126–50.

16. Dolores G. Morris, "Weaker Assertion→ Stronger Argument," *The Gospel Coalition*, March 8, 2023, https://tinyurl.com/yjhe9cm6.

17. Nathan L. King, *The Excellent Mind: Intellectual Virtues for Everyday Life* (Oxford: Oxford University Press, 2021), 115.

18. Travis Kerns, "'The Chosen' and the Sufficiency of Scripture," *G3 Blog*, February 1, 2023, https://tinyurl.com/yc3tseh5.

Chapter 4

1. For example, Friedrich Hayek speaks of "the individualist tradition which has created Western civilization" (*The Road to Serfdom* [Chicago: University of Chicago Press, 1965], 20). Colin Morris likewise speaks of western individualism as "an eccentricity among cultures" (*The Discovery of the Individual, 1050–1200* [Toronto: University of Toronto Press, 1987], 2)

2. See, for example, G. K. Chesterton, *Orthodoxy* (London: Lane, 1908), esp. ch. 8, "The Romance of Orthodoxy."

3. David Tracy, *The Analogical Imagination: Christian Theology and the Culture of Pluralism* (New York: Seabury, 1981).

4. Tracy, *Analogical Imagination*, 104.

5. Andrew M. Greeley, *The Catholic Imagination* (Berkeley: University of California Press, 2000).

6. See Karal Ann Marling, *Merry Christmas! Celebrating America's Greatest Holiday* (Cambridge: Harvard University Press, 2000), 44–45.

Chapter 5

1. Westminster Assembly, "The Shorter Catechism," in *The Westminster Confession of Faith and Catechisms* (Lawrenceville, GA: Christian Education & Publications, 2007), Q&A 1.

2. Thomas Aquinas, *Summa Theologica*, trans. Fathers of the English Dominican Province (New York: Benziger Brothers, 1911–1925), 2-1.44.1.

3. Todd W. Hall (with Miriam Elizabeth Lewis Hall), *Relational Spirituality: A Psychological-Theological Paradigm for Transformation* (Downers Grove, IL: IVP Academic, 2021), 11–42.

4. M. Elizabeth Lewis Hall, "What Are Bodies For? An Integrative Examination of Embodiment," *Christian Scholar's Review* 39 (2010): 171–72.

5. Brian A. Primack, Ariel Shensa, Jaime E. Sidani, Erin O. Whaite, Liu Yi Lin, Daniel Rosen, Jason B. Colditz, Ana Radovic, and Elizabeth Miller, "Social Media Use and Perceived Social Isolation among Young Adults in the U.S.," *American Journal of Preventive Medicine* 53 (2017): 1–8.

6. Sara Konrath, "The Empathy Paradox: Increasing Disconnection in the Age of Increasing Connection," in *Handbook of Research on Technoself: Identity in a Technological Society*, ed. Rocci Luppicini (Hershey, PA: IGI Global, 2012), 204–28;

Christopher Terry and Jeff Cain, "The Emerging Issue of Digital Empathy," *American Journal of Pharmaceutical Education* 80 (2016): 58.

7. All quotations of Scripture in this chapter are from the ESV.

8. M. Elizabeth Lewis Hall, Eric Silverman, Shane J. Sacco, Crystal Park, Jason McMartin, Kelly Kapic, Laura Shannonhouse, Jamie Aten, and Lindsay M. Snow, "Intimacy with God: Development of an Emic Christian Measure and Relationship to Well-Being," *Journal of Psychology and Christianity* 41 (2022): 36–53.

9. Hall, "What Are Bodies For?," 165–66.

10. John Bowlby, *Attachment*, vol. 1 of *Attachment and Loss* (New York: Basic Books, 1969).

11. Lee A. Kirkpatrick and Phillip R. Shaver, "Attachment Theory and Religion: Childhood Attachments, Religious Beliefs, and Conversion," *Journal for the Scientific Study of Religion* 29 (1990): 315–34; A. Birgegard and P. Granqvist, "The Correspondence between Attachment to Parents and God: Three Experiments Using Subliminal Separation Cues," *Personality and Social Psychology Bulletin* 30 (2004): 1122–35; Marie-Therese Proctor, "The God Attachment Interview Schedule: Implicit and Explicit Assessment of Attachment to God" (PhD diss., University of Western Sydney, 2006).

12. Todd W. Hall and Beth Brokaw, "The Relationship of Spiritual Maturity to Level of Object Relations Development and God Image," *Pastoral Psychology* 43 (1995): 373–91; Hall, *Relational Spirituality*, 138–73.

13. Jane R. Dickie, A. L. Eshleman, Dawn M. Merasco, Amy Shepard, Michael Vander Wilt, and Melissa J. Johnson, "Parent-Child Relationships and Children's Images of God," *Journal for the Scientific Study of Religion* 36 (1997): 25–43.

14. Pehr Granqvist, Tord Ivarsson, Anders G. Broberg, and Berit Hagekull, "Examining Relations among Attachment, Religiosity, and New Age Spirituality Using the Adult Attachment Interview," *Developmental Psychology* 43 (2007): 590–601.

15. Daniel J. Siegel, *The Developing Mind: How Relationships and the Brain Interact to Shape Who We Are*, 3rd ed. (New York: Guilford, 2020), 169–72.

16. Matthew is portrayed as someone on the autism spectrum. Research has demonstrated that people with autism are more likely to develop avoidant attachment, perhaps because of the disruptions autism presents to parent-child attachment. See Elena Gallitto and Craig Leth-Steenson, "Autistic Traits and Adult Attachment Styles," *Personality and Individual Differences* 79 (2015): 63–67.

17. Daniel Kahneman, *Thinking, Fast and Slow* (New York: Farrar, Straus and Giroux, 2011), 19–30; Hall, *Relational Spirituality*, 97–137.

18. Hall, *Relational Spirituality*, 97–137.

19. Wilma Bucci, Bernard Masit, and Sean Murphy, "Connecting Emotions and Words: The Referential Process," *Phenomenology and the Cognitive Sciences* 15 (2016): 359–83.

20. Hall, *Relational Spirituality*, 233–40.

21. Alice Y. Kolb and David A. Kolb, "Learning Styles and Learning Spaces: Enhancing Experiential Learning in Higher Education," *Academy of Management Learning & Education* 4 (2005): 193–212; Margot Pearson and David Smith, "Debriefing in Experience-Based Learning," in *Reflection: Turning Experience into Learning*, ed. David Boud, Rosemary Keogh, and David Walker (London: Routledge, 1985), 69–84.

Chapter 6

1. Adrian Ashford, "'The Chosen' Creator Dallas Jenkins on Hit Christian Show's Success, North Texas Set," *Dallas Morning News*, January 25, 2024, https://tinyurl.com/2n8x2nxe.

2. See Paul J. Pastor, "Dallas Jenkins: Seeing in the Dark," *Outreach Magazine*, July 11, 2023, https://tinyurl.com/ypm682ce. Jenkins explicitly cites Aristotle's analysis of drama, explaining that "it also happens to be a great framework to understand the story of the Gospels, the story of the Bible, God's story of humanity."

3. In his desire to be true to the biblical stories in his own retelling of those stories, Jenkins works in ostensive parallel with the biblical authors themselves. For both Jenkins and the Bible's own storytellers, the desire is to present what Hans W. Frei has called a "realistic narrative." According to Frei, "realistic narrative, if it is really seriously undertaken and not merely a pleasurable or hortatory exercise, is a sort in which style as well as content in the setting forth of didactic material, and in the depiction of characters and action, the sublime or at least serious effect mingles inextricably with the quality of what is casual, random, ordinary, and everyday. The intercourse and destinies of ordinary and credible individuals rather than stylized or mythical hero figures, flawed or otherwise, are rendered in realistic narratives. Furthermore, they are usually rendered in ordinary language" (*The Eclipse of Biblical Narrative: A Study in Eighteenth and Nineteenth Century Hermeneutics* [New Haven: Yale University Press, 1974], 14–15).

4. Frei, *Eclipse of Biblical Narrative*, 11.

5. As an illustrative contrast with modern hermeneutical methods, Lewis Ayres

observes that Christians in the patristic period did not make the methodological distinction between exegesis and theology that one finds in modern scholarship. Because "the narrative structure of faith shaped Christian discussions of human nature and transformation in teleological directions," according to Ayres, "Christian narratives thus also shaped epistemological concerns.... In the divinely governed drama of redemption Christians explore and debate the transformation that constitutes Christian life by attention to the scriptural text." See Lewis Ayres, *Nicaea and Its Legacy: An Approach to Fourth-Century Trinitarian Theology* (Oxford: Oxford University Press, 2004), 38–39.

6. Adolf von Harnack, *What Is Christianity?*, trans. Thomas Bailey Saunders (Philadelphia: Fortress, 1986), 12.

7. Justin Taylor, "An Interview with Dallas Jenkins on the First Multi-Season Drama about the Life of Christ," *The Gospel Coalition*, December 17, 2018, https://tinyurl.com/2exsrny2.

8. One might identify a fourth misguided approach to biblical renarration, namely, those uses that trivialize the Bible's art form by exploiting and repurposing its narrative elements for ends either dissonant with or opposed to that of the biblical stories themselves. This approach is typically political or commercial in intention, the latter of which often producing results that one might call cheesy. In fact, "cheesy" is a term Jenkins himself uses as something he means assiduously for *The Chosen* to avoid. See Ashford, "'The Chosen' Creator Dallas Jenkins."

9. Norm Macdonald, *Based on a True Story* (New York: Random House, 2016), 21. Of course, Macdonald was not speaking of the various ways one might approach Scripture. He was, though, telling a story.

10. Alasdair MacIntyre, *After Virtue*, 2nd ed. (Notre Dame: University of Notre Dame Press, 1984), 216.

11. MacIntyre, *After Virtue*, 218. See also Alasdair MacIntyre, *Whose Justice? Which Rationality?* (Notre Dame: University of Notre Dame Press, 1988), 349–69.

12. See esp. Alasdair MacIntyre, *Three Rival Versions of Moral Enquiry: Encyclopaedia, Genealogy, and Tradition* (Notre Dame: University of Notre Dame Press, 1990).

13. Here I am largely in methodological agreement with George A. Lindbeck, who commended a theology that "redescribes reality within the scriptural framework rather than translating Scripture into extrascriptural categories" (*The Nature of Doctrine: Religion and Theology in a Postliberal Age*, 25th anniversary ed. [Louisville: Westminster John Knox, 2009], 104). According to Lindbeck, "It is the text, so to speak, which absorbs the world, rather than the world the text."

14. See the claim, expressed in Vatican II's *Dogmatic Constitution on Divine Revelation*, that Scripture is the "foundation" of sacred theology (*Dei Verbum* §24), the principal character of the Bible being Jesus Christ "who fully reveals humanity to itself" (*Gaudium et Spes* §22).

15. Matthew Levering, *Scripture and Metaphysics: Aquinas and the Renewal of Trinitarian Theology*, Challenges in Contemporary Theology (Oxford: Blackwell, 2004), 241.

16. See Lindbeck, *Nature of Doctrine*, 99–110.

17. See the collection of essays on narrative theology in Stanley Hauerwas and L. Gregory Jones, eds., *Why Narrative? Readings in Narrative Theology* (Eugene, OR: Wipf & Stock, 1997), esp. the essay by Nicholas Lash, ("Ideology, Metaphor, and Analogy," 113–37). See also Garrett Green, ed., *Scriptural Authority and Narrative Interpretation* (Minneapolis: Fortress, 1987).

Chapter 7

1. All quotations of Scripture in this chapter are from the ESV.

2. Hannah Le Cras, "The Chosen and the Word," *TGC*, December 1, 2023, https://tinyurl.com/3wb8c24z.

3. The Synoptic Gospels do not include the raising of Lazarus. Raymond Brown, *The Gospel according to John I–XII*, AB 29 (Garden City, NY: Doubleday, 1966), 1:429, discusses the prominence John ascribes to the raising of Lazarus as the decisive event prompting the march toward Jesus's death.

4. *Embrimaomai* has been used for "the snorting of horses," which suggests a quality of physical expression to this troubled state. For a discussion of how this term can connote both grief and anger, see Edward Klink, *John*, ZECNT (Grand Rapids: Zondervan, 2016), 507–8.

5. For example, Craig Keener, *The Gospel of John: A Commentary*, 2 vols. (Grand Rapids: Baker Academic, 2003), 2:846. Keener considers this the most fitting interpretation in view of Jesus's troubled anger in 11:33, 38. Jesus responds to the unbelief of those whom he expects to have it, comparing it to God's anger at Israel's unbelief amid his signs (Num 14:11). See also Rudolf Bultmann, *The Gospel of John: A Commentary*, trans. G. R. Beasley-Murray (Philadelphia: Westminster, 1971), 406.

6. Some find this theory unlikely, observing that Jesus's anger would be an unprecedented response since John's Gospel never portrays Jesus as impatient with

unbelief anywhere else; cf. Dorothy Lee, "Emotion, Beauty, and the 'Sublime' in the Gospel of John," *Australian Biblical Review* 71 (2023): 9.

7. Herman Ridderbos, *The Gospel of John: A Theological Commentary* (Grand Rapids: Eerdmans, 1997), 402–3; Marianne Thompson, *John: A Commentary* (Louisville: Westminster John Knox, 2015), 248–49; Klink, *John*, 508.

8. Frederick Dale Bruner, *The Gospel of John* (Grand Rapids: Eerdmans, 2012), 676, states, "The world's (and the Church's) anguish in the experience of death breaks Jesus' heart. The deep pain that death and the devil (who uses death so mercilessly) both bring to human hearts breaks Jesus' heart."

9. When this moment was addressed on *The Chosen* "Season 4, Episode 7 Aftershow" (https://tinyurl.com/3zxuj6m8), the actors recognized that while sometimes the nuances of a scene might allude to a particular intended meaning, often it can be variously interpreted by audiences.

10. Keener, *John*, 2:845, briefly suggests Jesus's grief in 11:33 is understandable given his impending death, citing 12:27; 13:21. Lee, "Emotion," 9, observes a "deeper level of grief and anger" extending beyond the Lazarus scene, citing parallels between Lazarus's tomb and Jesus's coming death, which suggests that Jesus may already consider himself marching toward the cross.

11. Brown, *John*, 1:429, observes how "the supreme miracle of giving life to man leads to the death of Jesus," which offers a "dramatic paradox" to round out Jesus's ministry.

12. John Chrysostom, "Sermon LXIII," in *Homilies* (London: Smith, 1883), 558; David Ford, *The Gospel of John: A Theological Commentary* (Grand Rapids: Baker Academic, 2021), 225. Brown, *John*, 1:435, points out that the same word (Greek: *tarassō*) used in Jesus's grief over Lazarus (John 11:33, 38) also expresses his grief anticipating Judas's betrayal (13:21) and the disciples' grief over Jesus's coming death (14:1, 27).

13. For more detailed descriptions of funerary customs, see Jeannine M. Hanger, *Sensing Salvation in the Gospel of John* (Leiden: Brill, 2023), 123.

14. N. T. Wright, *The Resurrection of the Son of God* (Minneapolis: Fortress, 2003), 443, suggests there would not be any smell since Jesus's prayer for Lazarus to remain "uncorrupt" was answered.

15. Brown, *John*, 1:427, observes that the verb John uses (*kraugazō*) occurs only eight times in the Greek Bible (six occurrences in John). Four times it describes the crowds calling for Jesus's crucifixion (John 18–19), which leads Brown to suggest a

contrast between the crowds shouting for Jesus's death and Jesus's shout bringing Lazarus to life.

16. For example, in Matt 26:6–13 and Mark 14:3–9, the woman pours the perfume over Jesus's head instead of his feet. For further comparison of these passages, see Jeannine M. Hanger, *Engaging Jesus with Our Senses: An Embodied Approach to the Gospels* (Grand Rapids: Baker Academic, 2024), 141–42.

17. Keener, *John*, 2:864.

18. Dominika Kurek-Chomycz, "The Fragrance of Her Perfume: The Significance of Sense Imagery in John's Account of the Anointing in Bethany," *Novum Testamentum* 52 (2010): 337.

19. Kurek-Chomycz, "Fragrance," 334–35. She also points out how Martha's mention of the stench of death is only one of four negative references to smell in the entire New Testament (Phil 4:18; 2 Cor 2:14–16; Eph 5:2).

20. Jane Webster, *Ingesting Jesus: Eating and Drinking in the Gospel of John* (Atlanta: Society of Biblical Literature, 2003), 93.

21. Lee, "Emotion," 11.

22. For a more detailed discussion of this dynamic, see Hanger, *Engaging Jesus with Our Senses*, 176–77.

Chapter 8

1. Rob Kuznia, "Nearly 10,000 Students See 'Schindler's List' in Free Educational Screenings," USC Shoah Foundation, December 5, 2018, https://tinyurl.com/4353cfdz; "Teach about Selma," *Teaching for Change*, June 18, 2017, https://tinyurl.com/9mcnmjdv.

2. Felicity Harley-McGowan, "The Passion," in *Routledge Handbook of Early Christian Art*, ed. Robin Jensen and Mark Ellison (London: Routledge, 2018), 290–93.

3. The proposed height of the cross is based on the average height of males and the dimensions of the Puteoli graffito; see Joan E. Taylor, *What Did Jesus Look Like?* (London: Bloomsbury, 2018), 158–60.

4. Emma Jones, "The Chosen: The Christian-Funded Hit about Jesus Taking the US by Storm," *BBC*, January 24, 2024, https://tinyurl.com/yc4n85jn.

5. Julia Duin, "Who Is Jesus? How Pop Culture and Makers of 'The Chosen' Help Define His Life amid Few Biographical Details," *Newsweek*, June 13, 2022, https://tinyurl.com/nuusnzba.

6. David Robb, "Jordan Walker Ross Says His Disability Took His Character on 'The Chosen' to New Level," *Deadline*, April 22, 2021, https://tinyurl.com/2em4c6ct.

7. E. Mary Smallwood, *The Jews under Roman Rule from Pompey to Diocletian: A Study in Political Relations*, 2nd ed. (Leiden: Brill, 1981), 151–52.

8. This trend has been seen for decades. See, e.g., Neil Postman, *Amusing Ourselves to Death: Public Discourse in the Age of Show Business* (New York: Penguin, 1985).

9. Patrick Gray, "Teaching the Bible with Film," in *Teaching the Bible through Popular Culture and the Arts*, ed. Mark Roncace and Patrick Gray, Resources for Biblical Study 53 (Atlanta: Society of Biblical Literature, 2007), 88–89.

10. "Director Ava DuVernay on sharing the story of 'Selma' and deconstructing American heroes," *PBS News*, January 8, 2015, https://tinyurl.com/57uwzh3b.

11. Quoted in Scott C. Esplin and Matthew J. Grey, "From Scripture to Screen: Films Depicting Jesus and the World of the New Testament," *Review Magazine*, winter 2021, https://tinyurl.com/yyww7trf.

12. This archive is available at https://tinyurl.com/4by7ehmx.

13. Morgan Jones, "Dallas Jenkins: Behind the Scenes of 'The Chosen,'" *All In* (podcast), July 29, 2020, https://tinyurl.com/bddfy7z4.

Chapter 9

1. For a representative sample of this criticism from the Catholic side (I am a Catholic theologian), see Leila Miller, "The False Christ of *The Chosen*," *Crisis Magazine*, February 19, 2024, https://tinyurl.com/3rf37na3.

2. Dallas Jenkins, creator and director of *The Chosen*, in the global livestream for S4E5 on June 16, 2024, put the matter this way in response to a viewer's question: "The canon, the world of our show [*The Chosen*], is its own world and we don't want to imply that our world is the accurate world and separate from the Bible, right? So, the Bible is where you're going to get history and truth.... The show is a TV show and it is inspired by truth, it is inspired by capital 'T' Truth and lowercase truth, but the majority of the show did *not* actually happen. The majority of the dialogue is not from history or the Bible. This is a piece of art, and so I want to make sure [that viewers] treat it that way." This video in its entirety was posted at https://tinyurl.com/28rcr9c8 (with the foregoing comments beginning at 1:56:11); it has since been edited and significantly pared down and so no longer shows these remarks by Jenkins.

3. See Augustine, *De diversis quaestionibus 83*, q. 80 (CCSL 44A, 236–37); and Thomas Aquinas, *Summa theologiae*, III.5.2 and 5.3.

4. For more on Docetism, see Fernando Ocáriz, Lucas F. Mateo-Seco, and José Antonio Riestra, *The Mystery of Jesus Christ: A Christology and Soteriology Textbook*, trans. Michael Adams and James Gavignon (Portland: Four Courts, 2011), 55–58. As the authors note, "Docetism was not a clearly defined sect. It was rather a tendency to be found in many sects, particularly Gnostic ones.... These [docetic] errors ... derive partly from Manichaean and Gnostic doctrines which regarded matter and more specifically the human body as something evil and therefore totally inappropriate for God to assume" (55–56).

5. All quotations of Scripture in this chapter are from the RSV.

6. See *Decrees of the Ecumenical Councils*, 2 vols., ed. Norman P. Tanner (Washington, DC: Georgetown University Press, 1990), 1:24.

7. *Decrees*, 1:86.

8. *Decrees*, 1:86.

9. For my publications on Christ's humanity, see *The Passions of Christ's Soul in the Theology of St. Thomas Aquinas* (Münster: Aschendorff, 2002); "Aquinas on Christ's Male Sexuality as Integral to His Full Humanity: Anti-Docetism in the Common Doctor," in *Thomas Aquinas and the Crisis of Christology*, eds. Michael Dauphinais, Andrew Hofer, OP, and Roger Nutt (Ave Maria, FL: Sapientia, 2021), 195–232; "The Maleness of Christ," in *The Clerical Sex Abuse Scandal: An Interdisciplinary Analysis*, ed. Jane F. Adolphe and Ronald J. Rychlak (Providence: Cluny, 2020), 347–63; "St. Thomas Aquinas, the Communication of Idioms, and the Suffering of Christ in the Garden of Gethsemane," in *Divine Impassibility and the Mystery of Human Suffering*, ed. James F. Keating and Thomas Joseph White, OP (Grand Rapids: Eerdmans, 2009), 214–45; "The Humanity of Christ, the Incarnate Word," in *The Theology of Thomas Aquinas*, ed. J. Wawrykow and R. van Nieuwenhove (Notre Dame: University of Notre Dame Press, 2005), 252–76; and "Anti-Docetism in Aquinas' *Super Ioannem*: St. Thomas as Defender of the Full Humanity of Christ," in *Reading John with St. Thomas Aquinas: Theological Exegesis and Speculative Theology*, ed. M. Dauphinais and M. Levering (Washington, DC: Catholic University of America Press, 2005), 254–76.

10. I borrow this phrase from Pope Benedict XVI. See Joseph Ratzinger/Pope Benedict XVI, *From the Baptism in the Jordan to the Transfiguration*, vol. 1 of *Jesus of Nazareth*, trans. Adrien J. Walker (New York: Image, 2007), 178. The passage, which matches closely with what we see depicted throughout *The Chosen*, merits

to be cited in its entirety: "We may presume that all of the Twelve were believing and observant Jews who awaited the salvation of Israel. But in terms of their actual opinions, of their thinking about the way Israel was to be saved, they were an extremely varied group. This helps us to understand how difficult it was to initiate them gradually into Jesus' mysterious new way, of the kinds of tension that had to be overcome."

11. In the global livestream for this episode on June 16, 2024, Dallas Jenkins acknowledges that it was Jonathan Roumie, the actor who plays Jesus, who recommended this line, "Also human" (https://tinyurl.com/28rcr9c8).

12. Miller, "False Christ of *The Chosen*," is fairly representative of this criticism.

13. In his short metaphysical treatise, *De ente et essentia*, ch. 5, Thomas Aquinas argues that risibility is an attribute following upon human rationality, that is, upon our rational soul or form, just as binary sexual difference (maleness and femaleness) marks an attribute that proceeds upon our animallike bodiliness (i.e., upon our matter).

14. In the global livestream for S4E8 on June 30, 2024, Dallas Jenkins invoked the self-emptying nature of the incarnation (kenotic Christology) that the Christ hymn of Philippians proclaims (Phil 2:6–11, esp. vv. 6–7) as a way of justifying the show's depicting Jesus having limited knowledge. While such a move is certainly theologically sound, the two-natures doctrine provides a more metaphysically or ontologically robust way of arguing the case. Indeed, even Jenkins himself is not immune to a momentary lapse into a kind of epistemological Monophysitism, as evidenced by his remark during the same livestream: "We [at *The Chosen*] portray Jesus as not one hundred percent of the time having one hundred percent full omniscience." This statement stands in need of slight emendation, since Jesus, in his human intellect (the intellect that served him in his earthly ministry), at no time ever enjoyed full omniscience—not even one percent of the time, to employ the terminology that Jenkins uses. This video in its entirety was posted at https://tinyurl.com/mpnd2k5h (with the foregoing comments beginning at 2:16:36); it has since been edited and significantly pared down and so no longer shows these remarks by Jenkins.

Chapter 10

1. All Scripture citations, unless otherwise noted, are from the RSV (emphasis added).

2. See Brendan Byrne, *Life Abounding: A Reading of John's Gospel* (Collegeville, MN: Liturgical Press), 53: "This theophany at Sinai provides a dramatic scriptural

background and contrast to the Cana miracle, which ends ... with the comment that here Jesus 'revealed his glory.'"

3. For the Sinai covenant as the "wedding of God and Israel," see Jon D. Levenson, *Sinai and Zion: An Entry into the Jewish Bible* (New York: HarperOne, 1987), 75–80.

4. *Mekhilta de-Rabbi Ishmael: A Critical Edition, Based on the Manuscripts and Early Editions*, trans. Jacob Z. Lauterbach, 2nd ed., 3 vols. (Philadelphia: Jewish Publication Society of America, 2004), 2:306.

5. For an extensive treatment of this theme, see Edward Sri, *Queen Mother: A Biblical Theology of Mary's Queenship* (Steubenville, OH: Emmaus Road, 2005). See also Brant Pitre, *Jesus and the Jewish Roots of Mary: Unveiling the Mother of the Messiah* (New York: Image, 2018), 74–86.

6. See the example of Bathsheba in 2 Kgs 2:12–25.

7. There is irony here in that Mary is the mother of the true bridegroom.

8. The Hebraism, "What is this to me and to you?" has three possible meanings according to Raymond Brown, *The Gospel according to John I–XII* (New York: Doubleday, 1966), 99. The first two meanings involve "some refusal of an inopportune involvement, and a divergence between the views of the two persons concerned." However, one meaning includes hostility to the asking party (e.g., Judg 11:12; 2 Chr 35:21; 1 Kgs 7:18; Mark 1:24), whereas the other includes simply a disengagement (e.g., 2 Kgs 3:13; Hos 14:8). Brown points to a third meaning that suggests that the concern is neither that of the one asking nor the one asked (e.g., 2 Sam 16:10). Brown excludes this meaning and opts for the second because Jesus mentions "*my hour.*" Yet Jesus's hour is also Mary's hour (Luke 2:34–35).

9. I am drawing here from Brant Pitre, *Jesus the Bridegroom: The Greatest Love Story Ever Told* (New York: Image, 2014), 39–45.

10. The Samaritan woman is not named in the biblical text. Photina is her name according to Eastern Christian traditions.

11. This mutual animosity dates back to the construction of a temple on Mount Gerizim ca. 400 BC and the Samaritans' refusal to recognize Jerusalem as the site of the only legitimate temple. See Colin G. Kruse, *The Gospel according to John: An Introduction and Commentary* (Grand Rapids: Eerdmans, 2004), 137–38.

12. According to Paul M. Hoskins, *Jesus as the Fulfillment of the Temple in the Gospel of John*, PBM (Milton Keyes: Paternoster, 2006; repr., Eugene, OR: Wipf & Stock, 2007), 119, John 1:14 "suggests that the incarnate Word fulfills an expectation whose fulfillment was expected to occur in the new Temple."

13. See Hoskins, *Jesus as the Fulfillment*, 125: "the glory of the Word" in John 1:14 "verifies that he [Jesus] takes the place of the Tabernacle and the Temple as the locus for the manifestation of the glory of God to his people."

14. Mary L. Coloe, *God Dwells with Us: Temple Symbolism in the Fourth Gospel* (Collegeville, MN: Liturgical Press, 2001), 206.

15. See Scott W. Hahn, "Temple, Sign, and Sacrament: Towards a New Perspective on the Gospel of John," *Letter and Spirit* 4 (2008): 107–43. Hahn remarks, "Arguably, the first image that this bloody stream from Christ would evoke for a first-century Jew was the brook Kidron, which flowed along the base of the Temple Mount. The brook was connected to the Temple altar by a guttering system that channeled down the enormous amounts of blood from the thousands of Passover lambs being slaughtered, producing a torrent of bloody water" (133).

16. Coloe, *God Dwells with Us*, 207.

17. See Johannes Beutler, *A Commentary on the Gospel of John*, trans. Michael Tait (Grand Rapids: Eerdmans, 2017), 121: "This has nothing to do with purely inner worship without liturgical assembly of the community, rites, and ministers, but with worship of the end time." See also Benny Thettayil, *In Spirit and Truth: An Exegetical Study of John 4:19–26 and a Theological Investigation of the Replacement Theme in the Fourth Gospel*, CBET 46 (Leuven: Peeters, 2007), 164: "Worship in Spirit and truth does not mean that all external forms of worship are rejected at the coming of Jesus. Rather, the emphasis here is on being in the person of Jesus in opposition to any geographical limitation of the worship of God." Brown, *John I–XII*, 180, similarly observes, "His statement has nothing to do with worshiping God in the inner recesses of one's own spirit; for the Spirit is the Spirit of God, not the spirit of man."

18. J. P. Heil, *The Gospel of John: Worship for Divine Life Eternal* (Eugene, OR: Cascade Books, 2015), 40.

Chapter 11

1. J. R. R. Tolkien did make illustrations of his creations, but only one appeared in the original edition of *The Lord of Rings* (London: Allen & Unwin, 1954–1955). It was not until after his death that the extent of his drawings and painting related to his writing became widely known. See Wayne Hammond and Christina Scull, *J. R. R. Tolkien: Artist and Illustrator* (London: HarperCollins, 1995). Peter Jackson worked primarily from the art of Alan Lee, whose illustrations appeared in the 1991 edition of *The Lord of the Rings* (published by Houghton Mifflin).

2. Section 6. For the text of the entire letter, see "Letter of His Holiness Pope John Paul II to Artists," https://tinyurl.com/27cd86bm.

3. John Paul II, "Letter to Artists," section 10.

4. Some scholars distinguish the "Jesus of history" from the "real Jesus." The former is that Jesus assessable by historiography, and the latter is the Jesus who lived a fully human life in a particular time and place. While I accept the usefulness of keeping in mind the limits of our reach into the past, it is nevertheless the case that the "real Jesus" is the object of historical research. It is not insignificant that this Jesus is also the object of Christian faith.

5. All translations in this chapter are from the NABRE.

6. Avery Dulles, *A History of Apologetics* (Washington, DC: Corpus Instrumentorum, 1971; repr., Eugene, OR: Wipf & Stock, 1999), 51–59.

7. Charles Talbert has provided judicious selection from Reimarus's massive original text in Herrmann Samuel Reimarus, *Fragments* (Minneapolis: Fortress, 1979). An even shorter version can be found in "The Gospels as Fraud," in *The Historical Jesus Quest: Landmarks in the Search for the Jesus of History*, ed. Gregory W. Dawes (Louisville: Westminster John Knox, 1999), 54–86.

8. This story has been told many times, but perhaps the most thorough is the two-volume work of Colin Brown (with Craig A. Evans), *A History of the Quests for the Historical Jesus* (Grand Rapids: Zondervan Academic, 2022).

9. Albert Schweitzer, *The Quest of the Historical Jesus: A Critical Study from Reimarus to Wrede*, trans. W. Montgomery (New York: Macmillan, 1957), 399.

10. Hilarin Felder, *Christ and the Critics: A Defense of the Divinity of Christ against Modern Sceptical Criticism*, 2 vols., trans. John L. Stoddard (New York: Benziger Brothers, 1924), 2:444.

11. Bultmann's masterwork here is his 1931 *Die Geschichte der synoptischen Tradition* (*The History of the Synoptic Tradition*, rev. ed., trans. John Marsh [London: Blackwell, 1971]).

12. Bultmann's most accessible presentation of this idea is found in *Jesus Christ and Mythology* (New York: Scribner's Sons, 1958).

13. The entirety can be found in Ernst Käsemann, "Re-opening the Quest," in Dawes, *Historical Jesus Quest*, 279–313; the translation is from Käsemann, *Essays on New Testament Themes*, trans. W. J. Montague (London: SCM, 1964), 15–47.

14. Käsemann, "Re-opening the Quest," 299, 310.

15. This conclusion was made most pointedly by Günther Bornkamm, *Jesus of*

Nazareth, trans. Irene McLuskey, Fraser McLuskey, and James M. Robinson (New York: Harper & Row, 1959).

16. Respectively, Edward Schillebeeckx, *Jesus: An Experiment in Christology*, trans. Hubert Hoskins (New York: Crossroad, 1979); Burton Mack, *A Myth of Innocence: Mark and Christian Origins* (Minneapolis: Fortress, 1988); John Dominic Crossan, *The Historical Jesus: The Life of a Mediterranean Jewish Peasant* (New York: HarperCollins, 1991).

17. Robert W. Funk, a professor of New Testament at the University of Montana, founded the Jesus Seminar in 1985. The idea was to gather exegetes and have them vote with differently colored beads—red for authentic, pink for authentic with reservations, gray for traces of authenticity, and black for "Jesus did not say this." This procedure is explained in Robert W. Funk, Bernard Brandon Scott, and James R. Butts, eds., *The Parables of Jesus: Red Letter Edition; A Report of the Jesus Seminar* (Salem, CA: Polebridge, 1988), ix–xv.

18. John P. Meier, *The Mission of Christ and His Church: Studies in Christology and Ecclesiology*, Good News Studies 30 (Wilmington, DE: Glazier, 1990), 34.

19. John P. Meier, *The Roots of the Problem and the Person*, vol. 1 of *A Marginal Jew: Rethinking the Historical Jesus* (New York: Doubleday, 1990), 6–9.

20. N. T. Wright, *Jesus and the Victory of God*, vol. 2 of *Christian Origins and the Question of God* (Minneapolis: Fortress, 1996), 87–88.

21. The best sustained modern argument for the Gospels, including John, having their origins in eyewitness testimony is Richard Bauckham, *Jesus and the Eyewitnesses*, 2nd ed. (Grand Rapids: Eerdmans, 2017). See also the provocative essays in Anthony Giambrone, *A Quest for the Historical Christ: Scientia Christi and the Modern Study of Jesus* (Washington, DC: Catholic University of America Press, 2022).

Chapter 12

1. For text and discussion, see J. K. Elliott, ed., *The Apocryphal New Testament* (Oxford: Clarendon, 1993), 3–16.

2. All quotations of Scripture in this chapter are from the NRSV.

3. Scholars debate the nature and significance of these "we passages," arguing variously that they indicate a first-person source or a convention found in ancient literary texts and thus without historical value. See, for example, Sean A. Adams, "The Relationships of Paul and Luke: Paul's Letters and the 'We' Passages of Acts,"

in *Paul and His Social Relations*, ed. Stanley E. Porter and Christopher D. Land (Leiden: Brill, 2013), 125–42.

4. Zachary K. Dawson, "Henry J. Cadbury and the Composition of Luke-Acts," in *Further Essays on Enduring Methods*, vol. 3 of *Pillars in the History of Biblical Interpretation*, ed. Stanley E. Porter and Zachary K. Dawson (Eugene, OR: Pickwick, 2021), 181.

5. Michael F. Bird, *The Gospel of the Lord: How the Early Church Wrote the Story of Jesus* (Grand Rapids: Eerdmans, 2014), 217.

6. Jean Owens Schaefer, "Saint Luke as Painter: From Saint to Artisan to Artist," in *Artistes, artisans, et production artistique au Moyen Âge*, ed. Xavier Barrai i Altet (Paris: Picard, 1986), 413–27.

7. Many such manuscripts survive from the Middle Ages. See Georgi Parpulov, *Middle-Byzantine Evangelist Portraits: A Corpus of Miniature Paintings* (Berlin: de Gruyter, 2022).

8. This tradition goes back at least to the fifth century, in the Acts of John by Prochorus. See R. Alan Culpepper, *John, the Son of Zebedee: The Life of a Legend* (Columbia: University of South Carolina Press, 1994), 303.

9. See M. R. James, *The Apocryphal New Testament* (Oxford: Clarendon, 1924), 187–93; James M. Robinson, ed., *The Nag Hammadi Library in English* (Leiden: Brill, 1998), 104–23.

10. See, for example, Paul J. Achtemeier, *The Inspiration of Scripture: Problems and Proposals* (Philadelphia: Westminster, 1980).

11. It is not made clear how long after the death. There is a note of melancholy, which might indicate that the interviews take place on Holy Saturday before Jesus rises from the grave, but other hints suggest that any sadness is a longing to have Jesus in their company as he was before the cross.

Chapter 13

1. The quotation is from Isa 43:1, as delivered by Jesus in this episode of *The Chosen*. All other quotations of Scripture in this chapter are from the NIV.

2. A personal favorite comes in S3E6, where Big James attempts to remember Joanna's name and says the name "Junia" instead, a subtle reference to the Junia mentioned by Paul in Rom 16:7 and the argument made by some scholars that Joanna and Junia might have been the same person. See, for example, Richard Bauckham,

Gospel Women: Studies in the Named Women of the Gospels (Grand Rapids: Eerdmans, 2002), 165–86.

3. *Confessions* 1.1 (trans. Maria Boulding).

4. Charles Taylor, *A Secular Age* (Cambridge: Belknap, 2007). A more accessible introduction to Taylor's thesis on the secular and its impact on Christian belief can be found in James K. A. Smith, *How (Not) to Be Secular: Reading Charles Taylor* (Grand Rapids: Eerdmans, 2014).

5. Taylor says that this new dominant social imaginary, which he labels "the immanent frame," is "something which permits closure [to the transcendent], without demanding it"; see Taylor, *Secular Age*, 544. So, it is possible to live in a secular age and remain open to transcendent interference, but the point of secularism is that it is also possible today to conceive of the world as purely natural, purely immanent, something that was virtually unthinkable only five centuries ago.

6. T. S. Eliot, *Four Quartets* (New York: Harcourt, 1943), 17.

7. Daniel Payne, "Anxiety and Depression Is Spiking among Young People: No One Knows Why," *Politico*, April 10, 2024, https://tinyurl.com/2dzxu6pt.

8. Access to the full report is available at https://tinyurl.com/33tb7v8k.

9. See Erin Smith and Daniel Payne, "What's Driving the Youth Mental Health Crisis? We Asked 1,400 Clinicians," *Politico*, April 10, 2024, https://tinyurl.com/42td6r8h. See also Jonathan Haidt, *The Anxious Generation: How the Great Rewiring of Childhood Is Causing an Epidemic of Mental Illness* (New York: Penguin, 2024).

10. Hartmut Rosa, *Social Acceleration: A New Theory of Modernity*, trans. Jonathan Trejo-Mathys (New York: Columbia University Press, 2013).

11. Rosa, *Social Acceleration*, 71–80.

12. Hartmut Rosa, *Resonance: A Sociology of Our Relationship to the World*, trans. James C. Wagner (Cambridge: Polity, 2019).

13. Rosa, *Resonance*, 184.

14. Rosa, *Resonance*, 163, 174. Rosa notes the meaning of the two terms "affect" (from Latin ad*facere* or af*ficere*—to do *to*) and *emotion* (from Latin e*movere*—to move out *from*).

15. Rosa, *Resonance*, 157.

16. Rosa, *Resonance*, 285, states, "*What we experience as beauty is the expression of the possibility of a resonant relationship to the world, a possible mode of being-in-the-world in which subject and world respond to each other.*"

17. See the roundtable discussion between Dallas Jenkins, Ryan Swanson (one of the show's writers), and Elizabeth Tabish (the actor who portrays Mary Magdalene) at https://tinyurl.com/8zmu92dk.

CHAPTER 14

1. Alice Von Hildebrand, *Remnant of Paradise: Selected Essays*, ed. John Henry Crosby (Steubenville, OH: Hildebrand, 2023), 67.

2. In a recent interview, Jonathan Roumie offers us a clue to his method: "I try to gently receive the encounter with the spirit of Jesus." The actor goes on to say, "I've been put here to play this character for a reason, I believe. And if that's to allow people to get closer to their faith and to develop a relationship with God, then what more could I ask for as an actor? How many times in an actor's career do you get an opportunity to have a real tangible impact on someone's life?" ("Jonathan Roumie: *The Chosen* 'Makes Me Want to Be a Better Version of Myself,'" *Movieguide*, February 2, 2024, https://tinyurl.com/ybcyhyt9).

3. For a thorough account of personalism in all its forms, see Thomas D. Williams and Jan Olof Bengtsson, "Personalism," *The Stanford Encyclopedia of Philosophy*, April 27, 2022, https://tinyurl.com/3v5a2vbz.

4. Karol Wojtyła [Pope John Paul II], "Subjectivity and the Irreducible in the Human Being," in *Person and Community: Selected Essays*, trans. Theresa Sandok, Catholic Thought from Lubin 4 (New York: Lang, 1993), 213.

5. Gabriel Marcel, *Faith and Reality*, vol. 2 of *The Mystery of Being*, trans. Rene Hague (Chicago: Regnery, 1951), 13.

6. Susan Selner-Wright, "Thomistic Personalism and Creation Metaphysics," *Studiea Gilsoniana* 7 (2018): 469–85.

7. Wojtyła, "Subjectivity and the Irreducible," 213.

8. Karol Wojtyła, *Love and Responsibility* (San Francisco: Ignatius, 1993), 41. Wojtyła points to this as the "personalistic norm" and considers it the premise underlying Jesus's commandment to love at Matt 22:36–40.

9. *Gaudium et spes* §24. This statement from the Documents of Vatican II (1965) is said to be definitive of the personalism at work in the Gospels and thus in church teaching.

10. Wojtyła, "Subjectivity and the Irreducible," 11. For a more complete account of Wojtyła's anthropology, see Deborah Savage, "The Place of Lived Experience in Karol Wojtyła's Account of the Person," *Wojtyła Studies* 1 (2024): 41–77.

Notes to Pages 155–167

11. See especially Karol Wojtyła's *Person and Act,* available in Antonio López et al., eds., *Person and Act and Related Essays,* vol. 1 of *The English Critical Edition of the Works of Karol Wojtyła/John Paul II,* trans. Grzegorz Ignatik (Washington, DC: Catholic University of America Press, 2021).

12. All quotations from Scripture in this chapter are from the RSV.

13. See Etienne Gilson, *Being and Some Philosophers* (Toronto: Pontifical Institute of Mediaeval Studies, 1949), 4–89. This is a reference to the real distinction made by Aquinas between essence and existence and provides an important point of contact between Wojtyła and Aquinas. See Wojtyła, "Thomistic Personalism," *Person and Community,* 165–75, esp. 170–71.

14. Thomas Aquinas, *Quaestiones disputatae de veritate* XXI, 2.

15. Selner-Wright, "Thomistic Personalism and Creation Metaphysics," 469–85.

16. Karol Wojtyła, *Faith according to St. John of the Cross,* trans. Jordan Aumann (San Francisco: Ignatius, 1981), 237–61.

17. Thomas Aquinas, *Summa theologiae* II-II.4.2.

18. Wojtyła, *Faith according to St. John of the Cross,* 237, 245, 264.

19. Roco Buttiglione, *The Thought of the Man Who Became Pope: John Paul II* (Grand Rapids: Eerdmans, 1997), 46–47.

20. See Wojtyła, *Faith according to St. John of the Cross,* 237–61.

21. George Weigel, *Witness to Hope: The Biography of John Paul II* (New York: Harper Collins, 1999), 86.

22. C. S. Lewis, "The Weight of Glory," *Theology* 43 (1941): 10.

Chapter 15

1. See "Universal Declaration of Human Rights," United Nations, https://tinyurl.com/5e4wpbea.

2. John F. Crosby, *The Personalism of John Paul II* (Steubenville, OH: Hildebrand, 2019), ix.

3. Martin Luther King Jr., "Letter from Birmingham Jail," in *Why We Can't Wait* (New York: Signet, 1964), 81–82.

4. Andrea Dworkin, *Letters from a War Zone* (Brooklyn: Lawrence Hill Books, 1993), 119.

5. Phillips Brooks, *The Influence of Jesus,* The Bohlen Lectures (New York: Dutton, 1879), 38–39.

6. See especially Brooks, *Influence of Jesus,* 37–39.

7. Phillips Brooks, "The Value of the Human Soul," in *Lectures on Preaching* (New York: Dutton, 1877), 256–57.

8. Dallas Willard, "The Soul Series, Part 2: The Sufficiency of God to Your Soul," Dallas Willard Ministries, 2019, https://tinyurl.com/3j4wmbmu.

9. Phillips Brooks, *Seeking Life and Other Sermons* (London: Macmillan, 1905), 134–35.

10. See Virgilio Elizondo, *Galilean Journey: The Mexican-American Promise*, rev. ed. (Maryknoll, NY: Orbis Books, 2000), esp. 57–58, 63, 81, 87, 93, 100, 122, and 128.

11. Elizondo, *Galilean Journey*, 57.

12. Goran Medved, "The Fatherhood of God in the Old Testament," *KAIROS—Evangelical Journal of Theology* 10 (2016): 212–13. Medved notes that God is said to be the Father of corporate Israel in Exod 4:22–23; Deut 1:31; 8:5; 14:1; 32:6; Isa 43:6; 63:8, 16; 64:8; Jer 3:4–22; 31:9–20; Hos 11:1–4; and Mal 1:6; 2:10; 3:17. God is said to be the Father of King David in 2 Sam 7:14 and 1 Chr 17:13.

13. Elizondo, *Galilean Journey*, 57–58.

14. Catherine L. McDowell, "In the Image of God He Created Them: How Genesis 1:26–27 Defines the Divine-Human Relationship and Why It Matters," in *The Image of God in an Image Driven Age: Explorations in Theological Anthropology*, ed. Beth Felker Jones and Jeffrey W. Barbeau (Downers Grove, IL: InterVarsity Press, 2016), 30.

15. See Meredith G. Kline, *Kingdom Prologue: Genesis Foundations for a Covenantal Worldview* (Overland Park, KS: Two Age, 2000; repr., Eugene, OR: Wipf & Stock, 2006), 45.

16. Kline, *Kingdom Prologue*, 45, as cited in Catherine L. McDowell, *The Image of God in the Garden of Eden: The Creation of Humankind in Genesis 2:5–3:24 in Light of the mīs pî pīt pî and wpt-r Rituals of Mesopotamia and Ancient Egypt* (Winona Lake, IN: Eisenbrauns, 2015), 132.

17. McDowell, *Image of God in the Garden of Eden*, 131.

18. McDowell, "In the Image of God He Created Them," 29.

19. The material in this paragraph is drawn from McDowell, "In the Image of God He Created Them," 38–39n29.

20. McDowell, "In the Image of God He Created Them," 39n29.

21. Catherine L. McDowell, "Human Identity and Purpose Redefined: Gen. 1:26–28 and 2:5–25 in Context," *Advances in Ancient Biblical and Near Eastern Research* 1 (2021): 43.

22. Henry Churchill King, *The Moral and Religious Challenge of Our Times: The*

Guiding Principle in Human Development; Reverence for Personality (New York: Macmillan, 1911), 206.

23. I thank Dolores Morris for alerting me to this worry.

24. See also Matt 9:20–22; Mark 5:25–34.

Chapter 16

1. My transcription from "The Women of the Chosen," https://tinyurl.com/2n r2ndmj. All transcriptions used in this chapter have been lightly edited to remove incomplete thoughts with the goal of making it more reader friendly.

2. See, for example, Phyllis Trible, "Depatriarchalizing in Biblical Interpretation," *Journal of the American Academy of Religion* 41 (1973): 30–48; Elisabeth Schüssler Fiorenza, *In Memory of Her: A Feminist Theological Reconstruction of Christian Origins*, 10th anniversary ed. (New York: Crossroad, 1983); and Lilly Nortjé-Meyer, "Retrieving the Voices of Women Sages in the New Testament and Early Christianity," *Journal of Early Christian History* 8 (2018): 1–6.

3. See J. Cheryl Exum, "Feminist Criticism: Whose Interests Are Being Served?," in *Judges and Method: New Approaches in Biblical Studies*, ed. Gale A. Yee, 2nd ed. (Minneapolis: Fortress, 2007), 66–67.

4. Gaye Strathearn and Angela Cothran, "Naomi, Ruth, and Boaz: Borders, Relationships, Law, and Ḥesed," in *Covenant of Compassion: Caring for the Marginalized and Disadvantaged in the Old Testament*, ed. Avram Shannon et al. (Provo, UT: Deseret Book, 2021), 184–85. Some scholars have argued that the book of Ruth in its canonical form serves to support the Davidic storyline. See, for example, Gale A. Yee, "Ruth," in *Fortress Commentary on the Bible: The Old Testament and Apocrypha*, ed. Gale A Yee, Hugh R. Page Jr., and Matthew J. M. Coomber (Minneapolis: Fortress, 2014), 351. Nevertheless, others argue that it may have originated in a female community. See, for example, Fokkelien van Dijk-Hemmes, "Ruth: A Product of Women's Culture?," in *A Feminist Companion to Ruth*, ed. Athalya Brenner, Feminist Companion to the Bible 3 (Sheffield: Sheffield Academic, 1993), 134–39. Some have also argued that other biblical texts may have been written by women. See, for example, Alice Ogden Bellis, *Helpmates, Harlots, and Heroes: Women's Stories in the Hebrew Bible* (Louisville: Westminster John Knox, 2007), 29, 193; Athalya Brenner and Fokkelien van Dijk-Hemmes, *On Gendering Texts: Female and Male Voices in the Hebrew Bible* (Leiden: Brill, 1993).

5. Judith Plaskow, *Standing Again at Sinai: Judaism from a Feminist Perspective* (San Francisco: HarperOne, 1991), 1–2.

6. Plaskow, *Standing Again at Sinai*, 2, emphasis added.

7. Unless otherwise noted, all biblical quotations come from the English Standard Version (ESV).

8. In the account of the creation of humans in Gen 2:18, 20, however, we have the additional information that the creation of woman was a divinely mandated "helper fit" for Adam. On this terminology, see Rebekah Call, "What Is a 'Helpmate'? Using Comparative Semitic Linguistics to Propose New Translations for *Ezer Kenegdo*" (PhD diss., Claremont Graduate University, 2023); Phyllis Trible, "Depatriarchalizing in Biblical Interpretation," *Journal of the American Academy of Religion* 41 (1973): 30–48.

9. For a discussion of the pivotal roles that Sarah, Rebekah, Leah, and Rachel play "as determiners of who receives the Israelite Deity's promise," see Tammi J. Schneider, *Mothers of Promise: Women in the Book of Genesis* (Grand Rapids: Baker Academic, 2008), 10–100.

10. There is a reconfiguring of the tribes, with Joseph's two sons given equal portions in the place of the Levites (Josh 13:33; 14:4).

11. Plaskow, *Standing Again at Sinai*, 1–2.

12. Sheena Orr, "Women and Livelihoods in 1st Century Palestine: Exploring Possibilities," *Expository Times* 121 (2010): 539–47; Tal Ilan, *Jewish Women in Greco-Roman Palestine* (Peabody, MA: Hendrickson, 1996); Lynn H. Cohick, *Women in the World of the Earliest Christians: Illuminating Ancient Ways of Life* (Grand Rapids: Baker Academic, 2009).

13. Amy-Jill Levine and Marc Zvi Brettler, *The Bible with and without Jesus: How Jews and Christians Read the Same Stories Differently* (New York: HarperOne, 2020), ix.

14. Luke's account of Mary and Joseph taking Jesus to the temple when Mary's time of purification is completed and their interactions with Simeon and Anna have so far not been included in the series (Luke 2:22–39).

15. For example, the woman with an issue of blood is named Veronica, the Samaritan woman at the well is called Photina, and Zebedee's wife is named Salome. A woman named Salome is mentioned in Mark's Gospel as a witness of Jesus's crucifixion (Mark 15:40) and is among the women who come to the tomb with spices to anoint Jesus's body (Mark 16:1). She is not to be confused with the daughter of Herodias who danced before Herod (Matt 14:1–12; Mark 6:14–29), whom Josephus identifies as Salome (*Antiquities* 18.136). She is also frequently mentioned in the lists of Jesus's disciples in noncanonical texts (e.g., Gospel of Thomas 61;

Clement, *Miscellanies* 3.13.92; Gospel of Nicodemus, second Greek form 10–11; Constitutions of the Holy Apostles 3.1.6). The canonical gospels never identify her as the wife of Zebedee or the mother of Big James and John, but a Christian tradition conflates Mark 16:1 and Matt 27:56 to identify their mother as Mary Salome (Papias, fragment 10.3 [*ANF* 1:155]). Tatian's Syrian *Diatessaron* (c. AD 160–175), however, makes a distinction between Salome and Mary the mother of James and John (52:21–23).

16. Joanna's story as portrayed in *The Chosen* includes details about her marriage with Chuza and her financial support for Jesus's ministry.

17. On the portrayal of Mary Magdalene in films, plays, TV documentaries, and novels, see Jane Schaberg, *The Resurrection of Mary Magdalene: Legends, Apocrypha, and the Christian Testament* (New York: Continuum, 2003), 70–74.

18. The Synoptic Gospels indicate that there were several women who went to the tomb that morning (Matt 28:1–8; Mark 16:1–8; Luke 24:1–12).

19. This may be a reference to a similar story recounted in Matt 26:6–13; Mark 14:3–9.

20. Schaberg, *Resurrection of Mary Magdalene*, 68, 82. For example, we see the conflation of Mary Magdalene with both Mary of Bethany and Luke's unnamed sinful woman in a homily by Gregory the Great in AD 591: "She whom Luke calls the sinful woman, whom John calls Mary, we believe to be the Mary from whom seven devils were ejected according to Mark" (*Homily* 33 on Luke 7), quoted in Susan Haskins, *Mary Magdalene: Myth and Metaphor* (London: HarperCollins, 1994), 96. Gregory interpreted the seven devils with the vices of "pride, greed, lust, envy, gluttony, anger, and sloth." Philip C. Almond, *Mary Magdalene: A Cultural History* (Cambridge: Cambridge University Press, 2023), 11.

21. S4E1 also suggests that Elizabeth could read. When Mary comes to visit her, she recounts that, since Zacharias was unable to speak after his encounter with the angel Gabriel in the temple, he wrote down his experiences for her, which she then memorized.

22. See William V. Harris, *Ancient Literacy* (Cambridge, MA: Harvard University Press, 1989), 13.

23. Harris, *Ancient Literacy*, 8, 330.

24. Meir Bar-Ilian, "Illiteracy in the Land of Israel in the First Centuries CE," in *Essays in the Social Scientific Study of Judaism and Jewish Society*, ed. Simcha Fishbane et al., 2 vols., Canada-Israel Conference on the Social Scientific Study of Judaism (New York: Ktav, 1990, 1992), 2:46–61.

25. Catherine Hezser, *Jewish Literacy in Roman Palestine*, Texts and Studies in Ancient Judaism 81 (Tübingen: Mohr Siebeck, 2001), 31–33. Pieter J. J. Botha has argued persuasively against the idea that Jews in first-century Palestine had a widespread, organized, and compulsory system of elementary schooling. See "Schools in the World of Jesus: Analysing the Evidence," *Neotestamentica* 33 (1999): 225–60.

26. Hezser, *Jewish Literacy*, 496–97.

27. In S4E1, Thomas has come around to Ramah's desire to learn to read and study Torah. In his marriage proposal to Ramah he asks, "Will you forever walk with me, and read with me, and rattle off endless rules and extenuating circumstances with me?"

28. Recent studies suggest that by the fourth century, Christian women, from the elite classes, are known for their knowledge of Scripture. See Carolyn Osiek, "Between the Holy and the Ordinary: Women's Lives in Early Christianity," in *Material Culture and Women's Religious Experience in Antiquity: An Interdisciplinary Symposium*, ed. Mark D. Ellison, Catherine Gines Taylor, and Carolyn Osiek (Lanham: Lexington Books/Fortress Academic, 2021), 8–10; Joy A. Schroeder and Marion Ann Taylor, *Voices Long Silenced: Women Biblical Interpreters through the Centuries* (Louisville: Westminster John Knox, 2022), 20–48.

Chapter 17

1. Kenneth Burke, *A Rhetoric of Motives* (Berkeley: University of California Press, 1969), 41.

2. Kenneth Burke, *Permanence and Change*, 3rd ed. (Berkeley: University of California Press, 1984), 282.

3. Bernard L. Brock, "Rhetorical Criticism: A Burkean Approach Revisited," in *Methods of Rhetorical Criticism: A Twentieth-Century Perspective*, ed. Bernard L. Brock, Robert L. Scott, and James W. Chesebro (Detroit: Wayne State University Press, 1990), 185.

4. Burke, *Permanence and Change*, 284.

5. Brock, "Rhetorical Criticism," 186.

6. Kenneth Burke, *Language as Symbolic Action* (Berkeley: University of California Press, 1966), 20–21.

7. Brock, "Rhetorical Criticism," 187.

8. Kenneth Burke, *A Grammar of Motives* (Berkeley: University of California Press, 1969), xv–xvi.

9. Walter. R. Fisher, *Human Communication as Narration: Toward a Philosophy of Reason, Value, and Action* (Columbia: University of South Carolina Press, 1987), xi, 58.

10. Walter R. Fisher, "Toward a Logic of Good Reasons," *Quarterly Journal of Speech* 64 (1978): 376–84.

11. Fisher, *Human Communication*, 66, 105–123.

12. Fisher, *Human Communication*, 109, 187–88.

13. I am reckoning the people behind the series—for example, its creator Dallas Jenkins, his writing and producing teams, along with a team of theological consultants—as a singular rhetorical storyteller who work together to craft the message of the program. While they are the primary rhetor acting on the show's viewers at the metalevel, I focus here on the program itself, so references to rhetorical action will be within the story rather than outside of it.

14. Dominick S. Hernandez, *Proverbs: Pathways to Wisdom* (Nashville: Abingdon, 2020), 129.

15. Hernandez, *Proverbs*, 106.

16. Some retellings of the story of Jesus have insinuated a romantic or perhaps even inappropriate relationship between Jesus and Mary Magdalene. *The Chosen* counters this idea by having Mary recount the moment Jesus rescued her and how he touched her hand. She states that people could be confused about what that would mean, but it was not at all what they might presume (S2E1).

Contributors

ROBERT K. GARCIA
Associate Professor of Philosophy
Baylor University
Waco, Texas

DANIEL M. GARLAND JR.
Assistant Professor of Theology
Ohio Dominican University
Columbus, Ohio

PAUL GONDREAU
Professor of Theology
Providence College
Providence, Rhode Island

PATRICK GRAY
Professor of Religious Studies
Rhodes College
Memphis, Tennessee

KENNETH GUMBERT
Associate Professor of Film Studies
Providence College
Providence, Rhode Island

M. ELIZABETH LEWIS HALL
Professor of Psychology
Biola University
La Mirada, California

TODD W. HALL
Professor of Psychology
Biola University
La Mirada, California

JEANNINE M. HANGER
Associate Professor of New Testament
Talbot School of Theology at Biola
    University
La Mirada, California

Contributors

JOHN HILTON III
Professor of Religious Education
Brigham Young University
Provo, Utah

DOUGLAS S. HUFFMAN
Professor of New Testament
Talbot School of Theology at Biola University
La Mirada, California

JAMES F. KEATING
Associate Professor of Theology
Providence College
Providence, Rhode Island

DAVID KNEIP
Associate Professor of Bible, Missions, and Ministry
Abilene Christian University
Abilene, Texas

DOLORES G. MORRIS
Department of Philosophy
University of South Florida
Tampa, Florida

JOY E. A. QUALLS
Associate Professor of Communication Studies
Biola University
La Mirada, California

DEBORAH SAVAGE
Professor of Theology
Franciscan University of Steubenville
Steubenville, Ohio

JESSE D. STONE
Theologian in Residence
OneHope
Pompano Beach, Florida

GAYE STRATHEARN
Professor of Ancient Scripture
Brigham Young University
Provo, Utah

T. ADAM VAN WART
Associate Professor of Theology
Ave Maria University
Ave Maria, Florida

Index

Abigail, 20, 101, 146, 180, 189, 194
Abraham, 168–69, 178, 189
Acts of John, 126, 224n8
Acts of Paul and Thecla, 126
Acts of Peter, 126
Acts of Pilate (a.k.a. Gospel of Nicodemus), 126, 204n2
Acts of the Apostles, 9, 43, 128–29, 130, 181
Acts of Thomas, 126
Adam, 172
allegory, 62
anachronism, 7, 12–13
Andrew, 54, 73, 182–83, 203n13
Annunciation, the, 88, 180, 181
anti-Marcionite prologues, 129
Apocryphon of James, 181
Apocryphon of John, 130–31, 181
Apollinarianism, 95, 97
Aquinas, Thomas. *See* Thomas Aquinas
Aramaic, 7, 127, 171, 206n15
Aristotle, 154, 157, 190
art, Christian, 93–94, 99–101, 104, 144
artistic license, 6–7, 9–13, 85, 87, 93, 104, 105, 164, 175, 189

attachment theory, 48–49, 51–56
audience surrogacy, 12
Augustine of Hippo, 15, 17, 20, 95, 140–41, 143, 158, 206n15, 207n25, 208n33
authenticity (defined), 5
autism, 9–10, 84, 203n14, 211n16

Bar-Ilien, Meir, 185
Barnaby, 10, 20
Bede, Venerable, 15, 20, 23, 206n19, 207n28, 208n33
Bethesda, pool of, 169–70
biblical inspiration, views of, 64–65, 119, 131
Book of the Secret Supper (*Cena secreta*). *See* Questions of John
Brettler, Marc Zvi, 179
Brock, Bernard L., 190
Brooks, Phillips, 167, 170
Bultmann, Rudolf, 121–22, 222
Burke, Kenneth, 189–92, 199

Cadbury, Henry J., 129
Cana, wedding at, 20, 105–10, 125, 196
Capernaum, 98, 139, 146, 148, 184, 194
Caravaggio, 93–94

237

Index

Catholicism, 37–39, 42, 47, 63, 97, 102, 116–17, 150–51, 155
Chalcedon, Council of (AD 451), 94, 97–98, 101–3
character development, 6, 9–10, 56, 59, 82
characters, additional, 10–11
"Cherry-Tree Carol," 128
Chosen, The
   disclaimer screen, 4, 5, 87
   "Jewishness" of, 12–13
   and Scripture, 4–5, 36
   women in, 83, 110–14, 158–61, 165–66, 173–74, 176–87, 188–200
Chosen, The, episode references
   S1E1, 4, 53, 98, 99, 139–40, 148, 151, 158, 183, 188, 195
   S1E2, 11, 20, 27, 98, 99, 189, 193–94, 206n17
   S1E3, 20, 95, 98–101, 145, 180
   S1E4, 55, 148
   S1E5, 20, 106–10, 196, 206n17
   S1E6, 54
   S1E7, 54, 58, 132, 158
   S1E8, 57, 110–14, 146, 151, 156, 158, 166–67, 182, 189, 193, 197
   S2E1, 23, 132, 196, 233n16
   S2E2, 14, 15–24, 32, 184–85, 199, 206n17
   S2E3, 54, 180–81, 196
   S2E4, 89
   S2E5, 11, 27, 32, 33, 41, 102, 169, 196, 206n17
   S2E6, 41, 53, 54, 147, 193, 195–96
   S2E7, 102, 206
   S2E8, 23, 53, 102, 131, 196, 206n17
   Christmas special episode, 41, 131–32, 180
   S3E1, 32, 54, 198, 203n13
   S3E2, 11, 33, 54, 147
   S3E3, 23, 196
   S3E4, 158
   S3E5, 11, 148, 158, 174, 198
   S3E6, 12, 53, 198, 224n2
   S3E7, 12, 55
   S3E8, 12, 55, 200, 206n17
   S4E1, 148, 180, 206, 231n21, 232n27
   S4E2, 19, 55
   S4E5, 99, 217n2
   S4E7, 12, 69, 70, 148, 206n17
   S4E8, 69, 70, 206, 219n14
Christmas, 42
christological doctrine, 94
Church of Jesus Christ of Latter-day Saints, x, 42
Chuza, 183, 231n16
Clement of Alexandria, 129
Constantinople, First Council of (AD 381), 94, 97
Constantinople, Third Council of (AD 680–681), 102
consubstantial, 97, 98, 101, 104, 190
Crosby, John, 163
Cyril of Alexandria, 15, 17, 20, 21

depersonalizing forces, 163
dialectical imagination, 38–43
Dinah, 20, 108
Dionysius Exiguus, 202n9
Dionysius of Alexandria, 130
dispensationalism, 40
divine hiddenness. *See* hiddenness
divine revelation, 141
divorce, 193
Docetism, 95–96, 99–102, 218n4
dramatism/dramatic theory, 189–90
dual processing theory, 48–49, 56–60
Dunn, J. D. G., 123
Duvernay, Ava, 81, 85
Dworkin, Andrea, 163

Eden (wife of Peter), 10, 32, 55, 125, 151, 156–57, 182, 189, 200
Eliot, T. S., 141
Elizabeth, 132, 180, 231n21
Elizondo, Virgilio, 171
Enlightenment, the, 38, 39, 49, 62, 67, 120

Index

Ephrem the Syrian, 15, 21
Epiphanius, 127–28
epistemic humility, 35–36
Epistle of the Apostles, 181
Essenes, 139
Eusebius, 127, 129, 130
evangelization, 151
evil, problem of, 26, 28–30, 34–35, 148
Exodus, book of, 157

faith, experience (or act) of, 158–60
Felder, Hilarin, 121
fictitious events and conversations, 11–12, 145, 147, 148
Fisher, Walter, 191
flashbacks, 23, 106, 133, 180
flash-forwards, 23, 131, 132, 134
flesh (*sarx, caro*), 96
Frei, Hans W., 62, 212n3
Funk, Robert W., 223n17

Gabriel (angel), 180
Galilee, 194
Gen Z, 142
Gertler, Brie, 26–27
Gilson, Etienne, 156–57, 160
God
    barriers to intimacy with, 49–51
    fatherhood of, 170–75
    as incorporeal, 49–50
Gospel of John, 11, 14–24, 69–80, 105–14, 129–30, 133, 146, 184, 203n11
Gospel of Luke, 9, 78–79, 102, 128–29, 165, 168, 173–74, 180–81, 183–84
    infancy narrative, 108, 132
    prologue, 119, 135
Gospel of Mark, 121, 134
Gospel of Mary, 181
Gospel of Matthew, 127, 188
Gospel of Nicodemus. *See* Acts of Pilate
Gospel of Pseudo-Matthew, 128
Gospel of the Ebionites, 128
Gospel of the Forty Days, 130
Gospel of the Hebrews, 128
Gospel of the Nazarenes, 128
Gospel of Thomas, 134, 181
Greatest Story Ever Told, The (1965), ix, 134
Greeley, Andrew, 38–39
Gregory of Nyssa, 130–31
Gregory the Great, 231n20
Grey, Matthew J., 86
Guffey, Father David, 4

Hagar, 189
Hahn, Scott W., 221n15
Harnack, Adolf von, 63
Harris, William V., 185
Hawks, Howard, 39
Hebrews, epistle to the, 100, 129
hiddenness, 26, 28–31, 33–35, 209
hierarchy, 190
historical fiction genre, 4, 70, 118, 125, 200
Hopkins, Gerard Manley, 141
Huffman, Douglas S., 70, 181
human nature, 65–67
    humans as storytelling animals, 65–66
human persons
    as children of God, 170–75
    as created in the image of God, 170–73
    individual value of, 162–75
hypostasis, 98

imagination, role of, 26–28, 35–36, 64, 70, 80, 118
incarnation, 50, 95–96, 99–101, 118, 149
Irenaeus, 97, 108, 129
Isaiah, 108–9, 140, 195
Ishoʻdad of Merw, 15, 18, 19

Jacob, 22, 110, 111, 114, 178
Jairus, 158–59, 198
Jairus, daughter of, 159, 194, 198
James (a.k.a. Little James), 9, 11, 33, 83, 147–49, 193
James, son of Zebedee (a.k.a. Big James), 23, 180, 194, 224n8, 231n15

Index

Jenkins, Dallas, 4, 39–41, 61–63, 82–83, 87, 90, 100, 103, 176, 212
   global livestreams, 217n2, 219
   and script consultants, 4, 233n13
Jenkins, Jerry B., 39, 201n2
Jerome, 127, 129
Jerusalem, 106, 111, 112–13, 184, 220n11
Jesse (paralytic), 169–70, 174
Jesus
   anointing of, 77–79, 165, 184
   ascension, 9, 31, 50, 130
   birth, birth narrative, 8, 41–42, 132–33, 181, 202n9
   crucifixion and death, 8, 82, 86, 112–13, 146, 149, 183, 207n32, 215n10
   divine nature, 6, 22, 97–98, 102–4
   humanity of, 6, 11–12, 73–74, 93–104, 118, 149
   Jewishness of, 12–13, 123–25
   relatability, 6–8, 52–53, 56, 74, 99, 101
   resurrection, 8, 9, 31, 62, 67, 119, 130, 134, 181, 184
   sinlessness, 93, 102
Jesus of Nazareth (1977), ix, 64
Joanna, 83, 183, 186, 194, 198, 224n2, 231n16
John, son of Zebedee, 124, 129–30, 132–33, 194, 231n15
John Chrysostom, 15, 17, 20, 21, 73, 207n32
John of the Cross, 156, 159–60
John Paul II (Karol Wojtyła), xi, 116–17, 152–53, 155–60
John the Baptist, 8, 32, 33, 95, 102, 107, 148, 203n13
Joseph (husband of Mary), 23, 102, 196, 230n14
Joseph of Arimathea, 146
Josephus, 139, 230n15
Joshua, 20, 101, 146
Judaism, 12–13, 90, 122, 123–24, 171, 195

Käsemann, Ernst, 122
Kerns, Travis, 36
King, Henry Churchill, 173
King, Martin Luther, Jr., 163
King, Nathan L., 35–36
King of Kings, The (1927), ix
kippah, 12
Kline, M. G., 172
Kurek-Chomycz, Dominika, 77

language translation, 7, 88, 202n6
Last Supper, 100
Lazarus, 69–77, 99, 148, 214–16
Lee, Dorothy, 77
Leonardo da Vinci, 4
Levering, Matthew, 68
Levine, Amy-Jill, 179
Lilith. *See* Mary Magdalene
Luke, 124, 128–29, 131–32

Macdonald, Norm, 64
MacIntyre, Alasdair, 65–66
Magnificat, 41, 88, 132, 134, 179
Marcel, Gabriel, 153, 155
Mark, 127
Martha, 71–74, 75–76, 180, 198
Mary, mother of Jesus, 41, 99–100, 102, 107–9, 128–30, 131–32, 133, 179–81, 196
Mary Magdalene, 27, 40–41, 131–32, 133, 134, 147–49, 179, 182–86, 193–96
   in S1E1, 140, 158, 188
Mary of Bethany, 180, 184, 186, 198
Matthew, 12, 54, 84, 124, 149, 183, 185, 193, 195–96
   ancient traditions regarding, 127–28
   as author, 131, 133
   as autistic, 9–10, 84, 211n16
McDowell, Catherine, 172–73
Meier, John P., 123
Messiah, 19, 20–21, 27–28, 31–36, 40, 111, 114, 166, 194, 199
Meyer, Ben F., 123

miracles, 7–8, 10, 27, 55, 72, 115, 147–48, 179, 184
Monophysitism, 95, 97–98, 101–4, 219n14
Moses, 20, 107, 130, 157, 180
Moshe bar Kepha, 15, 17, 21, 207n32

narrative theology, 68
Nathanael, 12, 14–23, 32–33, 158, 205–7
Nazareth, 19–21, 23, 194, 197, 205–7
Nicaea, Council of (AD 325), 98
Nicodemus, 11, 32, 57–58, 132, 139, 146–47, 149, 158, 184, 193
Nonnus of Nisibis, 15, 17, 22

O'Keefe, John J., 23
Origen, 97, 105, 127, 204n3, 208n36

Papandrea, James L., 24
Papias, 127
paralytic at pool of Bethesda. *See* Jesse (paralytic)
Passion of the Christ, The (2004), ix, 100
Patel, Paras, 9, 84
Paul, 95–96, 119, 128, 129, 131, 203–4n15, 224n2
pedagogy, the use of film in
  advantages of, 81–84
  challenges of, 84–87
Peter, 10, 11, 32–33, 54–56, 71, 156, 174, 188–89, 196, 200
  mother-in-law of, 156–57, 182–83, 188–89
  wife of. *See* Eden (wife of Peter)
Petty, Michael John, 6
Pharisees, 139, 165
Philip, 14, 15, 17–21, 23, 54, 206n15
Photina, 10, 57, 110–14, 164, 166–67, 180, 186, 193–94, 197, 220n10
Pilate's wife (a.k.a. Claudia), 194, 198
Pirandello, Luigi, 67
Plantinga, Alvin, 29
Plaskow, Judith, 177–78
plausibility (defined), 5

Prochorus, 130, 224n8
prodigal son, 173
Protestantism, 37–40, 48–49, 63
Protestant Reformation, 38, 42
purification, 190

Questions of John (*Interrogatio Iohannis*), 130
Quintus, 139

Ramah, 180, 184–86, 193–95, 199
Rea, Michael, 29
redemption, 190
Red River (1948), 39
Reimarus, Herrmann Samuel, 119–20, 222n7
relatability (defined), 5–6
Reno, R. R., 23
Revelation, book of, 129–30
rhetoric/rhetorical theory, 189–93, 198–99
ritual impurity, 158
Roman Catholicism. *See* Catholicism
Rosa, Hartmut, 142–45
Roumie, Jonathan, 6, 7, 94, 148–49, 151, 156, 158, 219n11, 226n2
Russell, Bertrand, 26
Ruth, book of, 177

sacramental imagination, 37–43
Sadducees, 139
Salome, 194, 230–31
Samaritans, 110–11, 220n11
Samaritan woman at the well. *See* Photina
Sanders, E. P., 123
Sanhedrin, 8, 146
Schindler's List (1993), 81
Scholasticism, 159
Schweitzer, Albert, 120–21
script consultants, x, 3–4, 13, 233n13
selectivity of episodes, 8–9
Selma (2014), 81, 85
Seth, 172

Index

Shabbat, 193–95
Shema prayer, 146
Sheva Brakhot (the seven blessings), 106
Shmuel, 79
Shula, 10
Simon Peter. *See* Peter
Simon the Pharisee, 165
Simon the Zealot, 9, 27–28, 32, 33, 149, 169–70
Sobel, Rabbi Jason, 4
soteriological principle, 96–97
spirituality, split between theology and, 49
spork, 97
Step'anos Siwnets'i, 15
Strauss, David Friedrich, 120, 121
Susanna, 183

Tabish, Elizabeth, 84, 226n2
Tamar (Ethiopian disciple), 193–94, 198
Tatian, 231n15
Taylor, Charles, 141, 143–44
technology, 142
tenebrism, 94
Tertullian, 128
Thaddeus, 158, 193
Theodore of Mopsuestia, 15, 17, 21
Thettayil, Benny, 221n15

Thomas, 185–86, 194, 199
Thomas Aquinas, 48, 66, 95, 154–55, 157, 159, 219n13, 227n13
Thomism, 156, 157, 159
timeline compression, 4, 9, 83, 87, 188, 203n12
Tolkien, J. R. R., 116, 128, 221n1
Torah, 180, 185, 193, 195, 199
Tracy, David, 37–39

United Nations' "Universal Declaration of Human Rights," 163

Veronica, 10, 148, 158–60, 170, 173–74, 180, 186, 194, 197–98, 230n15
Von Hildebrand, Alice, 151
Von Hildebrand, Dietrich, 151

Westminster Catechism, 47
Willard, Dallas, 168
woman at the well. *See* Photina
woman with the flow of blood/hemorrhaging woman. *See* Veronica
Wordsworth, William, 140
Wright, N. T., 123–24, 215n14

yarmulke, 12

Zealots, 139
Zohara (wife of Nicodemus), 139